THE NORTH AMERICAN FOLK MUSIC REVIVAL: NATION AND IDENTITY IN THE UNITED STATES AND CANADA, 1945–1980

The North American Folk Music Revival: Nation and Identity in the United States and Canada, 1945–1980

GILLIAN MITCHELL
University of Wales, Bangor, UK

ASHGATE

Published by
Ashgate Publishing Limited
Gower House
Croft Road
Aldershot
Hampshire GU11 3HR
England

Ashgate Publishing Company
Suite 420
101 Cherry Street
Burlington, VT 05401-4405
USA

Ashgate website: http://www.ashgate.com

British Library Cataloguing in Publication Data
Mitchell, Gillian
   The North American folk music revival : nation and identity
   in the United States and Canada. – (Ashgate popular and
   folk music series)
   1.Folk music – United States – 20th century – History and
   criticism 2.Folk music – Canada – 20th century – History
   and criticism 3.National characteristics, American
   4.National characteristics, Canadian
   I.Title
   781.6'21'009045

Library of Congress Cataloging-in-Publication Data
Mitchell, Gillian.
   The North American folk music revival : nation and identity in the United States and Canada, 1945–1980 / Gillian Mitchell.
      p. cm.—(Ashgate popular and folk music series)
   Includes bibliographical references.
   ISBN-13: 978-0-7546-5756-9 (alk. paper)
   ISBN-10: 0-7546-5756-6 (alk. paper)
   1. Folk songs, English—United States—History and criticism. 2. Folk songs, English—Canada—History and criticism. I. Title. II. Series.

   ML3550.5.M58 2007
   781.62'100904—dc22
                                                                              2006016619
   ISBN 978-0-7546-5756-9

Printed and bound in Great Britain by MPG Books Ltd, Bodmin, Cornwall.

Contents

General Editor's Preface

The upheaval that occurred in musicology during the last two decades of the twentieth century has created a new urgency for the study of popular music alongside the development of new critical and theoretical models. A relativistic outlook has replaced the universal perspective of modernism (the international ambitions of the 12-note style); the grand narrative of the evolution and dissolution of tonality has been challenged, and emphasis has shifted to cultural context, reception and subject position. Together, these have conspired to eat away at the status of canonical composers and categories of high and low in music. A need has arisen, also, to recognize and address the emergence of crossovers, mixed and new genres, to engage in debates concerning the vexed problem of what constitutes authenticity in music and to offer a critique of musical practice as the product of free, individual expression.

Popular musicology is now a vital and exciting area of scholarship, and the *Ashgate Popular and Folk Music Series* aims to present the best research in the field. Authors will be concerned with locating musical practices, values and meanings in cultural context, and may draw upon methodologies and theories developed in cultural studies, semiotics, poststructuralism, psychology and sociology. The series will focus on popular musics of the twentieth and twenty-first centuries. It is designed to embrace the world's popular musics from Acid Jazz to Zydeco, whether high tech or low tech, commercial or non-commercial, contemporary or traditional.

Professor Derek B. Scott
Chair of Music
University of Salford

Acknowledgements

I wish to express my gratitude to the many people who have helped me in the research and writing of this book. To Dr Neil Rosenberg, the external examiner of my doctoral thesis, for his advice and assistance at the preliminary stage of research and for his helpful and extensive comments on the finished thesis; to John Leeder, for helping me to track down a number of interviewees; to Brian Walsh, Merrick Jarrett, Michael Van Dusen, Nicholas Jennings, the late Estelle Klein, Ken Whiteley, Brian Hollander, Happy Traum, Tom Pacheco, Arthur Wenk and Richard Flohil for taking the time to share their reminiscences of the folk revival with me; to Rob Bowman, Bob Bossin, Peter Goddard and Scott Richards for the information they provided on the Canadian music scene; to all those who provided suggestions during the thesis research process, particularly Dr Judith Cohen, Dr Pauline Greenhill, and Dr Terry Donaldson; to the staff at the American Folklife Center, Library of Congress, Washington, DC, and at the National Library and Archives of Canada, Ottawa, for their help during my research visits there, and to Rennie Cantine and family for their hospitality during my visit to Woodstock, New York.

I also wish to thank Edward McGhee for sharing his opinions on the folk music revival in Britain and in North America, and for his encouragement of my interest in popular music history, and the members of the communities of Wycliffe College, Toronto, and St Brendan's, Saltcoats, Scotland, particularly Mrs Isabel Garrett and Miss Bernadette Doyle, for their support, generosity and kindness.

I wish especially to thank my committee members Dr John Ingham and Dr Cecilia Morgan for their insightful suggestions and feedback, and my supervisor, Dr Elspeth Brown, for her extensive and helpful comments on the various drafts of the thesis, and for her generosity and hospitality; these were greatly appreciated. I am also most grateful to Dr Wil Griffith, Prof. Duncan Tanner, Dr Ceri Sullivan and all colleagues at the Department of History and Welsh History, University of Wales, Bangor, for their help and support, and to Mrs Stephanie Dolben of WISCA at the University of Wales, Bangor, for her assistance in the preparation and formatting of the manuscript.

Lastly, the greatest debt of gratitude is owed to my family – to my parents, John and Rose Ann Mitchell, my sisters Hilary and Roslyn, my brother-in-law John, and my uncle, Thomas Kirk, for their unfailing encouragement and support. It is to them that this work is dedicated, with much love.

Introduction

The folk music revival, a movement which emerged, essentially, in the 1940s and reached its apex in the mid-1960s, has been an enduring source of fascination for academics and music enthusiasts alike. Many of the most influential of the revival musicians continue to enjoy illustrious careers as esteemed 'elders' of the contemporary music scene, all, in their own way, reflecting certain key aspects of the revival in their performances. While performers such as Joan Baez, Pete Seeger and Tom Paxton remain committed to the questioning, radical political stance of the folk revival, Bob Dylan, Paul Simon and Neil Young, nurtured in the intellectually stimulating, thoughtful atmosphere of the revival, have honed their song-writing skills to the extent that they have now become recognised as masters of their art. Interest in the most prominent and successful of the revivalists has been considerable, with Martin Scorsese's insightful documentary on Bob Dylan, *No Direction Home*, representing one of the most recent analyses of the folk revival and one of its principal participants.[1] The quirks and eccentricities of the movement have not gone unnoticed in recent years, however. Christopher Guest's affectionately amusing 'mockumentary' about the revival, *A Mighty Wind*, also exposed many of the absurdities of the movement – such as the political 'hang-ups' of many of the revivalists, and the proliferation, in the 1960s, of commercialised folk groups whose often embarrassingly sanitised, stylised music represented an attempt by record companies to 'cash in' on the popularity of folk music.[2] Scholarly interest in the folk revival, though evident from the 1960s onwards, was reawakened in the nineties by a series of seminal publications which reminded readers that the movement possessed a tremendous variety and complexity which stretched far beyond either the most celebrated or the most commercial performers of the revival.[3] Essentially, the movement represented a large umbrella under which gathered a plethora of musicians, students, academics, political and social activists, special-interest groups of various kinds, and admirers, young and old. Budding composers of anti-nuclear and civil rights protest songs, earnest graduate students with a passion for obscure Appalachian string-bands, and those interested in topping the charts with a new folk ballad, thereby becoming the next Kingston Trio, all found a place within the

---

1   *Bob Dylan: No Direction Home*, directed by Martin Scorsese (2005)
2   *A Mighty Wind*, directed by Christopher Guest (2003)
3   See Neil Rosenberg (ed.), *Transforming Tradition: Folk Music Revivals Examined* (Urbana, IL and Chicago, IL, 1993); Robert Cantwell, *When We Were Good: Class and Culture in the Folk Revival* (Cambridge, MA 1996); and Ronald D. Cohen, *Wasn't That a Time! First-Hand Accounts of the Folk Music Revival* (Metuchen, NJ and London, 1995) and the most recent and detailed work to date, Ronald Cohen, *Rainbow Quest: The Folk Music Revival and American Society, 1940–1970* (Amherst, MA and Boston, MA, 2002). These works, and their significance, will be discussed again later in the introduction.

revival during its halcyon days in the late 1950s and early 1960s.[4] Scholars like Neil Rosenberg and Ronald Cohen have demonstrated the passion for musical diversity and catholicity exhibited by the revivalists; their desire to uncover and appreciate the immense variety of North American, and world, folk music was all-consuming, and outlasted the many commercial 'fads' for which the movement is frequently ridiculed today.

The aim of this study is to uncover the meaning behind this diversity via an analysis of the conceptualising of national identity and the nation in the folk music revival movement, not merely in the United States but also in English-speaking Canada in the post-1945 era, with a particular focus on the apex of the movement in the 1960s.[5] The study illustrates the shifts in thinking about the nation which occurred within the folk music world of Canada and America at this time. During the early 1960s, the folk revival in both countries adopted an optimistic, pluralistic and inclusive 'North American' focus, in which the continent was perceived and celebrated as a diverse patchwork quilt of cultures. However, by late in the decade, as the revival became increasingly integrated into 'mainstream' popular music, and as the political climate changed, this optimistic concept became outdated; in Canada, folk music, in its many forms, was frequently considered a quintessentially 'Canadian' mode of expression, while, in the US, folk artists lost their faith in the forces of social change and retreated from their nation into personalised worlds of self-analysis and introspection. The study both outlines, in detail, the nature of these shifting concepts of the nation, and explains the reasons why such ideas were formulated, and why they altered over time.

Background: The Folk Revival Movement of the Post-1945 Era

It is no easy task to document or understand with precision the resurgence of interest in folk music in North America which became known as 'the folk revival'. This movement, was, indeed, prodigiously complex and factional, and members of the various factions were embroiled in bitter ideological combats. Even as the movement unfolded it was constantly attempting to define and redefine itself, and to arrive at an understanding of its almost bewildering eclecticism. The folk revival was profoundly political; its ideology, and the endless dialogue and discourse surrounding its existence and its meaning, are essentially of equal significance to historians as is the music itself.

To this day, scholars of the revival, many of whom were themselves musicians or participants, have been unable to reach a unified understanding of the movement. They continue to debate the appropriateness of the term 'revival' to describe the phenomenon, and puzzle over, among other issues, whether 'the revival' was really

---

4   The Kingston Trio had a 'number one' hit with their calypso-style version of the traditional song 'Tom Dooley' in 1958. Their success is said to have been the catalyst for the sudden rise in popularity of folk music, although they were later condemned by 'purist' revivalists for being too commercial in orientation.

5   Please note that, unless indicated, 'Canada' is meant to stand for 'English-speaking Canada'. The book does not discuss the folk music movement of Quebec in any detail.

several revivals or one movement; when exactly it began and ended; what precisely constituted 'folk music', what caused it to become popular, and, above all, what the folk revival *meant*, then and now.[6] The folk revival, nurtured in a politicised, controversial atmosphere, remains the subject of tremendous controversy and continues to pose many bewildering questions for scholars.

Attempting any study of the folk revival is, for these reasons, a daunting task. No one study can claim to be exhaustive, nor can it provide satisfactory answers to all the lingering queries of academics. To endeavour to compare the folk revival movements of Canada and the United States during this period is to complicate matters still further. While most academic studies of the revival have focused on America – the country in which the movement, in its post-World War II form, essentially began – and glanced occasionally at the United Kingdom, there has been remarkably little academic literature produced on the Canadian revival. Indeed, to date, there is yet to be published a full-length scholarly history of Canadian popular music, let alone on the folk revival in Canada. This disparity might suggest that a comparative study of the music of the two nations is bound to put Canada at a disadvantage.

Comparing Canada and the United States: Advantages and Difficulties

In general, there is still much resistance to the idea of historical and cultural comparison between America and Canada at the academic level.[7] It is an accepted truism that the majority of such protests are voiced by Canadians, rather than by Americans; some of this animosity results from reflexive or 'knee-jerk' sentiments of anti-Americanism, but many also perceive that such studies must necessarily be of a one-sided nature, to the detriment of Canada. As one writer has remarked, the quest to rationalise and explain the differences between Canada and America is largely a preoccupation of Canadians; he states that '[t]he United States is so vast, so distant from the rest of the world, and so successful that its self-fascination blocks out much room for thinking about others.'[8] Traditionally, Americans have had little reason to study or reflect upon their northern neighbours, while Canadians are ever conscious of the actions of the United States, and are perpetually anxious to demonstrate that they are 'not Americans'. This last point illustrates yet another complication: Canada and America, while different in terms of national origins, politics, foreign affairs and government, also share many profound similarities. Among other things, both countries were founded upon European emigration and

---

6   See the essays in Rosenberg (ed.), *Transforming Tradition*, and the detailed first-person reminiscences in Cohen (ed.), *Wasn't That a Time!*.

7   There are some exceptions to this. For example, Francis M. Carroll, *A Good and Wise Measure: The Search for the Canadian-American Boundary, 1783–1842* (Toronto, 2001) and Sheila MacManus, *"The Line Which Separates": Race, Gender, and the Alberta-Montana Borderlands, 1862–1892* (PhD Thesis, York University, Canada, 2001). There are some comparative essays in Canadian and American musicology in Timothy J. McGee (ed.), *Taking a Stand: Essays in Honour of John Beckwith* (Toronto, 1995), pp. 149–218.

8   Jeffrey Simpson, *Star-Spangled Canadians: Canadians Living the American Dream* (Toronto, 2000), p. 4.

colonisation at a fatal cost to the aboriginal peoples who had originally settled there; both boast, today, a tremendous ethnic diversity, and both have grown to become powerfully wealthy capitalist nations. Nevertheless, of the two, America has, historically, proven the more thrusting and the more overtly unified in terms of a politically and publicly endorsed national culture. Since the late nineteenth century, the United States has played an increasingly important role in world affairs, while Canada, evolving slowly from British colonial status, has had no such clear self-definition. As Seymour Martin Lipset has argued, 'Americanism became and has remained a political ideology. There is no such ideology of Canadianism.'[9] Existing in the shadow of the more aggressive United States, Canadians have tended to define their identity as a 'non-identity'; lacking the self-evident political or cultural basis for a unified, public national identity, the country has sought to proclaim itself a 'mosaic' of multiculturalism, a vibrant whole made up of equal but contrasting parts. The Canadian government has, since the 1960s, done much to endorse such a notion and implement it both in law and in education.[10] Feelings of animosity towards the United States frequently underlie much discussion of Canadian identity; a sense of threat from America is often perceived, and the domination of American popular culture in Canada is much lamented and attemptedly counteracted with domestic initiatives.[11]

As a result, Canadian scholars, in particular, are often loath to undertake any comparative study of the two countries, especially when the study involves an aspect of popular culture, such as music. They believe that not only would such an undertaking put Canada at a disadvantage, but that it would also impose upon Canada an 'American perspective' which is both damaging and limiting.

This study will treat notions such as these as evolving historical ideas which have which underwent important alterations in the period 1960–80. Furthermore, the study will focus as much on the concept of Canada and America as *ideas* as on their existence as political and geographical entities. Essentially the aim of the study is to discuss the two countries and their music, not in exhaustive detail, but in terms of the changing ways in which the countries were, conceptually, understood and discussed as 'imagined communities' by the musicians, commentators and communities on whose lives, opinions and work the study focuses.[12]

Defining Nation and Nationalism

Benedict Anderson's concept of the "imagined community" is vital to this study, and, indeed, to any history which involves discussion of nationalism or national

---

9   Seymour Martin Lipset, *Continental Divide: The Values and Institutions of the United States and Canada* (New York, 1990), p. 42.

10   For example, Prime Minister Lester B. Pearson and his successor, Pierre Trudeau, were both active in the promotion of a multicultural and bilingual Canada during the 1960s.

11   See J.L. Granatstein, *Yankee Go Home? Canadians and Anti-Americanism* (Toronto, 1996).

12   Benedict Anderson, *Imagined Communities: Reflections on the Origin and Spread of Nationalism* (London and New York, 1991).

identity. Benedict Anderson considers the nation, not as an ancient entity constructed on a basis of ethnic or linguistic unity, or as simply a country or geographical area which has achieved political statehood. Rather, for Anderson, the nation is an 'imagined' concept, the consequence of great social, political and cultural changes which took place in the early modern era. In the formulation of his arguments, Anderson owes much to Eric Hobsbawm and Terence Ranger's *The Invention of Tradition,* an anthology of essays which demonstrates the ways in which certain national institutions, pageants (such as those of the British monarchy), and nationalist movements (such as those of Scotland and Wales) relied on notions of the past which were essentially, fabrications.[13] These 'invented traditions' were often created during times of turbulence – particularly during the last 200 years – when societies coping with rapid modernisation needed a 'past' upon which to lean. The revelation that apparently timeless traditions could be inventions was a crucial one for historians, and it is certainly fundamental to the work of Anderson.

Anderson demonstrates that, until the Middle Ages, the life of all communities, in Europe and beyond, was governed and defined both by religion and by a political order based on dynastic inheritance.[14] Ancient religious texts, and deep-seated beliefs concerning social hierarchy, provided the context for people's existence. However, by the late fifteenth century, this context had begun to alter considerably. The exploration of places beyond the 'known' world gave geography, and a sense of physical context, a new significance for people. Furthermore, as the Reformation and the increased use of the printing press caused Latin to be replaced by vernacular languages, people became aware of their specific differences and of the pluralistic nature of the world. The old order based on generalised, religious universalism was no longer in existence, and, according to Anderson, people found new ways to understand and 'imagine' their place in the world and their relationship to one another. It was the new system of 'print capitalism', more than anything else, which helped people to redefine themselves. Novels and newspapers were read with increasing frequency, providing new insights and new ways of thinking and imagining. It was within this context – a context of greater specificity, a new geographical awareness, and changing insights on the world – that the idea of a new kind of 'imagined community' – the nation – came into being in the eighteenth century.

Significantly, Anderson considers that the nation-based 'imagined community' was a product of the Americas which was transplanted to Europe. Encouraged by the new kinds of discourses which existed in the print capitalist world, Americans were able to imagine new realities for themselves – realities of republicanism, nation-states, popular sovereignty, national flags and common citizenship.[15] These notions would, eventually, travel to Europe, and would be adopted grudgingly by aristocratic leaders who feared popular uprisings.[16]

---

13   Eric Hobsbawm and Terence Ranger (eds), *The Invention of Tradition* (Cambridge, 1992).

14   Anderson, *Imagined Communities*, pp. 9–36.

15   Ibid., pp. 47–65

16   Ibid., pp. 83–111.

Therefore, for Benedict Anderson, a nation – indeed, any kind of community which is larger than a small village where all inhabitants are actually acquainted – is 'imagined'. However, contrary to the view of Ernest Gellner, an earlier scholar, the 'imagining' of a nation does not make that nation unreal.[17] Rather, it 'creates' the nation and brings it into being. When discussing America, Canada, and, indeed, North America as a whole, therefore, the theories of Benedict Anderson, theories which treat nations as ideas rather than as fixed concepts, are particularly apt.

During the turbulent years of the 1960s and 1970s, both Canada and America underwent dramatic and significant changes of many kinds; in both countries, various political, social and cultural changes brought about a re-evaluation of national identity, a re-evaluation which was reflected in both Canadian and American musical culture. It is, thus, upon the *idea* of nation, on the changing discourse surrounding such an idea, and on the ways in which music reflects and promotes such an idea, that the study is primarily focused.

Furthermore, just as it is important to address the issue of what precisely constitutes a 'nation', so too does the idea of 'nationalism' play an important role in the study. This is particularly true in the context of Canada in the late 1960s, but it also affects the discourse surrounding the United States throughout the twentieth century. Anthony D. Smith has created a 'working definition' of nationalism which asserts that '[nationalism is] an ideological movement for attaining and maintaining autonomy, unity and identity on behalf of a population deemed by some of its members to constitute an actual or potential "nation".'[18] Smith also demonstrates that nationalism can be 'cultural' (i.e. based on a claim of ethnic, linguistic, or general cultural unity) or 'political' (centred around a desire to create a separate nation-state), or indeed both.[19]

That the United States has been, and continues to be, nationalist, is almost a truism. The country fought for political self-determination, and has continued to reaffirm its cultural identity in a nationalistic manner, through a variety of movements from racist Nativism and the ideology of 'Manifest Destiny' to multiculturalism and 'American exceptionalism'. However, some scholars suggest that, in the case of Canada, such nationalism has not been so much in evidence. One contemporary examination of the potential for nationalism in Canada has stated that '[i]n many ways the term Canadian nationalism is an oxymoron. The geographical size of Canada and the diversity of its people have conspired to inhibit any strong manifestation of nationalism.' According to this account, Canada contains four distinct groups of peoples – the First Nations, the Anglophone Canadians, the *Quebecois*, and recent immigrants – and, with the exception of the immigrants, it could be argued that 'each of the other three groups

---

17   Ibid., p. 6. See also Paschalis M. Kitromilides and Georgios Varouxakis, 'The "Imagined Communities" Theory of Nationalism', in Athena S. Leoussi (ed.), *Encyclopedia of Nationalism* (New Brunswick, NJ, 2001), p. 137.

18   Anthony D. Smith, 'Nationalism', in Leoussi (ed.), *Encyclopedia of Nationalism*, p. 224.

19   Ibid., p. 223.

considers itself a distinct nation.'[20] The only *bona fide* nationalism to be found in Canada, in the view of this account, is that of Quebec. Other nationalistic expressions of Anglophone Canada are virtually all 'anti-American' in tone: 'What has spurred Canadian nationalism more than anything else has been a fear that once cultural and economic sovereignty disappear, political independence will soon follow.'[21]

While there is no doubt that anti-Americanism has been an integral part of English-Canadian nationalism, it is not thoroughly accurate to state that there has been no other form of nationalism worth considering in the short history of Anglo Canada. The study reveals that, like American nationalism, expressions of Canadian nationalism have existed, and have undergone many transitions. Most significant to this study is the surge of nationalistic spirit which arose in Canada during the years surrounding 1967, the year in which the country celebrated the Centennial of Confederation. During this era, for example, the nationalism exhibited in the country was, though not without anti-American overtones, often highly optimistic and future-focused in its outlook. It celebrated a country which was diverse and multicultural (this aspect was stressed partially because of rising *Quebecois* dissent) and which possessed, and could enhance much further, a rich cultural life. The quest to produce music that was distinctly 'Canadian' became especially significant in Canada during the late 1960s, and this would have a crucial impact on folk and popular music in the country.

Therefore, shifts in thinking about national identity and the nation in both Canada and America from the early to the late 1960s form a crucial foundation of this study. In comparing Canada and America, the aim is not to make evaluations as to which country produced 'better' music, or which revival was more 'authentic'. While the concerns of Canadians regarding the perceived threat of their mighty southern neighbour, and the many ways in which Canadians did emulate and embrace American culture, are vital considerations, ultimately the study aims to look at the various ways in which the two countries thought about and perceived themselves and their folk music, and each other, during a particularly eventful period of history.

Defining 'Folk' and 'Folk Music'

Defining a category such as 'folk music' with precision presents further difficulties. Similar to the treatment of Canada and America, the aim here is not to elucidate every sub-category contained within the *genre* of 'folk music', but rather to examine the changing ways in which this highly evocative yet ambiguously defined generic category has been defined and redefined, particularly in the popular imagination. During the 1960s and 1970s, just as thinking about national identity altered in Canada and America, common understanding of 'folk music' shifted and broadened significantly. The 'folk revival' movement, which reached its zenith during the

---

20 'Canadian Nationalism', in Alexander J. Moytl (ed. in chief), *Encyclopedia of Nationalism: Volume II: Leaders, Movements and Concepts* (San Diego, CA; San Francisco, CA; New York; Boston, MA; London; Sydney; Tokyo, 2001), p. 68. (No author is credited for this entry.)

21 Ibid., p. 69.

early 1960s, was the principal reason for this; it was at this time that, in the words of musician John Cohen, folk music 'interfaced with popular culture' and became entangled with the growing phenomenon of adolescent and youth musical culture.[22]

To arrive at a precise definition of the generic category of 'folk music' is no easy task, although the term is widely used, and is often superficially understood to signify music that is in some way belonging to a particular ethnic, regional or historical group, or music which employs 'traditional' or acoustic instrumentation to give it a quieter, simpler texture than the sounds of rock music. Musical instruments associated with the folk tradition vary according to country and/or region. However, in the North American context, and, particularly in the context of the folk revival of the 1960s, those instruments which were most frequently used included acoustic guitar, harmonica, banjo, mandolin, autoharp, violin, and accordion.

An intuitive, simplistic understanding of folk music as merely 'traditional' and 'acoustic', however, belies the more complicated history of the use of the general term 'folk' as an adjective and category within the study of culture. 'Folk' is essentially a constructed term, a European invention of the industrial era. According to Simon J. Bronner, the nineteenth-century British antiquarian scholar William J. Thoms was the first to employ the term 'folklore' in his writings.

Thoms advocated the studying of 'the lore of the people' and the viewing of traditional 'custom' as 'a primitive predecessor of civilised "manners"' to illustrate "the irrationality of the "lower stages of progress"' and emphasise 'the rude or crude otherness of the folk'.[23] Bronner links Thoms' interest in 'the folk' to the nineteenth-century preoccupation with the 'primitive' and with theories of race and origin.

Prior to this, however, in the late eighteenth century, the German nationalist and philosopher-historian Wilhelm Gottfried von Herder had indicated the importance of peasant customs and lore to the creation of a nationalistic pride and culture. In his view, the tales and music of 'the folk' could 'provide the vitality and spirit which make for a truly national [culture]'.[24] Thus, from the late eighteenth century onwards, 'folk' was a term associated with a scholarly, upper-class understanding of 'lower classes' or 'ordinary people', apparently depending, as Bronner has indicated, upon their 'otherness'. While William Thoms considered them as an inferior category of people whose behaviour was retrogressive and linked to the 'primitive', and von Herder viewed them admiringly, if perhaps condescendingly, as the picturesque creators of a 'raw' national culture, both men perceived 'the folk' as 'essentially those who preserved an older way of life within an urban and literate society', as an unlearned, pre-industrial group of people whose customs and culture would not, and should not, change even as the dynamic, industrialising society altered around them.[25] Although the culture of 'the folk' was considered vital to the understanding

22	John Cohen, 'Overview', in Cohen (ed.), *Wasn't That a Time!*, p. 25.

23	Quoted in Simon J. Bronner, *Following Tradition: Folklore in the Discourse of American Culture* (Logan, UT, 1998), p. 16.

24	Gene Bluestein, *The Voice of the Folk: Folklore and American Literary Theory* (Cambridge, MA, 1972), p. 6.

25	Ian McKay, *The Quest of the Folk: Antimodernism and Cultural Selection in Twentieth-Century Nova Scotia* (Montreal & Kingston; London; Buffalo, NY, 1994), p. 12.

of a nation's character – von Herder would claim that 'peasant customs said more about what was intrinsic to the "people" or the "nation" than did the customs of, say, workers or the aristocracy' – this theory of its importance was entirely the creation of privileged men, without the contribution or the agency of 'the folk' themselves. [26]

This one-sided understanding of the significance of 'the folk' would continue throughout the nineteenth century and into the twentieth century, when the activities of the major pioneers in folksong collecting were at their peak. The American ballad collector Francis James Child, the British collector Cecil Sharp, and later, in the United States, John A. Lomax and, in Canada, collectors such as Helen Creighton, would all approach their subjects with various preconceived notions about folk culture and about what constituted a useful and 'pure' example of the music of their respective nations. Francis James Child, whose study of British folk ballads culminated in the publication of the highly-influential *English and Scottish Popular Ballads* in 1898, decreed that there were in existence 305 ballads in the British Isles which were 'pure' and 'authentic' examples of songs emanating from an ancient, illiterate culture. All others encountered, he appeared to suggest, must be 'corruptions' from the 'modern era'. Child's canon would be, for many years, the perceived authority on British folksong and also the ultimate example of approach to folksong collecting. His biases would reflect in the work of subsequent collectors such as Helen Creighton and George Lyman Kittredge. The work of John Lomax is considered a departure from such strictures – he focused on the collection of what he perceived to be quintessentially 'American' music, in particular, cowboy songs and African-American music – but revisionists of his career, such as Jerrold Hirsch, have detected in his work much of the latent racism, 'conservative romanticism' and concern with 'purity' which have also been perceived in the work of the earlier, more overtly Anglo-centric collectors.[27]

From the 1930s onwards, the understanding of the concept of 'the folk' began to broaden, particularly in the North American context. Amidst the difficulties of the Great Depression, the various Federal Cultural Projects encouraged a re-emphasis on the variety of American regional and ethnic cultures.[28] Meanwhile, the 'Popular Front' policy of the Communist Party in this period began to extol the virtues of the people's customs and culture rather than view such things as submissive means of escaping harsh reality.[29] During this time, the advent and increasing influence of mass communications also enabled more performers to be heard by larger numbers of people, and so folk music began to leave the pages of the academic thesis and become part of performance culture, particularly in America. ('Purists', who continued to extol the virtues of the conservative approach of Child et al., would take

---

26 Ibid., p. 12.

27 Jerrold Hirsch, 'Modernity, Nostalgia, and Southern Folklore Studies: The Case of John Lomax', *Journal of American Folklore*, 105 (1992): 183–207.

28 Simon J. Bronner, *American Folklore Studies: An Intellectual History* (Lawrence, KS, 1986), p. 97. See also Alfred Haworth Jones, 'The Search for a Usable American Past in the New Deal Era', *American Quarterly*, 23/5 (1971): 710–24.

29 See Michael Denning, *The Cultural Front: The Labouring of American Culture in the Twentieth Century* (London and New York, 1996).

issue with such 'popularisers', continuing to insist that the songs must be performed by singers originating from the same culture as the music; such attitudes would continue to exist throughout the duration of the 1960s revival.)

It was in the left-leaning, less rigid subcultural climate of the decades surrounding the Second World War that the folk music revival, which would reach its apex in the 1960s, began to take shape. Folk music was, by the post-war period, firmly established as the favoured musical form of the left-wing intellectuals of the urban north, and groups such as the Almanac Singers, featuring Pete Seeger and Woody Guthrie, and solo singers such as Paul Robeson, Burl Ives and 'Aunt' Molly Jackson, performed at, and participated in, workers' rallies and union meetings. 'Hootenannies' and square dances were already a fixture in urban left-wing circles during the 1940s. People's Artists Inc. was formed in 1946 to promote folk music as the chosen expressive form of the 'progressive entertainer' and to organise with more efficiency the participation of folk singers in political rallies and workers' demonstrations.[30] Groups such as The Weavers, which also featured Pete Seeger, reflected the popularisation of folk song, made possible by the efforts of People's Artists and by the growing influence of sound recordings; The Weavers also boasted a markedly internationalist and eclectic perspective in their choices of music, performing Israeli, South African and American songs. Meanwhile, Woody Guthrie, proudly proclaiming his identity as a 'dustbowl balladeer' from Oklahoma, reflected the nascent pride in regional origins which originated in the Depression years.

The grip of Anglo-centric scholars and folklorists upon folk music scholarship and activity was beginning to lessen by this period too. By mid-century, people from a wider variety of social and ethnic backgrounds would become crucial influences on the development of folk music scholarship, recording and performance, and would play a central role in the folk revival of the post-war years. Among these people, there was a particularly large number who were of (frequently left-wing and secular) Jewish origin, from Moses Asch, the founder of Folkways Records, to record producer Kenneth Goldstein, and Israel Young, who began the Folklore Center on MacDougal Avenue, Greenwich Village, in the late 1950s. Although such figures entered the world of folk music proudly aware of their Jewish roots, they did not promote a personally ethnocentric understanding of folklore, but were, rather, interested in 'dedicat[ing themselves] to the process by which others mediated understandings across cultural boundaries'.[31]

In the 1960s, when the folk revival was in its 'boom' period, to employ the term used by Neil Rosenberg, Ellen Stekert, a folklorist and participant in the folk revival, outlined a new definition of folk music to accommodate the eclecticism and fluidity, and the differences of opinion and controversy, which characterised the movement from the 1940s onwards.[32] She outlined four principal strands within the generic category of 'folk' as it existed in 1966, identifying firstly the 'traditional

---

30   Serge Denisoff, *Great Day Coming: Folk Music and the American Left* (Urbana, IL; Chicago, IL and London, 1971), pp. 118–19.

31   Peter D. Goldsmith, *Making People's Music: Moe Asch and Folkways Records* (Washington, DC and London, 1998), p. 5.

32   Neil Rosenberg, Introduction to Rosenberg (ed.), *Transforming Tradition*, p. 2

singers', those who could be said to belong clearly to, and musically represent, a particular regional and ethnic tradition, then she spoke of the 'imitators' who desired to dedicate their lives to replicating the sounds, the lifestyle, and the appearance of the traditional singers. The 'utilizers' were the popularisers, those who had adapted 'folk' styles to make them palatable to an urban audience, and, finally, the 'new aesthetic' performers were those who built on the foundations of traditional folk music to create their own, unique, eclectic style, partly 'art music' and partly 'folk music'.[33]

Arguably, the 'new aesthetic' group of which Stekert wrote, a group consisting of performers such as Joan Baez, Judy Collins, Peggy Seeger, and their successors, such as James Taylor, Paul Simon, Janis Ian and Don McLean, among many others, was essentially responsible for the ultimate widening of the definition of 'folk music'. Their compositions, often employing folk song structures and traditional instrumentation, but nonetheless new, married the traditional idea of the folk song to the modern idea of commercial popular music.

Thus, tracing the historical development of the idea of 'folk' and 'folk music' reveals that the term has been fluid and that its meaning has changed and altered over time. It is perhaps most useful, then, for the purposes of this study, to accept a definition of folk music which is in the spirit of that of Ellen Stekert – broad, fluid and perhaps at times contradictory. However, a sense of the development of, and the changes in, the definition of 'folk music' as a category is equally essential to this study, as conflicts between the historically minded preserver and the adventurous creative punctuated the folk revival from the 1950s until well into the 1970s and even beyond.

Understanding the Relationship between National Identity and the Folk Revival

Neither the Canadian nor the American folk revivalists considered the movement to be purely 'American', despite its origins in the United States. Rather, the folk music revival began, basically, as a North Eastern American urban phenomenon, and spread from city to city throughout the entire continent and beyond, to Western Europe. In the early 1960s, folk music was very much an urban neighbourhood phenomenon, rooted in specific locales; as Nicholas Jennings has pointed out, the cities, though inspired by similar music, were each unique, and this resulted in the creation of equally distinct folk music neighbourhoods and culture.[34] A study of two of the most important folk music centres of the 1960s, Greenwich Village, NYC and Yorkville in Toronto demonstrates this clearly.

Participants of the folk revival were drawn generally from similar backgrounds in both Canada and America – folk music enthusiasts were usually young people of middle-class background, many of whom were university students. In 1945, both Canada and America had emerged from war considerably wealthier than the

---

33   Ellen Stekert, 'Cents and Nonsense in the Urban Folksong Movement: 1930–66', reprinted in ibid., pp. 84–107.

34   Nicholas Jennings, in discussion with the author, 2 December 2002.

countries of Europe and East Asia which had been embroiled in the conflict. One indirect consequence of this was the creation of a post-war generation of North American children brought up in affluence and aware of their collective identity as a generation. In the early decade, these children of the 'baby boom' were infected by the idealistic, liberalist tenor both of contemporary politics and of folk music culture, which made them anxious to discard the increasingly commercialised rock 'n' roll music of their early teens and embrace the music of social significance.[35]

It could be argued that the social protest aspect of folk music was largely an American export to Canada, furthered in Canada by the many visits of socially conscious American singers such as Joan Baez, Richie Havens and others to Canadian coffee-houses, and by the messages found in revival periodicals such as *Sing Out!* or the song compilation periodical *Broadside*.[36] This contention, as well as the precise extent and nature of the impact of liberal politics and social protest on the Canadian revival, will be investigated thoroughly in the study. However, the revival was more than mere political protest. It was also, simultaneously, a rediscovery (albeit partly the result of the left-wing celebration of 'the people's music') of apparently 'obscure' forms of folk music, often from less economically developed, but culturally 'rich', areas such as the Maritime Provinces in Canada or the Appalachians in America. This was an interest which captured the imaginations of Canadians and Americans alike.

Indeed, vital to any understanding of the folk music revival in America and Canada is recognition of the important role played by regionalism, and the concept of region, in folk music activity in the post-war period. Regionalism complicates any simplistic understanding of nationhood; it is a geographically based and place-specific interpretation which illustrates the limits of viewing America and Canada as binary opposites or as purely political entities. There are persuasive studies which argue that those wishing to seek and explain differences within North America should first examine the considerable regional variations of the continent (which manifest themselves from east to west rather than from north to south) rather than continue to insist that the existence of the Canadian-US border holds the answer to their queries. For example, the journalist Joel Garreau wrote in 1981 about the 'nine nations of North America', dividing the continent according to its distinctive geography, from the coastal regions of New England and the Canadian Maritimes to the mountainous landscape of British Columbia and the American Rocky Mountains.[37]

In both America and Canada, the concept of the region played a vital role in the urban rediscovery of folk music in the post-war period. In the years preceding, and during, the peak period of the folk revival, performers and enthusiasts exhibited a

---

35   See Robert Cantwell, 'When We Were Good: Class and Culture in the Folk Revival', in Rosenberg (ed.), *Transforming Tradition*, p. 42.

36   The Canadian revival periodical, *Hoot!*, was markedly less political than the American periodicals. It is also worth noting, however, that *Broadside* contained many protest songs by British writers concerning British social and political situations.

37   Joel Garreau, *The Nine Nations of North America* (New York, 1981). Jeffrey Simpson discusses the merits of Garreau's semi-serious work in *The Star-Spangled Canadians*, pp. 40–42.

fascination for the regions of their continents, and for the musical 'treasures' that the more remote places might hold. Ian McKay has noted the fascination for the Maritime Provinces held by many central Canadians, and the fixation which urban American youth from the northern cities exhibited for the South, especially the Appalachian region, and the West, is well documented.[38] The resurgence of interest in folk music and 'the folk' was crucially bound up with a 'sense of place', a sense of regional diversity.[39] Revivalists, many of whom, both Canadian and American, were, as has been stated, civil rights and social activists with idealistic dreams of an integrated society, set much store by the concept of unity in diversity, and so the exhaustive exploration of regions and provinces of their countries was a natural manifestation of their idealistic politics. While the political folk revivalists were critical of the policies of their native land, ultimately their explorations of cultural and regional diversity represented, in many ways, a pride in the cultural wealth of their nation, and an optimistic faith that political and cultural change could be attained through working within the existing system.

The impulse to explore and uncover regional music was also the legacy of the earlier, pioneering folklorists such as Barbeau, Creighton, Lomax and Charles Seeger; many young revivalists, Canadian and American – Sheldon Posen, Pauline Greenhill, Ellen Stekert, Neil Rosenberg, Ronald Cohen and Archie Green to name but a few – would go on to pursue doctoral studies and academic careers in folklore as a result of their experiences in the revival. Many of the especially dedicated revivalists devoted themselves to the mastery of one particular type of music – be it Bluegrass, Gaelic singing, Elizabethan balladry or Appalachian fiddle music – and allowed themselves to be absorbed into the culture and world of their chosen style of music. This process, which Stekert called 'imitation', was, and remains, controversial – debates over the 'authenticity' of such musicians and their art continue among scholars and in folk music circles, forming one of the most crucial aspects of folk revival discourse.[40]

By the late 1960s, in both countries, this fixation with regional and cultural diversity as an expression of national pride and idealism would become, overall, less important in folk music expression as political events changed revivalists' perceptions of their native countries. The folk revival, as a cohesive movement, (if, indeed, it had ever existed as such), would splinter, and the meaning of folk music would alter to signify very different things for Canadians and Americans. If, in the early 1960s, Canadians and Americans had seemed vaguely similar in their overall political beliefs and aims, by the late decade the two nations were perceiving each another very differently. While generational conflict and internal strife, largely caused

---

38 Mackay, *The Quest of the Folk*. See also David Whisnant, *All That is Native and Fine: The Politics of Culture in an American Region* (Chapel Hill, NC and London, 1983), and Benjamin Filene, *Romancing the Folk: Public Memory and American Roots Music* (Chapel Hill, NC and London, 2000).

39 Barbara Allen and Thomas J. Schlereth, *Sense of Place: American Regional Cultures* (Lexington, KY, 1990).

40 See, for example, the essays by Sheldon Posen, Burt Feintuch and Neil Rosenberg in Rosenberg (ed.), *Transforming Tradition*.

by the Vietnam War, brought about a crisis in the United States, the celebration of one hundred years of Confederation afforded Canada the opportunity to redefine herself and reflect on the meaning of her existence as a nation.

In 1967, Canada celebrated the centennial of the Confederation, an event which was commemorated by an unprecedented surge of 'euphoric nationalism'.[41] This was the first major Canadian national celebration which was not tied in some way to the country's British roots, and the commemorations emphasised the country's youth, future promise and potential – Expo 67, hosted very successfully by Canada in Montreal, was perhaps the epitome of the underlying theme of the celebrations. The prevalence of such a positive outlook in Canada marked a sharp contrast to the growing dissent and discord in the United States in the late 1960s.[42] Draft resisters began to flee from America to Canada, while those young people who remained at home began to express dissatisfaction with their country's actions in Vietnam, expressions which grew increasingly hate-ridden, and which reached a bloody climax at the Chicago Democratic Convention of 1968. While Canada was attaining a newfound strength, American society was apparently disintegrating, 'split asunder' as never before.[43]

By the late 1960s, the cultural meanings surrounding one's identity as a 'Canadian' or as an 'American' had altered profoundly, and the effects of such an alteration on the folk revival movement, and on folk music in both countries, would be equally momentous. Anti-authoritarian sentiment among the young in the US helped to bring about an end to the folk revival in its early-decade, idealistic format; simultaneously, as folk music entered the mainstream pop culture, largely after Bob Dylan's notorious 1965 Newport performance, it became part of the general *melange* of styles that formed 'rock' music, and, by the early 1970s, the meaning of 'folk' had changed again.

The climate of optimistic nationalism in Canada would have a similar, disintegrating effect on the Canadian revival. In the years surrounding the Canadian Centennial, the growing nationalistic desire to ameliorate the underdeveloped state of the Canadian domestic music industry led to the passage of the Canadian Radio Television Communications Commission's 'Canadian Content' regulation in 1971. The regulation stipulated that some thirty per cent of all music played on radio stations should be 'Canadian' in origin. The Commission believed firmly that such a move would naturally create and nurture a distinctive and recognisably 'Canadian' popular music. While the legislation assisted many musicians to pursue their careers from within their native land, the creation of a viable music industry inadvertently brought

---

41   Robert A. Wright, 'Dream, Comfort, Memory, Despair: Canadian Popular Musicians and the Dilemma of Nationalism, 1968–1972', in Beverley Diamond and Robert Witmer (eds), *Canadian Music: Issues of Hegemony and Identity* (Toronto, 1994), p. 283.

42   This 'positive outlook', as will be demonstrated in Chapter 4, was not shared by all Canadians, although the media promoted Centennial fervour rigorously. Aboriginal peoples and the poorest communities, as well as Quebec separatists, had little to celebrate in 1967.

43   Douglas T. Miller, *On Our Own: Americans in the Sixties* (Lexington, MA, 1996), p. 176.

about an overriding concern, even obsession, with the creation of a 'Canadian sound' in popular music, a preoccupation that remains to this day.

In many respects, it was the success of Canadian folk musicians that had brought about the creation of the 'Cancon' ruling; nationalists pointed to the success of erstwhile Yorkville 'new aesthetic' performers such as Neil Young, Joni Mitchell, Gordon Lightfoot and the Tysons both to illustrate Canadian musical success, and to lament the fact that these talented artists had been forced to seek recording contracts in the United States. The idea that the 'folk sound' bespoke something 'uniquely Canadian' was born during this nationalist period and continues to be expressed even today, even though many of the most successful Canadian new aesthetic musicians are often ambivalent to such an association. However, the centralisation of the music industry in Canada, and the popularisation of folk music during the 1970s had a fatal impact on the Canadian folk revival. As the Canadian music industry became increasingly focused on the creation and maintenance of national trends in music, the early folk revival's embracing of regionalism and eclecticism, and the energy of local folk music scenes, waned. As in America, folk music, as defined during the revival, became an ingredient of mainstream popular music, and those who sought to maintain the eclectic spirit of the old revival began to look elsewhere for inspiration.

The interest in revivals of specific musical styles would continue throughout the rise and fall of the revival movement, but it was in the early 1970s that these revivals would grow particularly strong and would find a showcase at an ever-increasing number of folk festivals across the continent. Arguably, the revival of interest in such styles of music as Klezmer or Bluegrass or Maritime music during the 1970s did not represent a continuation of the enquiring eclecticism of the early years of the previous decade, but was, rather, largely symptomatic of the reactionary self-absorption of the so-called 'me decade'. It appeared, in some ways, to be a personal quest for roots and a display of nostalgia for the romanticised world of one's forebears, real or adopted, as well as a reaction against the alleged, often-lamented banality of the music industry and its heavily commercialised character.

To outline the link between national identity and the folk revivals in America and Canada is to narrate a complicated tale, a tale considerably more nuanced and complex than the brief outline provided above. However, the various chapters of the study are intended, collectively, to paint a detailed picture of an eclectic movement and its effects on the culture of two similar, yet different, nations.

Chapters

The structure of the study is basically chronological, with the development of the revivals in Canada and America traced from the immediate post-war years to the late 1970s. The majority of the work focuses, however, on the 1960s. The first chapter outlines the origins of the revival in Canada and America from the late nineteenth century onwards, looking at the activities of early folklore enthusiasts of Canada and America and their philosophies on their subject as well as on their native land. In addition, this chapter endeavours to uncover the roots of the discourse linking national, and regional, identity to folk music. The second chapter discusses the immediate background to the so-called 'great boom' of folk music in North America in the post-war period, and outlines some of the major characteristics of the pre-1965 revival in Canada and America. Particular attention is paid to the regional and multicultural focus of much of the folk music during this time, and to the cultural and social reasons for this focus, as well as to the extent to which such reasons applied, or otherwise, in Canada. Owing to the proliferation of local folk music 'scenes' during the early 1960s, Chapter 3 is devoted to a comparison of some of the most important of these, with a particular focus on Greenwich Village, NYC, and Yorkville, Toronto, two of the major magnets for young North American folk enthusiasts during this period, and on the unique culture, or subculture, which these neighbourhoods helped to foster within their respective cities. It could be argued that the folk music communities of these cities represented attempts to manifest the revival's ideas of 'unity in diversity', and true community, in reality. Chapter 4 chronicles the changes which were undergone by both folk music and American and Canadian society after 1965, and the impact which these had on the respective revival movements and on the understanding of what folk music meant to each society. This chapter also discusses the resurgence of interest in ethnic music, and the cultural significance of such a renaissance for society and culture in the 1970s. The fifth and final chapter provides an epilogue in its examination of the development of the idea of the folk since the 1970s, particularly the consequences and significance of the development of 'world music'.

Resources on the Folk Revival

There exists a wealth of primary material both on the folk revival and on overlapping and related subjects. The American Folklife Center in the Library of Congress in Washington, DC, holds much vital information on the revival, including rare periodicals such as *Promenade* (from the 1940s), and *The Little Sandy Review* (from the late 1950s and early 1960s), numerous song books and anthologies from the revival era, and a large collection of vertical files on many of the figures, major and minor, of the movement. Among the most notable holdings of the Folklife Center are correspondence between folklore collector John Lomax and the performer Leadbelly, both of whom were foundational figures in the development of the revival; selected letters of folk musician Woody Guthrie, and an invaluable series of extensive tape-recorded interviews between folklore student Richard Reuss and Israel Young, owner of the Folklore Center in Greenwich Village and general commentator on the revival movement. These interviews were recorded sporadically between 1965 and 1969, and contain a wealth of vital and original information and insights.

The recordings of the principal artists of the revival are still widely commercially available. More obscure recordings can be found in major music libraries. The Central Branch of the Toronto Public Library holds a particularly impressive collection of old LPs of folk musicians, as does the National Library of Canada, which is legally required to hold copies of virtually any recording with Canadian participants.

Periodicals and magazines are another vital primary source, from magazines specifically about the revival, such as *Sing Out!*, *Broadside*, the more commercial *Hootenanny* and the Canadian *Hoot!*, to more general music magazines such as *Rolling Stone*, *Billboard* or the Canadian *RPM*, to newspapers and magazines which carried extensive coverage of the music 'scene' such as *Time*, *Newsweek*, *Village Voice*, *Maclean's*, *Saturday Night* and the *Toronto Telegraph*.

While previous research on the American revival has made available a wealth of information, primary and secondary, and made archived primary sources easier to trace, the lack of scholarship on the Canadian side makes the location and finding of primary sources more problematic. The National Library of Canada, Ottawa, contains a large collection of vertical files on many of the prominent Canadian folk musicians. The University of Toronto's Music Library holds a considerable number of Canadian Music Periodicals from the 1960s and 1970s. Clipping files on folk artists and folk music are also to be found in the Central Branch of the Toronto Public Library, and the Urban Affairs Branch of the Toronto Public Library contains information and articles on the history of Yorkville, the 'folk music neighbourhood' of Toronto. The Canadian Broadcasting Corporation (CBC) Archives also hold some interesting material – particularly television and radio news items on Yorkville and on the CRTC 'Canadian Content' ruling – much of which is now accessible online.

Perhaps the richest primary source at the revival historian's disposal is that of first-hand accounts. Folk revival musicians and participants can provide highly articulate and thoughtful accounts of their involvement in the movement which often skilfully weave personal anecdotes with more general observations and theories about the significance and the meaning of the revival. Again, several American first-person accounts and anthologies of reminiscences have been published, but no such comprehensive or scholarly compilation exists on the Canadian side.[44]

I have conducted a number of interviews with Canadian revival musicians and participants, including musician and Mariposa Festival co-ordinator Ken Whiteley, participant and 'Yorkville-goer' Brian Walsh, musician Michael Van Dusen, festival organiser and journalist Richard Flohil, Mariposa organiser Estelle Klein, and participant and author Nicholas Jennings. Jennings himself has done much to promote the memory of Yorkville; he gathered a number of important interviews when researching his popular history of Yorkville, *Before the Gold Rush*, some of which appear, in edited versions, in his book, others which he described to me during my own interview with him.[45] Other musicians and revival participants have provided more brief recollections via e-mail or telephone – these include Merrick Jarrett, a revival musician from the Prairies, Arthur Wenk, a musician who was active in student protest in the United States, Judith Cohen, a former Montreal revival

---

44   For example, Cohen (ed.) *Wasn't that a Time!*, Robbie Wolliver's *Bringing it All Back Home* (New York, 1986), and Eric Von Schmidt and Jim Rooney, *Baby Let Me Follow You Down: The Illustrated Story of the Cambridge Folk Years* (Garden City, NY, 1979). The only exception on the 'Canadian side' is a rather random, but interesting anthology of stories told at the Mariposa Folk Festival. See Bill Usher and Linda Page-Harpa, *For What Time I Am In This World: Stories from Mariposa* (Toronto, 1977).

45   Nicholas Jennings, *Before the Gold Rush*.

participant who now teaches at York University, Toronto, and John Leeder, former editor of the *Canadian Folk Music Bulletin*. Folksinger and former editor of *Sing Out!* Happy Traum, *Woodstock Times* editor and former revival participant Brian Hollander, and musician Tom Pacheco have discussed their roles in the movement, and Edward McGhee, a Scottish folk revival participant with a strong interest in the music of the North American revival, provided some insights on the movement from a 'trans-Atlantic' perspective.

Many newspapers and magazines of the 1960s and 1970s also contain interviews with revival musicians. The Toronto Public Library's vertical files hold a number of newspaper interviews with such musicians as Ian Tyson, Gordon Lightfoot, Neil Young and Stan Rogers. *Maclean's*, an influential Canadian periodical, also interviewed musicians sporadically. *Rolling Stone* magazine published particularly insightful interviews throughout the late 1960s and early 1970s; subjects of 'The Rolling Stone Interview' included David Crosby, Joan Baez, Bob Dylan, Paul Simon and many other significant former folk revival musicians.

Existing Scholarship

The first academic histories of the American folk revival were written in the immediate aftermath of the 1960s. These largely emphasised the left-wing nature of folk music activity and linked its growth in popularity to the social and political changes of the 1960s. R. Serge Denisoff's *Great Day Coming: Folk Music and the American Left* was a particularly formative work, a concise history which traced the roots of 'folk consciousness' to the rural South and in the Communist subcultures of the urban North, and recounted the development of the revival from the Depression Era to the end of the 1960s and the decline in popularity of *Sing Out!* as the ideals of the original revival lost touch with a changing reality.[46] Also in 1971, Richard Reuss completed his doctoral thesis on American folk music and left-wing politics from the 1920s to the 1950s; his work stopped short of discussion of the revival's 'great boom' of the 1960s, but, in doing so, made it very evident that the seeds of the revival had been sown by the urban left-wing intellectuals of the northern cities, and thereby emphasised the political aspects of folk music activity above all else.[47]

In 1976, Jerome Rodnitzky published *Minstrels of the Dawn*, his study of four of the central figures of the 'folk-protest' movement – Joan Baez, Phil Ochs, Pete Seeger and Bob Dylan. For Rodnitzky, who had already published a short work on folk music and left-wing politics, 'popular protest music' had been 'a radical politico-cultural influence since 1945', and he lauded the four subjects of his study as masters of protest song and heroes of a generation.[48] Little was said, in any of these works, about the complexity of the revival or about its many components as

---

46   R. Serge Denisoff, *Great Day Coming*.

47   Richard A. Reuss with JoAnne C. Reuss, *American Folk Music and Left-Wing Politics, 1927–1957* (Lanham, MD and London, 2000), adapted from Richard Reuss's doctoral dissertation, submitted to Indiana University in 1971.

48   Jerome L. Rodnitzky, *Minstrels of the Dawn: The Folk-Protest Singer as a Cultural Hero* (Chicago, IL 1976). See 'Popular Music as a Radical Influence, 1945–1970', in Leon

outlined by Stekert in the mid-1960s; as early histories, these works essentially outlined and analysed the basic developments of the movement – its origins, its initial success and its crumbling after the failure of peaceful protest tactics and the advent of folk-rock.

The next major wave of scholarship on the revival occurred in the early 1990s. As those revival participants who had been inspired by the movement to enter academia began to reach middle age, they attained new perspectives on the revival and were now able to view it with hindsight and with the benefit of their scholarly expertise in the fields of folklore and musicology. The major publication of this decade was the volume of essays edited by folklorist Neil Rosenberg, entitled *Transforming Tradition: Folk Music Revivals Examined*. Many of those contributing to this volume, including Rosenberg, had also participated in the Indiana University Conference of May 1991, given in memory of the late folklore scholar Richard Reuss, in which revival stalwarts recounted their memories of the revival. Far from being fond, anecdotal reminiscences and random memories, the speeches given at the conference were both personal and scholarly in tone. Speakers such as Joe Hickerson outlined the many areas of the revival which were yet to be examined by scholars, while other participants passionately, even bitterly, re-aired debates which were now thirty years old.[49] However, the papers presented at the conference, collated in the volume *Wasn't That a Time!*, represented a marked shift in focus from early scholarship on the revival. Perhaps because those who participated in the conference had all been active in the 1960s revival, they approached their subject with a degree of passion and a precision, an attention to detail, that was missing from the 'overview approach' taken by earlier works. A wide spectrum of people gathered for the conference – from performers such as John Cohen, the Kossoy sisters and Len Chandler, to magazine founders and editors, such as Irwin Silber of *Sing Out!* and Jon Pankake of the eccentric *Little Sandy Review*, to stalwarts of the New York scene, most notably Israel Young, founder of the significant Folklore Center of Greenwich Village. All of those who participated had different, yet complementary, stories to narrate, and all were important figures in the revival; equally important, however, was the fact that these individuals had not become 'celebrities' like Seeger, Dylan or Baez, on whom earlier scholars had focused. Although essentially a primary source, comprised of first-hand accounts, *Wasn't That a Time!* helped to shape the future direction of revival scholarship. Those who were now creating the narrative were all, with few exceptions, former revivalists with some exposure to academia and/or scholarly methodology. Their work would be tinged with passion and commitment, and sometimes with bias and prejudice, but, above all, these scholars were able to provide a more nuanced, more detailed, and less celebrity-focused approach to the history of the revival.

Borden Blair (ed.), *Essays on Radicalism in Contemporary America* (Walter Prescott Webb Memorial Lectures) (Austin, TX and London, 1972).

49   John Cohen and Lou Gottlieb re-engaged in the 'purist/commercialist' debate. Transcripts of speeches given at the conferences are found in Cohen (ed.), *Wasn't That a Time!*.

Transforming Tradition is, arguably, the epitome of this approach. It, too, is the work of a number of very different scholars with differing approaches, but its essay-volume format enables a wide range of varied, yet complementary, subjects to be discussed. It is this work which makes full use of Ellen Stekert's model for understanding the folk revival; not only does the book reprint her 1966 essay, with an updated commentary by Stekert herself, but it also borrowed from her multi-faceted understanding of the revival as the theoretical foundation of the book. *Transforming Tradition* discusses, in turn, the 'new aesthetic' (that is, the work of those who adapted the folk genre to their own purpose) and 'named-systems revivals' (revivals of specific types of music, including as Bluegrass, the Blues, and Northumbrian pipe music).[50] The inclusion of the latter is especially important, as, hitherto, there had been little discussion of this aspect of the revival by scholars.[51] One particularly important issue for the contributors is the concept of 'authenticity' in the revival: this focuses on debates regarding which party has 'the right' to sing certain types of music and of questions arising from an imitator's performance of traditional music belonging to another culture. Theoretically sophisticated, prodigiously detailed and furnished with an excellent bibliography, *Transforming Tradition* firmly established new foundations on which to construct future folk revival scholarship.

Since the publication of *Transforming Tradition*, two full-length monographs on the revival have been published. The first, Robert Cantwell's *When We Were Good: Class and Culture in the Folk Revival*, was published in 1996, mingling historical detail of the revival with very personal, quasi-artistic interpretation.[52] In 2002, Ronald D. Cohen published *Rainbow Quest: The Folk Revival and American Society*.[53] The fruit of many years of labour, the book is Cohen's *magnum opus*, representing, once again, both his position as a revivalist and his viewpoint as a scholar. The book is, again, impressively detailed, although it is, essentially, a reasonably straightforward, chronological history of the movement.

Other scholars have written extensively on the revival as part of broader histories or of studies with a slightly different focus. One of the most important of such works is Benjamin Filene's *Romancing the Folk: Public Memory and American Roots Music*, published in 2000.[54] Again focusing primarily on the concept of 'authenticity', Filene discusses the work of folklorists, record producers and leading musicians of the twentieth century in shaping public understanding of what constitutes 'true' folk music. Included in his study are discussions of the careers of Pete Seeger and Bob Dylan, and an account of the complex relationship between John and Alan Lomax and the African-American singer Huddie Ledbetter ('Leadbelly'), all of which are central to the folk revival.

---

50   Stekert would have called 'named systems' revivalists 'imitators'. The term 'named systems' was devised by Neil Rosenberg.

51   Some histories of individual named-systems revivals had been published, however, such as Neil Rosenberg's excellent *Bluegrass: A History* (Urbana, IL and Chicago, IL, 1985).

52   Cantwell, *When We Were Good*.

53   Cohen, *Rainbow Quest*.

54   Filene, *Romancing the Folk*.

There exists a proliferation of studies on all aspects of American popular music, and many of these discuss issues relating to the folk revival. Some of the most significant of these include Bill C. Malone's *Country Music, USA*, a comprehensive survey of the genre which discusses revival-influenced country performers such as Ricky Skaggs and Emmylou Harris, and Charlie Gillett's *The Sound of the City*, which remains a seminal study of the various influences found within rock music.[55] There have also been some studies of individual 'named systems' revivals, in particular, Neil Rosenberg's study of Bluegrass and Mark Slobin's recent examination of the development of Klezmer music in America.[56] Victor Green's *A Passion for Polka* is a study of old-time ethnic music in America which has some bearing on aspects of the various ethnic music revivals of the 1970s.[57]

As has been stated, there has been little written on the Canadian folk revival. Essays by Pauline Greenhill, Sheldon Posen and Anne Lederman in *Transforming Tradition* concern Canadian subjects, but there exists no comprehensive survey of the Canadian movement, even in article format.[58] Robert A. Wright's excellent essay 'Dream, Comfort, Memory, Despair: Canadian Popular Musicians and the Dilemma of Nationalism' remains one of the few works to incorporate any discussion of the Canadian revival. His focus, however, is on those prominent Canadian musicians such as Joni Mitchell, Neil Young and Gordon Lightfoot, who were lauded by the press for their 'Canadianness' yet had, fundamentally, attained success by co-opting and adapting the American folk-protest tradition to create their own unique, ambivalent, neither pro-Canadian nor anti-American, perspectives on the contemporary political scene. Wright's argument is a very important one, and one which will be discussed later in the study. However, his work continues to stand alone as one of the few attempts to analyse and understand the Canadian folk scene at this time. Barry K. Grant's "Across the Great Divide: Imitation and Inflection in Canadian Rock Music" is, like Wright's essay, a piece on general popular music, but it, too, concerns itself with many of the new aesthetic folk performers, including Gordon Lightfoot and Neil Young, illustrating the ways in which Canadian performers exhibit their identity by displaying the fact that they are 'not American'.[59] Again, Grant's theory will be discussed in greater detail later in the study. However, these general accounts of Canadian folk music in short articles essentially represent the extent of scholarly discussion of the revival. A large amount has been produced on Canadian folk and

---

55   Charlie Gillett, *The Sound of the City: The Rise of Rock 'n' Roll* (New York, 1971).

56   Mark Slobin (ed.), *American Klezmer: Its Roots and Offshoots* (Berkeley, CA, 2002).

57   Victor Green, *A Passion For Polka: Old-Time Ethnic Music in America* (Berkeley, CA, 1992).

58   I. Sheldon Posen, 'On Folk Festivals and Kitchens: Questions of Authenticity in the Folksong Revival'; Pauline Greenhill, '"The Folk Process" in the Revival: "Barrett's Privateers" and "Baratt's Privateers"'; Anne Lederman, '"Barrett's Privateers": Performance and Participation in the Folk Revival'. These last two essays both concern a song popularised by Canadian folk musician Stan Rogers. All appear in Rosenberg (ed.), *Transforming Tradition*.

59   Barry K. Grant, 'Across the Great Divide: Imitation and Inflection in Canadian Rock Music', *Journal of Canadian Studies*, 21/1 (1986).

popular music by more general writers, however. Much of this is of dubious quality: popular histories such as Martin Melhuish's *Oh What a Feeling* or the volume of reminiscences *Shakin' All Over* are largely anecdotal and unquestioningly laudatory in their tone, and the large number of artist biographies published by Quarry Press in Kingston are of a similar nature.[60] Nicholas Jennings's history of Yorkville is the exception in this body of popular literature; well researched and written, it is a worthwhile and important account of the neighbourhood during its years as a centre for folk and rock 'n' roll music.

Other scholarly works have skirted around the topic of the folk revival without discussing it directly, but serve as important signposts and foundations for building knowledge. Ian McKay's *Quest of the Folk*, an account of the reinvention of Nova Scotia as a romanticised, pre-modern wilderness, is one such example. The book contains an extensive analysis of the career of folklorist Helen Creighton, whose collections of Maritime folk music, later published, would become important to revivalist musicians and scholars alike. McKay's work also recounts Creighton's brief dealings with Pete Seeger and her loathing of his left-wing sympathies. His book is important not only in its discussion of Canadian folklore as a developing discipline, but also for its treatment of issues of authenticity and agency surrounding Maritime culture.

Other scholarly studies which are useful in understanding the Canadian revival include Doug Owram's *Born at the Right Time: A History of the Baby Boom Generation in Canada* and Denis W. Johnston's *Up the Mainstream: The Rise of Toronto's Alternative Theatres*.[61] Although both these works deal with very different subjects in considerably different ways, both address the central issue of the relationship between youth in Canada and America during the 1960s, assessing the extent to which the former imitated the latter, and the differences exhibited between the two. Johnston's study also includes some discussion of the impact of draft-resisters on Torontonian, and Canadian, society, and, conversely, on the appeal of Canada for dissenting young Americans during the late 1960s.[62]

This study makes two major contributions to revival scholarship. First, it provides a trans-national focus for the folk revival, examining conditions in both America and Canada, and, second, it focuses centrally upon a particular theme – that of nation and national identity – as a lens through which to view the North American revival movement. The study owes much to the detailed approach taken by Ronald Cohen in *Rainbow Quest*, and, in particular, to the content and style of *Transforming Tradition*. This essay anthology illustrates, with depth and skill, the nature and extent of the folk revival's many facets and aspects. However, the central theme of 'nation'

---

60   Peter Goddard and Philip Kamin (eds), *Shakin' All Over: The Rock 'n' Roll Years in Canada* (McGraw-Hill/Ryerson Press, 1989); Martin Melhuish, *Oh What A Feeling: A Vital History of Canadian Music* (Kingston, Ont., 1996).

61   Doug Owram, *Born at the Right Time: A History of the Baby Boom Generation in Canada* (Toronto; Buffalo, NY; London, 1996) and Denis W. Johnston, *Up the Mainstream: The Rise of Toronto's Alternative Theatres* (Toronto, 1991).

62   See also Frank Kusch, *All American Boys: Draft Dodgers in Canada from the Vietnam War* (Westport, CT, 2001).

and 'national identity' provides a new means of interpreting and rationalising the tremendous diversity of the movement.

Most significant, however, is the fact that this study focuses on both Canada and America. Not only is it hoped that this will help to contribute something of substance to the little-examined field of Canadian folk revival studies, and Canadian popular music studies in general, but it is also hoped that the adoption of a North American focus, rather than confirming fears that such a focus will put Canada at a disadvantage, will, on the contrary, enrich and enhance understanding of both the United States and Canada during what was a pivotal time in their respective, and shared, histories.

Chapter 1

Defining the People's Songs: National Identity and the Origins of the North American Folk Music Revival to 1958

Introduction

This chapter both provides some of the background to the blossoming of the folk revival's 'great boom' in the late 1950s, and examines some of the earlier associations, forged by folklorists, scholars, artists and performers, between the concepts of nation and national identity and folk music. The folk revival of the late 1950s and early 1960s in both Canada and America promoted a view of nation as mosaic of eclectic regional and ethnic cultures and tremendous variety. This chapter endeavours to illustrate how this vision emerged in both countries.

First, this chapter discusses the development of an 'American' focus for folklore studies in the United States – this was an important progression which helped to pave the way for the folk revival. Before the early decades of the twentieth century, when fieldworkers and folklore specialists began to realise that there was a 'folk culture' in America worthy of study, specialists in the United States had been greatly influenced by the Harvard literature scholar Francis James Child. He died before being able to complete his own critical introduction to his study of English and Scottish ballads, and some of his pupils, interpreting his findings, were led to the conclusion that any vernacular music of worth in America had been transplanted from Britain. Child created a canon of ballads which met very narrow criteria which he had established, and he appeared to dismiss all other songs and musical forms of America as inferior. Thus, the idea that all American folk music worthy of consideration was inherently 'British' prevailed into the twentieth century.

Such a British-centric view of folk culture also prevailed at this time in Canada, a country fully independent yet still emotionally and culturally tied to its former motherland. The folklore of Helen Creighton and other Maritime specialists promoted the notion that, in this region above all, British customs and culture had been carefully preserved.

Challenges to the primacy of British-centric interpretations of folklore were mounted by various folklore fieldworkers who became active in the early decades of the twentieth century. Most prominent of these fieldworkers in America was John A. Lomax. Through his studies of Texas cowboy musical culture, other working-class cultures and songs of the South and West, and – particularly significantly – the music of the Southern African-Americans, Lomax illustrated not merely that these regions of the United States were rich in folklore heritage, but also that this folklore was alive and thriving, as opposed to being confined to the pages of a history textbook. Lomax also, through focusing on the 'folk' of the Western and Southern states, helped to begin a trend in folklore activity which would influence the folk music revival: namely, he assisted in the creation of the belief that it was in these regions, among black and white communities, that 'America's folk' were to be found.

The idea that the South and the West were major sources of distinctly 'American' folklore would also be enhanced by cultural activities and theories during the devastating economic depression of the 1930s. Historians have noted that, during the Depression, a mood of introspection and self-analysis prompted a new focus on American culture, particularly that of the 'ordinary people'.[1] The cultural 'projects' of the Roosevelt government's New Deal programme, organised by the Works Progress Administration (WPA), reflected this new direction. The Federal Writers' Project published guides to every individual state which were rich in detailed information on culture, geography, history and folk customs. Painters and musicians working for the WPA drew inspiration from folk idioms and local cultures. Again, it was upon the South and West that artists and public focused in particular; this region, which was affected badly by the economic blight, was recast in this period as the home of America's suffering but noble 'folk', a people who had held on to their simple values and customs. This focus would play an important part in the folk revival in subsequent decades.

However, the Federal Writers' Project was not merely concerned with the domestic American 'folk'. Another of the most significant of its contributions to the folk music revival of the 1950s and 1960s was its groundbreaking emphasis on a broader interpretation of America's ethnic and racial diversity. Through various publications and studies, the FWP aimed to paint as detailed a picture of the United States as possible – one which acknowledged and celebrated the ethnic variety of the country, and which took interest in the culture and customs of, among others, African-Americans, Chicanos, and the many peoples of Europe who had emigrated to America. More than any other participant of the Project, it was folklorist and collector Benjamin Botkin who promoted and explored this diversity and multiplicity. His several volumes of American folklore, multi-regional and multicultural in approach, were popular and highly influential. They also helped to shape an optimistic, celebratory and eclectic approach to folklore which would be adopted by the folk revival of subsequent decades.

In the Canadian context, the work of prominent folklorist Marius Barbeau, and events such as the multi-ethnic 'railway concerts', served to challenge the myth of British primacy over Canadian culture, and to acknowledge, recognise and even celebrate the growing diversity of the country. Although the concerts did not acknowledge non-Caucasian groups in Canada, they did highlight *Quebecois* culture, Ukrainian and Polish culture in the Prairie Provinces, and the cultures of some of the

---

1   See Jerrold Hirsch, *Portrait of America: A Cultural History of the Federal Writers' Project* (Chapel Hill, NC and London, 2003); Jerre Mangione, *The Dream and the Deal: The Federal Writers' Project, 1935–1943* (Boston, MA and Toronto, 1972); and Michael Denning, *The Cultural Front: The Labouring of American Culture in the Twentieth Century* (London and New York, 1996).

ethnic groups of Britain (Scottish and English) in Ontario. The concerts, therefore, helped to establish the notion that Canada was a mosaic of many peoples.

Finally, in examining the immediate context for the revival, this chapter discusses the adoption of folk music by the urban left-wing movements from the 1930s onwards. Again, this group would look to the American regions for inspiration – the South-west, Midwest, and the Southern states. In lauding American indigenous customs and culture, the left-wing activists sought heroic worker-figures from these regions, and focused on musicians such as Woody Guthrie, who had grown up in poverty in Oklahoma, and who composed songs on themes of social justice and workers' rights. Urban musicians in Canada and America – including significant numbers of Jewish North Americans – began to experiment with folk music styles, and by the late 1950s, the seeds of the folk music revival of the subsequent decade had been sown.

This chapter provides a synthesis of many of the cultural forces, activities and events which were foundational to the post-1945 folk revival in both Canada and America. This chapter also demonstrates that, in diverse ways, folklore collectors and scholars, Federal Arts Project Workers and inter-war, leftist folksingers promoted a vision of North America as a place of great cultural diversity. They professed a love for the detailed and the specific in their explorations of the many cultures of their nations. This vision of the nation as a tapestry of diverse, rich cultures would become central to the post-Second World War folk music revival.

The Ballads of Francis James Child: British-American Folk Music

Although the theories of Johann Gottfried von Herder, which maintained that the 'ordinary people' and their customs revealed more about a country's national character than did any expressions of 'high art', were admired by writers and scholars in both Britain and the United States, it was not until the latter half of the nineteenth century that folklore began to gain in popularity as a subject of study in America itself.[2] Influenced by the activities of British folksong collectors, particularly Cecil Sharp, scholars such as Francis James Child and his pupil, George Lyman Kittredge, began to involve themselves in the study and classification of folksongs. The rise in popularity of folksong collecting and scholarship at this time could certainly be attributed, in part, to the sentiments of general *malaise* brought about by rapid social and economic change and unprecedented industrial growth. According to the scholar T.J. Jackson Lears, this uneasiness manifested itself in a surge of anti-modernism in (principally) British and American literature and the arts, of which the 'rediscovery' of 'the folk' was a significant part, as were, among other things, a resurgence of interest in such subjects as Arthurian legends and mythology, medieval romance and chivalry, interest in the 'Orient', and handcrafts.[3] Thus, according to Lears,

---

2   Simon J. Bronner, *Following Tradition: Folklore in the Discourse of American Culture* (Logan, UT, 1998), p. 16; Gene Bluestein, *The Voice of the Folk: Folklore and American Literary Theory* (Cambridge, MA, 1972), p. 12.

3   T.J. Jackson Lears, *No Place of Grace: Antimodernism and the Transformation of American Culture, 1880–1920* (New York, 1981).

troubled and disorientated upper middle-class writers and intellectuals found value in an idealised concept of a pure folk culture which had remained grounded in rural values and had survived the onslaught of industrialism.

Partially as a result of such anti-modernist intellectual and psychic trends, turn-of-the-century American academics and writers were inspired to participate in the exploration of folklore. However, other particular concerns and biases were initially inherent in their interpretations of the subject. The publication of Harvard academic Francis James Child's *The English and Scottish Popular Ballads* in 1898, a significant milestone in folksong scholarship in both Europe and in America, provided a list of some 305 British ballads which the author deemed 'pure' and 'authentic' examples of the genre.[4] This group of classified ballads became known as 'the Child ballads', and would cast a formidable shadow over subsequent folk music studies both in North America and in Europe. Pupils of Child, such as George Lyman Kittredge, came to the conclusion that Child believed the ballad to be an historical artefact, unable to be surpassed by subsequent song traditions. As Simon J. Bronner has shown, Child and his pupils were greatly influenced by the methodology and theories of the Brothers Grimm from Germany, whose renowned collection of fairy tales was inspired, in part, by the belief that 'the folk tradition' had been the victim of modernism, and was now extinct. The collected folksongs, therefore, belonged to a now-vanished past; they were 'remnants of ancient types rather than examples of living performances'.[5]

Because Child was the first English Literature professor of Harvard University, his theories wielded considerable influence. Folklorists of future generations would be obliged either to concur or to disagree with the concept of what folklorist D.K. Wilgus termed the 'Child/Other dichotomy' when discussing the folk music of Britain and America.[6]

Child's canon also helped to perpetrate the notion that the purest forms of American vernacular music were those ballads which had been transplanted to America, and which were still preserved in remote parts of eastern America, particularly the 'Anglo-Saxon' populated Appalachians. Many early folklorists exhibited no interest in, or appreciation for, American adaptations of British songs, hybrid songs, or the songs of other immigrant, ethnic and racial groups. Some interpretations of Child's canon, as Benjamin Filene has noted, would help to maintain the myth, also propagated by British folksong collector Cecil Sharp in his own work in Appalachia, that American culture was basically British in its roots and development.[7]

Of equal significance, however, was the fact that, for folklorists of the Child/ Sharp school, this 'pure' and 'British' folk music existed particularly abundantly in the Appalachian region of the South. In maintaining the image of the sparsely

---

4   Francis James Child, *The English and Scottish Popular Ballads*, edited by Helen Child Sargent and George Lyman Kittredge (Boston, MA, 1904).

5   Bronner, *Following Tradition*, p. 223.

6   Ian McKay, *The Quest of the Folk: Anti-modernism and Cultural Selection in Twentieth-Century Nova Scotia* (Montreal; Kingston; London; Buffalo, NY, 1994), p. 20. See also Benjamin Filene, *Romancing the Folk*, (Chapel Hill, NC and London, 2000), p. 21.

7   Filene, *Romancing the Folk*, p. 25.

settled, rural Appalachian region as an insulated bastion of English and Scottish culture, Cecil Sharp, William Wells Newell, and other Child followers assisted in the creation of a pervasive and lingering myth regarding this portion of the country, a myth that would be preserved well into the inter-war period.[8] Furthermore, as will be demonstrated, the South became a favourite region for folk music collectors throughout the twentieth century, and during the folk music revival of the post-Second World War era.[9] It is, therefore, to the followers of Sharp and Child that the special interest in the South, an interest which would prove so central to folk music studies and revivals throughout the twentieth century, can directly be traced.

The reasons for folklorists' insular and conservative focus on the 'British' culture of the Appalachians may, perhaps, lie in the highly polarised attitude towards 'high' and 'low' culture in existence at the turn of the twentieth century. As Lawrence Levine has shown convincingly in his influential study *Highbrow/Lowbrow: The Emergence of Cultural Hierarchy in America,* from the second half of the nineteenth century onwards, a formerly fluid and classless approach to the arts in America became polarised and highly stratified.[10] Levine argues that, after the mid-century, riots and unrest at operas, plays and other cultural events created an enhanced sense of class identity and urged cultural promoters to cater more exclusively for the rich. As a result, art forms such as opera and classical music became 'high culture', the property of the upper classes in America; European, rather than indigenous American, performers were preferred, and domestic cultural forms were frequently denigrated and considered inferior. It is possible to take issue with Levine's sweeping view of the construction of nineteenth-century culture, but it could be plausibly argued that an increasing sense of elitism surrounding the arts may have prompted turn-of-the-century Child followers to sort vernacular songs into categories of 'acceptable' and 'unacceptable', based on criteria partially borrowed from nineteenth-century beliefs concerning what was 'proper' in American art. As Benjamin Filene has shown, Child's refusal to consider the 'broadsides' (printed popular songs distributed among the people in early modern Britain) in his collection may have been based on such a concept; because they had been printed, they did not possess the 'purity' of the

---

8   David Whisnant's study, *All That is Native and Fine: The Politics of Culture in an American Region* (Chapel Hill, NC and London, 1983), deals with the history and development of this perception of the Appalachians. See also Jane Becker, *Selling Tradition: Appalachia and the Construction of an American Folk, 1930–1940* (Chapel Hill, NC and London, 1998).

9   It should be pointed out, at this stage, that the South was not the only region to be romanticised and stereotyped as a stronghold of British culture during the early twentieth century. Dona Brown, in her work *Inventing New England: Regional Tourism in the Nineteenth Century* (Washington, DC and London, 1995), has shown that the tourist industry of New England was prone to mythmaking of a similar nature. This will be discussed again subsequently. However, as the remainder of this chapter, and the next chapter, will demonstrate, it was to the South and West that folklorists and post-war folk revivalists would continually turn for inspiration, and so a particular emphasis will be placed on Southern and Western myths and stereotypes.

10   Lawrence Levine, *Highbrow/Lowbrow: The Emergence of Cultural Hierarchy in America* (Cambridge, MA, 1988).

canonical ballads which dated from the pre-printing press era.[11] Child denounced broadsides as merely 'products of a low kind of *art*', and he maintained that 'most of them are, from a literary point of view, thoroughly despicable and worthless.'[12] Contemporary attitudes about what was proper and worthwhile in art certainly seemed to influence the supporters of the Child canon.

Child and his followers were also, undoubtedly, influenced by the growing sense of *malaise* in the United States concerning the diverse groups of peoples immigrating to the country in the decades surrounding the turn of the century. T.J. Jackson Lears discusses the 'racial and class anxieties' of middle- and upper-class Americans in the late nineteenth century; he notes that increasing immigration, as well as the belief that the 'Anglo-Saxon' race had become 'overcivilised' and alienated from its roots in a hardier, more rugged world, provoked fears of either 'race suicide' for British-Americans or the 'revolutionary overthrow' of the existing order by dissenting immigrant groups.[13] Folklorists such as Cecil Sharp responded to such anxieties by propagating the notion that the only American folk music worthy of consideration and study was that which could be traced directly to Great Britain. They excluded other ethnic and racial groups – such as Southern and Eastern European Jews and Catholics, African-Americans, Irish Catholics, and Chicanos – from the narrative of American folk culture, unwilling even to acknowledge their validity.

Nation and Regional Folklore in Turn-of-the-Century Canada

Canadian folklorists working at the turn of the century would also exhibit a strong preoccupation with the 'Britishness' of the folklore of their country. This is, perhaps, not surprising; middle-class, Protestant Canadians at the turn of the twentieth century were strongly conscious, and proud, of their 'British' identity. Their links to Britain were, of course, tangible: since the Confederation of the Canadian provinces in 1867, the country had remained a dominion of Britain. Furthermore, while immigration of non-British groups was steadily increasing in Canada, the English, Scottish and Protestant Irish influences on the culture of the English-speaking portions of the country remained dominant.

However, for Canadians from the most influential sectors of society, to call oneself a British subject was more than merely adopting a derivative identity. Carl Berger's seminal study of Canadian imperialism during the period 1867–1914 has shown that, for some Canadians, belief in the British Empire was by no means incompatible with the expression of fervent Canadian nationalism. Indeed, according to Berger, 'for imperialists the sense of nationality and the ideal of imperial unity were interlocked and identical.'[14] The imperialists, who were largely white, male Protestants of

---

11   This was the interpretation of pupils such as George Lyman Kittredge; whether Child intended this meaning is subject to debate, according to D.K. Wilgus. See *Anglo-American Folksong Scholarship*, p. 33.

12   Quoted in Filene, *Romancing the Folk*, p. 13.

13   Lears, *No Place of Grace*, pp. 28–30.

14   Carl Berger, *The Sense of Power: Studies in the Ideas of Canadian Imperialism, 1867–1914* (Toronto and Buffalo, NY, 1970), p. 49.

British extraction, believed that the British Empire provided the best framework within which the Canadian nation could develop and grow. It would be within the Empire that Canada would attain maturity and strength – sufficient strength to ward off threats, real or imagined, from the uncouth republic to the south.[15] As Berger notes, 'Canadian imperialism rested on an intense awareness of Canadian nationality combined with an equally decided desire to unify and transform the British Empire so that this nationality could attain a position of equality within it.'[16] Thus, to be Canadian, and to be a British Subject simultaneously, was not a contradiction for imperialists who believed that the mother country could help to fulfil the ambitions and potential of the former colony.

The imperialists promoted a dual vision of themselves as British and Canadian, and, as a natural consequence of this, they considered their Canadian identity to be synonymous with their ethnic identity as Britons. Berger points out that one of the strongest advocates for Imperialism was the United Empire Loyalist Association (UELA), a group which grew in strength and in influence during the late nineteenth century, and which served to promote strongly the 'Britishness' of Canadian nationalism at this time. The centenary of the Loyalist landings in Canada was celebrated in 1884, and commemorations were held across the country, particularly in Ontario and in the Maritimes.[17] The UELA became inundated with applications for membership from people who desired to partake in the 'indigenous British-Canadian national feeling' prompted by the celebrations.[18] Norman Knowles, who has studied the ways in which the Loyalists have been invented and reinvented over time, notes that, in the late nineteenth century, the group was conceptualised by its descendents as 'a principled and cultured elite', a superior and learned body of people who removed themselves from the corruptions of revolutionary America to seek refuge in the more civilised, British North.[19] Those who celebrated in 1884, and those who flocked to join the UELA, endorsed this ideal vision of their ancestors and expressed pride in the cultivated 'Britishness' which they had allegedly exhibited. Therefore, largely unquestioned assumptions of the white, Protestant, British-centric character of English-speaking Canada permeated the culture of the nation in the late nineteenth century.

It was at this time, at the turn of the century, that the first fruits of the labours of Canadian folklore enthusiasts and specialists were in evidence. Their foci and interests were narrow and place-specific, and were not, at this stage, concerned with wider or national perspectives. However, much of their work would exhibit, by default, an overwhelming preoccupation with British folk culture in Canada. Like Sharp, Canadian folklorists had their favourite regions, areas of the country which

---

15 During the 1870s, as Berger notes, Canada languished in economic depression, which forced the country to acquiesce to a Reciprocity Treaty with America; this eliminated tariff barriers between the countries, provoking fears that the annexation of Canada by America could follow. (See *The Sense of Power*, pp. 3–5.)

16 Ibid., p. 49.

17 Many Loyalists, who remained faithful to the British crown during the American Revolution for a variety of reasons, left America and moved to Canada.

18 Berger, *The Sense of Power*, p. 78.

19 Norman Knowles, *Inventing the Loyalists* (Toronto; Buffalo, NY; London, 1997), p. 5.

they perceived as treasure-troves of unique folklore. Of all regions to be scrutinised, the Maritime Provinces, considered to be among the most prominently 'British' of the provinces in culture and character, were dominant. From the 1890s onwards, Newfoundland academics and writers composed short studies of the rich culture of their native region; Ernest S. Kirkpatrick compiled a volume of *Tales from the St. John River* in 1904; Mary Fraser and Archibald MacMechan completed work on the folklore of Nova Scotia in the 1920s and 1930s.[20] These folklorists presented a view of the Maritimes that shared many characteristics with the conservative folklorists' perception of Appalachia – the Maritime Provinces were, in their view, rural, unspoiled strongholds of a preserved British culture.

To suggest that Canadian folklorists working in the early decades of the century were solely concerned with Anglo-centric folklore is to overlook the important work completed by the influential folklorist Marius Barbeau, who specialised in Native culture and in the tales and songs of his native Quebec, or of Franz Boas, who studied Native cultures on the Pacific north-west coast of Canada, adopting the American anthropological models of study.[21] Nevertheless, in spite of the varied interests exhibited by folklorists such as Barbeau and Boas, Canadian folklore collectors were generally biased in favour of music and lore which could be traced to Great Britain.

One of the most influential and prominent of the Canadian Maritime folklorists of the early twentieth century was Helen Creighton.[22] A specialist in the culture of Nova Scotia whose career was at its peak in the 1920s and 1930s, she seemed, at least in the view of historian Ian McKay, to be the very embodiment of many of the presumptions and biases of Canadian folklore enthusiasts at this time. According to McKay, she was one of a number of Canadian Maritime folklorists who remained staunchly 'more conservative, more Anglocentric, and more fiercely essentialist' than any others in their approaches to folklore. McKay states that Creighton's focus on Nova Scotia was of a profoundly anti-modernist nature; her biased and prejudiced approach to folksong collecting helped to create a lingering but false image of Nova Scotia as a place of pre-industrial 'innocence', a homogeneous Scottish province which had been little affected by change, and which consisted largely of fishermen and rural workers imbued with an ancient but nobly primitive cultural and musical tradition.[23] In many respects, therefore, if Ian McKay's analysis is accurate, Creighton was to Nova Scotia as the Sharp/Child school was to Appalachia.[24]

---

20   Archibald MacMechan, *Tales of the Sea* (Toronto, 1947); Ernest Stanley Kirkpatrick, *Tales of the St. John River and Other Stories* (W. Briggs, 1904).

21   These are just a representative few of the many scholars and writers mentioned in Carole Henderson Carpenter, *Many Voices: A Study of Folklore Activities in Canada and their Role in Canadian Culture* (Ottawa, 1979), pp. 21–87.

22   For samples of Creighton's work, see Pauline Greenhill, *Lots of Stories: Maritime Narratives from the Creighton Collection* (Ottawa, 1985) and Rosemary Bauchman (ed.), *The Best of Helen Creighton* (Hantsport, Nova Scotia, 1988).

23   McKay, *The Quest of the Folk*, pp. 43–152.

24   Interestingly, in her memoir, *A Life in Folklore*, Helen Creighton declared that she had managed to find, in Nova Scotia, some 43 variants of the elusive Child Ballads; she considered this 'a feather in her cap'. (See Bauchman (ed.), *The Best of Helen Creighton*, p. 97.)

While some folklorists have considered McKay's revisionist study of Creighton to be excessively detractive, it sheds some light on the nature and scope of folklore studies in Canada.[25] Folklore activity was thriving, and studies of regional and community folklore abounded – and the activities of Canadian folklorists tended, through examination of specific regions such as the Maritimes and Ontario, to betray the belief that British culture remained the predominant, and most worthwhile, influence upon Canadian folklore.

The Fieldworkers' Visions

Francis James Child's disciples and Canadian folklorists such as Helen Creighton may have betrayed similar biases and prejudices regarding the culture of their respective regions and countries of study. However, while Child was a scholar of the printed word, who analysed his ballads as texts rather than as living entities, Helen Creighton, from the subsequent generation, was an active collector and fieldworker. Many fieldworkers, aided by the newly-available tape-recording machine, helped to revolutionise folklore studies and collecting during the early twentieth century, principally through their frequent perception of folk song as a dynamic and vibrant force.[26] Rather than study a printed text or second-hand recording, they travelled around to collect songs and interact with the traditional singers. They revelled in the uncovering of obscure and 'hidden' cultures of Canada and America, rejecting the bald theorising of academics in favour of a love of specificity, interaction and detail.

Fieldworkers, as will become evident, would exert a pivotal influence on the urban folk music revival movement of the 1940s onwards. This was particularly true of American folklore collectors such as Carl Sandburg, John and Alan Lomax, and, subsequently, Pete Seeger.[27] Their adventurous collecting trips became sources of great inspiration to urban young people, in both Canada and America, who yearned for authentic experience.[28] Their collections of songs also formed the backbone of the repertoire of the urban folk revival performer. Furthermore, they helped to reinforce the regionalist and eclectic perspective which the subsequent revival would

---

25   The concerns of folklorists regarding the treatment of their 'ancestor figure' Creighton are outlined in Archie Green's review of *Quest of the Folk* in *Canadian Historical Review* 77/1 (1996): 122–5. A different, feminist, scholarly perspective on Creighton was attained by Diane Tye in her article '"A Very Lone Worker": Woman-Centred Thoughts on Helen Creighton's Career as a Folklorist', *Canadian Folklore Canadien* 15/2 (1993): 107–17. This article focused on the position of female fieldworkers like Creighton in a world of academic folklore and anthropology which was dominated by men.

26   However, Creighton did not possess this fieldworker's vision of vibrant folklore. In spite of her fieldwork, she remained convinced that Nova Scotian folklore should be static and preserved.

27   Carl Sandburg, song collector and poet, first published his anthology of folksong, *American Songbag* (San Diego, CA; New York; London, 1990, 2nd edn) in 1927.

28   John Lomax's autobiography was, in fact, entitled *Adventures of a Ballad Hunter* (New York, 1947).

come to possess, because their art lay in uncovering the obscure, hidden details of American culture. Not content to accept the notion that 'the true folk' were only to be found in Appalachia, they wandered beyond the boundaries which had been imposed, travelling throughout the South, and also in the West and South-west. In doing so, they began to redefine the American folk. No longer were the white Appalachian balladeers the only worthwhile 'folk' of America; John Lomax would boldly challenge such a notion by advocating firmly that African-Americans were of fundamental significance to American folk music. Lomax was by no means a selfless or unbiased racial egalitarian. However, his recognition of the central importance of the music and culture of black Southerners would change the course, and scope, of folk music studies in America, and would, ultimately, have a profound impact on the post-Second World War folk music revival.

The work of the Lomaxes and Carl Sandburg in folk music collecting also offered new methods of understanding folk music's 'sense of place'. The Lomaxes and Sandburg saw 'a folk' that was on the move, migrating throughout the southernmost and westernmost regions of the country. This more fluid interpretation of 'the folk' would come to influence the music of the post-Second World War folk revival considerably.

The Work of John Lomax

Of the various fieldworkers who were active in the early portion of the twentieth century, it was arguably John Lomax (1867–1948) who would become the most significant, as far as influence on the subsequent folk music revival was concerned.[29] Having spent much of his childhood in Texas, John Lomax grew up with a fascination for the music of the cowboys who worked in the area surrounding his home. His abiding love for the culturally distinctive music styles of his native land led him to a view of folksong that was in direct contradiction to the views of Child and his disciples. As Benjamin Filene has said, folk traditions, to Lomax, did not have to be ancient remnants of a past world – nor did they remain static. Lomax believed that 'traditional American music remained vibrant, creative, and essential to American life.' He also rejected the reliance upon written text which had been so central to the Child tradition, and conducted his folksong research by undertaking 'fieldwork' trips and tape-recording traditional performers – a technique which served to enhance further the impression of folk music as living and vibrant.[30] Lomax also, ostensibly, 'democratised' American notions of folk music by insisting upon the merits of the songs of the 'ordinary American people', and he exhibited a particularly strong interest in songs associated with occupations. He was eager to track down the music of, among others, miners, railroaders, soldiers, sailors, down-and-outs, and cowboys, and to understand them, if not completely on their own terms, then on terms which were broader in definition than those of Francis James Child. Child was concerned with song texts and their relationship to British-American culture, but Lomax was

---

29   Much of my discussion of Lomax and his dealings with Leadbelly is informed by Benjamin Filene's excellent study, *Romancing the Folk,* pp. 47–75.

30   Ibid., p. 55.

better able to accept folk music as the music of human individuals who were more than merely retainers of borrowed traditions.

The biggest contribution made by John Lomax to the growing understanding of American folk music was his recognition of the importance of African-American music. Lomax was not the first folklorist to recognise the worth and significance of African-American music, but his unique field recordings emphasised the richness and vibrancy of this vital and distinctive cultural group.[31] Lomax maintained that African-American music was *central* to any understanding of national folksong, and in the 1920s and 1930s, accompanied by his son Alan (who would become a key figure in the folk revival from the late 1950s onwards), John Lomax made a tour of black communities in the South, searching tirelessly for musicians and informants. He even extended his search to chain gangs and maximum security prisons. It was in the Georgia State Penitentiary that Lomax found his most valuable source of African-American folksong: the convict Huddie Ledbetter, otherwise known as Leadbelly, who was serving a sentence for murder. After his release from prison, Leadbelly went to New York with John Lomax in the early 1940s, where he was provided with a recording contract and confronted with the increasing adulation of a new audience.[32] This audience was comprised of those who would eventually give rise to the folk revival movement – they were largely white, urban, middle-class intellectuals with left-wing sympathies, and, for them, Leadbelly was a hero, a walking songbook and the embodiment of their romanticised perception of the oppressed but noble Southern black man. He brought American folk music to life, and inspired many of his audience members – including singers such as Theodore Bikel and Pete Seeger – to become performers in their own right, thus aiding in the growth of the embryonic folk revival movement.

The work of John Lomax did indeed play a vital role in gaining appreciation for the music and culture of the 'ordinary people', especially that of the hitherto marginalised African-American communities. He urged folklore enthusiasts and students to accept American music on its own terms rather than constantly compare it unfavourably with older European traditions. The scholar Gene Bluestein, writing in the 1970s, praised Lomax for this contribution, pronouncing him a champion of the highest democratic values and recognising his emphasis on 'the virtues of the common man and the dignity of oppressed groups such as the Negro'.[33] Later scholars, however, took a closer look at some of Lomax's motivations and found some darker forces at work. Jerrold Hirsch, while acknowledging Lomax's importance in promoting African-American music, believed that his autobiographical account *Adventures of a Ballad Hunter* (1947) revealed a portrait of a fundamentally racist, paternalistic Southerner who was prepared to champion the rights of black people as long as they posed no threat to the racial status quo. He believed in the fundamental

---

31   Among the previous text-based collections of African-American folksongs were *Slave Songs of the United States* (1867) by William Francis Allen, Charles Pickard Ware, and Lucy McKim Garrison, and *The Book of Negro Spirituals* (1825) by James Weldon Johnson. See D.K. Wilgus, *Anglo-American Folksong Scholarship Since 1898*, p. 64 and p. 353.

32   This story is told in Filene, *Romancing the Folk,* pp. 47–75.

33   Bluestein, *The Voice of the Folk*, p. 105.

inferiority of black people and, though he admired their culture and hoped to see their difficult lot improved, he could not accept the idea that they deserved complete equality with whites.[34] Benjamin Filene, in examining in detail the intricacies of the relationship between Leadbelly and Lomax, has uncovered stories of financial and cultural exploitation. For example, Leadbelly, whom Lomax used as a house servant in New York, was ultimately forced to threaten Lomax with violence in order to recover his share of the profits from his recordings. Other stories reveal that Leadbelly was denied his own voice as an artist when in New York; Lomax had him perform in convict clothing or in work overalls in order to play the role of a dangerous, emotionally driven, racialised folk stereotype.[35] In his introduction to the anthology of Leadbelly's song, John Lomax recounts his initial encounters with Leadbelly, who was, he states, 'a friendless penitentiary Negro' when they first met; according to Lomax, the world of violence and murder from which Leadbelly came represented a veritable 'black epic of horrifics'.[36] There is much evidence to substantiate the claims of Hirsch and Filene that, to the Lomaxes, Leadbelly was an exotic being, a man whose misfortunes could be commodified and put to valuable use. However, the extent to which Lomax recognised and documented fully the music of African-Americans was highly significant, in spite of his biases and intentions.

Searching for 'the True Folk' in the South and the West in the 1920s and 1930s

In addition to his explorations of African-American folklore, John Lomax was also deeply interested in the music and culture of his native Texas. According to his biographer Nolan Porterfield, Lomax was fascinated by 'the image/mirage of Texas in its epic sense – rough and sprawling, dynamic, discordant, and glorious'.[37] This fascination set Lomax on the trail of other kinds of (principally white) American 'folk'. He set about exploring the music and lore of, among others, 'the cowboy, the miner, the tramp, the lumberjack, the Forty-niner, the soldier, [and] the sailor'.[38] The

---

34   Jerrold Hirsch, 'Modernity, Nostalgia, and Southern Folklore Studies: The Case of John Lomax', *Journal of American Folklore* 105 (1992): 183–207.

35   Filene, *Romancing the Folk*, pp. 47–76. Israel Young, a central figure in the New York folk scene, stated in an interview of 1965 that Leadbelly had been 'exploited' by the left: 'he'd be working for nothing … They'd be paying him nothing all the time. And he was really starving all the time' (1965, Interview by Richard Reuss. Tape-recording, 8 July. Box 1, Tape AFS 19,800. From the collection of the American Folklife Center, Washington, DC) The American Folklife Center also possesses a collection of handwritten letters between the Lomaxes and Leadbelly, including correspondence which discusses briefly a performance of Leadbelly's at the Village Vanguard in Greenwich Village, New York (no date provided). This correspondence is now available online at <http://lcweb4.loc.gov/service/afc/afc1933001> (accessed 17 February 2004).

36   John A. Lomax and Alan Lomax (editors, compilers and transcribers), *Negro Folk Songs as Sung By Lead Belly* (New York, 1936), p. x.

37   Nolan Porterfield, *Last Cavalier: The Life and Times of John A. Lomax* (Urbana, IL and Chicago, IL. 1996), p. 1.

38   John A. Lomax and Alan Lomax, *American Ballads and Folk Songs* (New York, 1994, original edn 1934).

songs of these groups were duly recorded and anthologised by Lomax and son.[39] The people who belonged to the 'categories' listed by Lomax were ordinary and poor, sometimes destitute, and their songs would never have met with the approval of more conservative folklorists – not merely because they were not Appalachian ballads, but also because the singers were migrants and travellers, people without clear or permanent roots. However, such people fascinated Lomax: their wanderings and isolation intrigued him. As Jerrold Hirsch states, 'from Lomax's point of view, American folklore was more than the remnant of Old World traditions. Rather, it was the creative response of the diverse American groups to their New World experience.'[40] Therefore, Lomax helped, once again, to create new ideas, and myths, about 'the folk' of the regions of America. He portrayed them as a group on the move, largely to be encountered wandering in the West or the South-west.

These myths of the folk persisted, as they were reinforced in the work of Carl Sandburg, a popular author who was a contemporary of Lomax and who was, by the 1920s, well established as a poet of the West.[41] Works such as *Slabs of the Sunburnt West*, published in 1922, presented poetic interpretations of many aspects of Midwestern and Western life, ranging from portraits of Chicago to depictions of Midwestern farmland and the Grand Canyon.[42] Sandburg's lifelong interest in Abraham Lincoln was reflected in his extensive historical biography of the former president, a work of some six volumes; the first two of these, entitled *The Prairie Years*, depicted Lincoln's youth in Illinois, and took pains to emphasise the 'earthiness' and folksy simplicity of the future president, 'set against an elaborate backdrop of his environment'.[43] Sandburg's 'mid-westernising' of Lincoln proved very popular, and his work was widely read. In the late 1920s, Sandburg turned folksong collector, and toured the country with a guitar, performing and amassing folk material of many varieties. Like John Lomax, Sandburg, too, was intrigued by the concept of migrating music – as his biographer Penelope Niven states, '[Sandburg] was curious about the vagrant past of songs which had made their way from overseas to the American highlands, prairies and frontier.'[44] The culmination of Sandburg's experimentations with folksong was the publication of *American Songbag* in 1927. Again, in words

---

39   See ibid.

40   Jerrold Hirsch, *Portrait of America: A Cultural History of the Federal Writers' Project* (Chapel Hill, NC and London: University of North Carolina Press, 2003), p. 29.

41   The importance of Carl Sandburg to the folk revival is discussed briefly in Ronald Cohen, *Rainbow Quest: The Folk Music Revival and American Society, 1940–1970* (Amherst, MA and Boston, MA, 2002), pp. 11–12. It should be noted, however, that Lomax and Sandburg are not the only collectors of regional folksong in this period. D.K. Wilgus gives a detailed listing of other folksong collectors working in the inter-war period in *Anglo-American Folksong Scholarship Since 1898*, pp. 123–239.

42   Carl Sandburg, *Slabs of the Sunburnt West* (New York, 1922).

43   Richard Crowder, *Carl Sandburg* (New York, 1964). For another dated but useful summary of Sandburg's interest in Western Americana, see Hazel Durnell, *The America of Carl Sandburg* (Washington, DC, 1965). Benjamin Filene also discusses Sandburg briefly in *Romancing the Folk*, pp. 44–5.

44   Penelope Niven, *Carl Sandburg: A Biography* (New York; Oxford; Singapore; Sydney/New York/Toronto, 1991), p. 444. For more information on Sandburg, see also Herbert

resembling those of Lomax, Sandburg stated that his anthology was 'not so much my book as that of a thousand other people, who have made its 260 colonial, pioneer, railroad, work-gang, hobo, Irish, Negro, Mexican, gutter Gossamer songs, chants and ditties'.[45] In Sandburg's list of people from whom his folksongs were taken, poor migrants of the Western frontiers were predominant. Southerners, South-westerners and 'ethnic' Americans also featured – all groups whose music had not been highly regarded until now. Therefore, like Lomax, Carl Sandburg helped to widen the boundaries of 'the folk', and also assisted in the creation of the idea that the 'true folk' of America were to be found in 'the regions' – especially the West, and also the Southern states.[46]

By the 1930s, the diversity and variety of American folk song had been widely acknowledged, and interest in the living performances of folksongs had eclipsed the overriding concern with text and melody exhibited by older folksong scholars. The Archive of American Folksong was established by the Library of Congress in 1928, and both its first director, Robert Winslow Gordon, and his successor, John Lomax, emphasised the importance of field recordings in demonstrating the breadth and variety of American folk song traditions.[47] The field workers' visions had, indeed, helped to transform understanding of, and appreciation for, American folk music.

The Great Depression, the Folk, and the Southern and Western States

The search for the 'true folk' of America would intensify in the 1930s, when, during the Depression, a new focus on the folk culture of America led many, especially from the urban North, to hanker after the mythical folk who wandered and subsisted somewhere in the semi-empirical, semi-mythical rural hinterland of the country. The cultural climate generated by the economic blight, and enhanced by the cultural 'projects' of Roosevelt's New Deal reforms, would celebrate 'the ordinary American', past and present, in a manner which almost bespoke a 're-Americanisation', or 're-democratisation' of art and culture. Once again, it was to the West and to the South that these Northerners would look most intently, encouraged by the regionalist art of

---

Mitgang (ed.), *The Letters of Carl Sandburg* (New York, 1968) and Philip R. Yannella, *The Other Carl Sandburg* (Jackson, MS, 1996), which discusses Sandburg's left-wing affinities.

45   Niven, *Carl Sandburg*, p. 453.

46   The geographical definitions of 'Southern states' and 'the West' at this time were often vague; however, generally, 'the South' refers to the ex-Confederacy states, including the upper South. 'The West' is even more imprecise – 'West' can encompass the desert South-west, the prairie Middle West, the plains of the North-west, and the far West of California. However, the historian Patricia Nelson Limerick accepts the vagueness of such a definition. 'West' she argues, was, literally, an ever-expanding term throughout the nineteenth century, and those regions which were considered 'western', from the Middle West to the Pacific, continue to share certain traits (including vast, federal-owned natural spaces, aridity, and orientation towards the Pacific rather than the Atlantic) which make them distinct from the East. (See 'The Realization of the American West', in Charles Reagan Wilson (ed.), *The New Regionalism* (Jackson, MS, 1998).

47   For a brief discussion of the Archive of American Folksong, see Cohen, *Rainbow Quest*, pp. 11–12.

Thomas Hart Benton, the work of New Deal photographers, and the Federal Writer's Project State Guides and folklore compendia.

The interest of Northerners in the South and West was part of what Alfred Haworth Jones has called 'the search for a usable past' during the New Deal era.[48] Jones argues that, in the disorientating climate of the Depression era, Americans who had hitherto been somewhat cynical about their country's culture suddenly developed a thirst for self-knowledge and a desire to learn more about the past as a means of understanding the difficulties of the present. Warren Susman has stated that, during the 1930s, the notion of 'being a culture' grew more important to Americans than ever before.[49] It was during this period that such volumes as the *Dictionary of American Biography* and the folklore-dominated *History of American Life* were published; their emphasis on the 'folksiness' and virtuous simplicity of the inhabitants of the American past represented, arguably, a significant challenge to the cultural elitism described by Lawrence Levine, a trend which had been present since the late nineteenth century – a 're-Americanisation' or 're-democratisation', in effect. As Jane Becker, a specialist in the development of the idea of the folk in the Appalachian region of the South, has argued, '[during the thirties], [m]iddle-class Americans were becoming more and more aware of the United States as a nation made up of local and unique communities with particular rituals, artistic forms, and ways of life that were very different from their own, and that perhaps had much to offer a national culture.'[50]

Jerrold Hirsch concurs with Becker's analysis, stating that the WPA writers 'saw cultural pluralism as a basis for national integration. They acknowledged and treasured particular cultural differences in America – regional, ethnic, and occupational – as a counterweight to the standardizing forces of modern life.'[51]

There were many types (and stereotypes) of 'folks' to be 'found' throughout America in the 1930s. Dona Brown's study of New England tourism shows that conservative stereotypes of 'quaint' New England, a bastion of Anglicised 'Yankee' manners and customs retained from the colonial era, persisted until the Second World War.[52] Jane Becker has also discussed the increasing interest of white Americans in

48 Alfred Haworth Jones, 'The Search for a Usable American Past in the New Deal Era', *American Quarterly* 23/5 (1971): 710–24.

49 Warren Susman, *Culture as History: The Transformation of American Society in the Twentieth Century* (New York, 1984, 2nd edn), p. 157.

50 Becker, *Selling Tradition,* p. 12.

51 Jerrold Hirsch, 'Cultural Pluralism and Applied Folklore: The New Deal Precedent', in Burt Feintuch (ed.), *The Conservation of Culture: Folklorists and the Public Sector,* (Lexington, KY, 1988), p. 51.

52 Brown, *Inventing New England.* Brown demonstrates that tourists in the inter-war decades continued to invest in the 'Yankee' myth of the region, unwilling to acknowledge the existence of immigrant communities in urban Lowell or Pawtucket, and desperate to go 'off the beaten track' to encounter a 'treasury of old Yankee artefacts and folkways' (pp. 201–13). See also Stephen Nissenbaum, 'Inventing New England', in Wilson (ed.), *The New Regionalism.*

the crafts of the South-western *pueblos*, a fascination linked to a romanticisation of the 'primitive'.[53]

However, when tracing the history of the post-Second World War folk revival, it is evident that the American South and the West attained a superlative degree of significance in the eyes of young folk music enthusiasts, and, for this reason, it is necessary to explore the roots of such a keen interest. Naturally, this interest resulted, in part, from the distinctive music styles which had emerged from these regions – the South was the cradle of many root genres from blues and string-band music to country music. The West, meanwhile, was the home of bluegrass and cowboy music, not to mention the birthplace of Woody Guthrie, the Oklahoman singer-songwriter who would become one of the 'father-figures' of the subsequent urban folksong revival.[54] It was not, however, merely the musical distinctiveness of these regions that was responsible for the Southern and Western fixations of urban folk fans in the 1950s and 1960s. The post-war folk revival inherited certain constructed notions about these regions – young people believed them to be 'the home of the folk', a land of authentic cultural richness and nobility amidst suffering and restless wanderings. These inherited ideas had originally surfaced amidst the cultural conditions created by the Great Depression of the 1930s. During the Depression, Americans sought authenticity, and their quest for 'a usable past' as gateway to a distinctive present led to their focus on the ordinary people of the South and the West, and their lore and culture.

During the Great Depression, many Northerners did exhibit a great curiosity about the South and West and the cultures of their various states. They were searching for a culture that was authentic and down-to-earth, an antidote to the sophistication and industrial clamour that seemed to have heralded the economic crisis in which they were now embroiled; eventually, they came to the conclusion that it was in the Southern states and the West that 'true American folk' were to be found. The South appeared, at least, to have retained its cultural distinctiveness and links with the past, while the West was still considered as uncharted territory, where simpler ways of life prevailed.

The various state guides commissioned and published by the Works Progress Administration (WPA) in this period helped to satisfy some of this hunger for knowledge of the South and the West. Within these guides, writers collated very detailed geographical, historical, cultural and folkloristic information about each state of America. The State Guides aimed to celebrate 'the ordinary people' as never before. The preface to the Mississippi State Guide, first published in 1938, professed that '[the] main emphasis has been placed on the typical and average people of the

---

53   Becker, *Selling Tradition*, pp. 12–13.

54   Bluegrass came from the Kentucky area, and first came to prominence in the 1940s via the music of Bill Munroe and duo Lester Flatt and Earl Scruggs; it was distinctive, above all, for the intricacies of its banjo and violin parts. Musicians would improvise extensively on 'country'-type themes. For more information, see Neil Rosenberg, *Bluegrass: A History* (Urbana, IL and Chicago, IL, 1985) and Robert Cantwell, *Bluegrass Breakdown: The Making of the Old Southern Sound* (Urbana, IL and Chicago, IL, 1984).

State, rather than the exceptional elements.'[55] All the State Guides were similar in their approach; the forgotten, hidden recesses of American life emerged in all their complexity and were lovingly related by the Federal Writers.

The accuracy of the Federal Writers' Project Guides as portraits of the American regions has been called into question by Jerrold Hirsch. Hirsch, who paints a convincing portrait of the Federal Writers' Project as a groundbreaking effort to explore and display the pluralism of American culture, felt that, in particular, the Southern State Guides failed to live up to such an experimental and novel agenda. He notes that, during the completion of the State Guides, conflicts arose between urban Northern writers with a liberal and multicultural outlook, and Southern writers whose views of their homeland were more conservative and insular. As a result, in Hirsch's view, the State Guides for the South made no effort to account for industrial growth or multiculturalism in the region, but clung to 'the plantation tradition' in their narratives, portraying the South as a region of happy-go-lucky, singing ex-slaves and impoverished 'crackers'.[56] Nevertheless, whatever the limitations of outlook or biases in the material presented therein, the Southern, and Western, State Guides provided a great deal of detailed information for Americans who were curious about the regions.

It was not merely the Federal Writers' Project, or the WPA arts projects generally, that promoted and reflected growing interest in the South and the West. Other cultural forms were also discovering the creative potential of folk material from these regions. An American Regionalist movement had existed in literature throughout the 1920s, and would continue to flourish in the 1930s through the works of authors such as John Steinbeck, Willa Cather, Mary Austin – all of whom wrote about the Western states – and William Faulkner, a Southern writer.[57] Simultaneously, in the field of social science, a number of scholars were arguing against a monolithic interpretation of the culture and outlook of the United States; they believed that America could not progress without an understanding and appreciation for the distinctiveness, roots and 'folk culture' of the various geographical regions of the United States. Regionalists, particularly the group of specialists led by Howard Odum of Chapel Hill University, were equally concerned with the eradication of poverty and ailments within the poverty-stricken parts of the country, particularly the South and the Midwest, and they exhibited a great interest in the poorer inhabitants of America – their heritage, their self-image and their beliefs.[58]

Ellen Graff's study of modern dance and left-wing politics in New York illustrates the extent to which dancers of the 1930s were inspired by folklore from the West and

---

55   Federal Writers' Project, *Mississippi: A Guide to the Magnolia State* (New York, 1949), Preface.

56   Hirsch, *Portrait of America*, pp. 179–94.

57   See Robert L. Dorman, *Revolt of the Provinces: The Regionalist Movement in America, 1920–1945* (Chapel Hill, NC and London, 1993), pp. 29–54.

58   For more information on the regionalists and their perspectives, see Howard W. Odum and Harry Estill Moore, *American Regionalism: A Cultural-Historical Approach to National Integration* (New York, 1938); Merrill Jensen (ed.), *Regionalism in America* (Madison, WI, 1951); Robert L. Dorman's study *Revolt of the Provinces*, and Wilson (ed.), *The New Regionalism*.

South. Ballets and dance sequences such as Agnes de Mille's *American Suite* (1939), featuring cowboy songs and folk tunes, Doris Humphrey's *Square Dance* (1938) and Jane Dudley's *Harmonica Breakdown* (1939), utilised American folk themes, while Lincoln Kirstein's Ballet Caravan, formed in 1936, devoted itself to the staging of American folk dance pieces, including *Billy the Kid*.[59] The radical dancer Sophie Maslow was particularly interested in American folk music, and staged a number of modern dance pieces with folk themes, including *Dust Bowl Ballads* (1941), based on the songs of Woody Guthrie (with whom Maslow collaborated while creating the piece).[60]

Similarly, visual artists of the 1930s were inspired and stimulated by the landscapes, natural and human-made, of the South and the West. Of all artists working in this period, it is the work of Thomas Hart Benton that is most associated with the culture of these regions. Benton, an itinerant artist throughout the 1920s and 1930s, painted scenes from all over the country, but came to focus particularly on the South and the West.[61] His style was fanciful yet grounded in regionalist realism; paintings such as *Cradling Wheat* (1938) and *Cotton Pickers* (1928–29) depicted occupational scenes, while others, such as *The Ballad of the Jealous Lover of Lone Green Valley* (1934) and *The Engineer's Dream* (1931) were more imaginative in scope and subject, depicting the individuals within the folklore of the region.[62] Simultaneously, many other artists, some of whom worked in the Federal Artists' Project, were similarly inspired to paint American folk themes of the South and West, and many of their works became murals, making bold public statements regarding the image of 'the folk' which they depicted. Murals such as Ward Lockwood's *Opening the West* and *Settling the West*, Harold G. Egan's *The Richness of the Soil*, and Laura Lewis's *Louisiana Farm*, exhibited similar tendencies to romanticise and glorify rural life and folk-life in the Southern states and in the West.[63] Therefore, artistic expression in 1930s America drew great inspiration from folk themes – and it seemed that, in many respects, 'folk' had become synonymous with 'Western' and 'Southern'.

Another vital factor in the mythologising and exoticising of the Southerners and Westerners during the Depression was the fact that the people of these regions were suffering, perhaps more keenly, and in larger numbers, than in any other part of America, and, almost perversely, this contributed to their mystique in the eyes of outsiders. In both the South and the West, agriculture was damaged considerably by the economic blight. Franklin Roosevelt's government identified the South as the nation's 'number one economic problem'. The region's one-crop economy was destroyed, and all agriculture severely blighted. Many black and white farm workers

---

59   Ellen Graff, *Stepping Left: Dance and Politics in New York City, 1928–1942* (Durham, NC and London, 1997), pp. 132–8.

60   Ibid., pp. 144–5

61   Benton describes his travels in these regions in an anecdotal fashion in his memoirs, *An Artist in America* (Columbia, MO, 1968, 3rd edn).

62   For these and other works, see J. Richard Gruber, *Thomas Hart Benton and the American South* (Augusta, GA, 1998) and Henry Adams, *Thomas Hart Benton: Drawing from Life* (New York, 1990).

63   Barbara Melosh, *Engendering Culture: Manhood and Womanhood in New Deal Public Art and Theatre* (Washington, DC and London, 1991), pp. 46–7, 58, 62.

would migrate from the region to the cities of the North, and legislation, such as Mississippi's Balance Industry with Agriculture Program of 1936, attempted to modernise and diversify the ailing economy of the region.[64] Meanwhile, in the West, crop blights on the prairies and dust storms in Oklahoma exacerbated the economic troubles of the region, and migration – to the cities of the North and to California – became the only solution for many of those who suffered.

During the 1930s, however, the rest of America would become privy to the most desperate sufferings of many Southerners and Westerners through the work of the many documentary photographers who toured these blighted regions. Through the distancing power of the lens, the images of the documentary photographers, though often harrowing and stark, became works of art which glorified and romanticised the stoicism of noble, suffering folk.

During the 1930s, many photographers, usually in the employ of the Farm Security Administration (FSA) of the New Deal, toured throughout the country to capture the images of the 'ordinary people'. Since the photography assignments of the FSA stretched into the early 1940s, many of the later images depicted reasonably prosperous, urban people.[65] However, those which would become most memorable, and most widely reproduced, were the photographs of the most impoverished families and areas of the South and the West. Ben Shahn photographed black cotton pickers from Arkansas at work and in their shack-like houses; John Vachon portrayed the poverty of Omaha, Nebraska, photographing beggars, disused grain elevators, flophouses and unemployed men who rode from place to place on freight trains. Dorothea Lange took photographs of the destitute migrants of Oklahoma, camped out in 'Hoovervilles' and striving to gain employment in California, and Arthur Rothstein captured the images of struggling tenant farmers in Alabama.[66]

Many of these photographs were widely circulated among the American public, via the publication of photographic anthologies in which captions were affixed to each individual picture. Although they purported to present straightforward, empirical evidence of rural and migrant poverty, the majority of the photographers were artists, not social scientists, and most were prepared to admit that an inexplicable fascination with the 'tragic beauty' of the poverty-stricken South drove them to document what

64   See Paul M. Gaston, *The New South Creed: A Study in Southern Mythmaking* (New York, 1970). An interesting study of the social consequences of industrialisation in the South is Jacquelyn Dowd Hall, James Leloudis, Robert Korstad, Mary Murphy, Lu Ann Jones and Christopher B. Daly, *Like a Family: The Making of a Southern Cotton Mill World* (Chapel Hill, NC and London, 1987). See also James C. Cobb and Michael V. Namorato (eds), *The New Deal and the South* (Jackson, MI, 1984).

65   For example, the 'Union Station' photographs of Jack Delano and the 'Small Town in Wartime' photographs of Marjory Collins. Many of these images are available online on the Library of Congress website <www.loc.gov>. See Carl Fleischhauer and Beverly W. Brannan (eds), *Documenting America, 1935–1943* (Berkeley, CA; Los Angeles, CA; London, 1988), pp. 252–93.

66   See ibid., pp. 76–89 for Shahn; pp. 90–113 for Vachon; pp. 114–27 for Lange; and pp. 146–59 for Rothstein.

they had witnessed during their travels.[67] The picture which came to typify the 'tragic beauty' of the photographs was Dorothea Lange's 'Migrant Mother', an image of a migrant woman who sits contemplatively, her face resting in her hand, looking at once worried and stoical while her children rest against her shoulders – the very image of the inner conflict which Roy Stryker, director of the photographic section of the FSA, described as 'dignity versus despair'.[68] As historian Lawrence Levine notes, 'it is significant that during these years the image of the victim was never sufficient; it had to be accompanied by the symbols of dignity, inner strength, and ultimate self-reliance.'[69] It is significant to note that the 'migrant mother' herself was never questioned about her feelings – nor did Lange widely publicise her name or details of her background.[70] She was to be considered a symbol of the triumph, amidst desperate struggle, of the ordinary Midwestern folk. Many of the photographers were overcome with the feeling that the symbolic and artistic potential of their subject-matter overrode their own concerns for their poverty. The writer James Agee, who toured the South with photographer Walker Evans collecting material which eventually comprised the anthology *Let Us Now Praise Famous Men* at the end of the 1930s, felt guilt-ridden yet helpless with regard to his perception of beauty in the sights he recorded.[71] Although he felt that he had 'only a shameful and a thief's right' to allow his art to intrude on the lives of his subjects, he and Walker Evans, in the opinion of William Stott, 'beautified into art [and] made an indelible music of [the lives of the poor]'.[72] *Let Us Now Praise Famous Men* was widely circulated, and inspired many imitations, some more scrupulous and genuine than others.[73]

These various books, however, became part of a major national fixation of the 1930s – the new emphasis on the rural hinterland of the South and West and its ordinary, distinctive, afflicted inhabitants. The books drew a very fine line between evoking genuine sympathy and exploiting suffering for the purpose of either art or sensation, or possibly both simultaneously. The rest of America was inexplicably drawn to such images of the South and the West, for their peculiarity, for their portrayal of a rural regions which had, apparently at least, maintained their distinctiveness, and for the impression which they gave that a life in poverty represented 'a superior,

67   William Stott, *Documentary Expression and Thirties America* (New York, 1973), p. 271. The photographs, and the circumstances which surrounded their creation, are also discussed intermittently in Dorman, *Revolt of the Provinces*, pp. 145–205.

68   Lawrence Levine, 'The Historian and the Icon', in Carl Fleischhauer and Beverly W. Brannan (eds), *Documenting America*, p. 36.

69   Ibid., p. 36.

70   In fact, the 'migrant mother' was a woman of Cherokee descent named Florence Owens Thompson.

71   James Agee and Walker Evans, *Let Us Now Praise Famous Men* (London, 1965, first British Commonwealth edn).

72   Ibid., Agee quote on p. 272; Stott commentary on p. 314.

73   Allegedly, another anthology, *You Have Seen Their Faces*, by Margaret Bourke-White and Erskine Caldwell (Athens, GA, 1995; original edn New York, 1937) contained photographs for which the authors had paid people to pose.

noble lifestyle'.[74] Beautiful suffering thus came to be perceived as being an intrinsic part of the lives of ordinary Westerners and Southerners, and during the Depression, this possessed a special appeal to those who viewed the anthologies of photographs divorced and softened, via the distancing power of the lens, from their context of brutal reality.

The Appeal of Southern and Western Music and Culture

The folk music of the Western and Southern regions was also reaching wider audiences in this period, owing to the growth of the recording industry and to the increasing significance of the radio. It was during this period that both *The Grand Old Opry* and *National Barn Dance* began on American radio, and record companies such as Victor, Okeh and Columbia issued recordings of 'old-time' or 'mountain' music: this style of music, traditional in sound, and featuring, typically, at least one singer accompanied by a fiddle, a banjo and a string bass, was popularised by such performers as The Carter Family, Jimmie Rodgers, and Lulu Belle and Scotty Wiseman. Largely as a consequence of the growth of radio and recorded sound, this musical genre did not remain static, but absorbed influences from other styles of music such as gospel, minstrel music, cowboy music and bluegrass from the West, and blues. The music resulting from this mixing of styles was often referred to as 'hillbilly music', and its sound possessed connotations of both the South and the West.

It is important to recognise that not everybody welcomed the increased hybridisation of Southern and Western folk music. In spite of the broadening of understanding of folk music attained by John Lomax, there remained those who clung to the Child/Sharp notion of the alleged 'purity' of Appalachian and Southern music. Folklore enthusiasts such as Sarah Gertrude Knott, who would be responsible for the first National Folk Festival of 1931, would cling desperately to the notion that Appalachian music was the pure-bred descendant of 'Anglo-Saxon' culture. Knott would ban from her festival all 'strange new music' that had, in her view, corrupted the traditions there, maintaining an emphasis on British ballads, sea shanties and morris dancing, all of which had allegedly been preserved intact for generations.[75] However, it was becoming evident that conservatism of this nature was losing ground in the climate of the inter-war period; such an approach could not hamper the fluidity, or the spread, of the eclectic mountain music of this period.

Significantly, 'hillbillies' and cowboy musicians proved to be commercially viable in more ways than one during the Depression. Wade Austin's research into Southern and Western 'B movies' of the 1930s uncovered a variety of minor yet popular 'hillbilly films' which reflected the growing popularity of country stars such as Gene Autry, 'the singing cowboy', and the Weaver Family. Although films such

---

74   Jack Temple Kirby, *Media-Made Dixie: The South in the American Imagination* (Baton Rouge, LA and London, 1978), p. 60.

75   Becker, *Selling Tradition*, p. 36. See also Chapters 1 and 2 of her book, and David Whisnant, an earlier study of cultural construction in Appalachia. Chapter 3, on the White Top Mountain Folk Festival, is of particular relevance here.

as *Mountain Music, Swing Your Lady, Down in Arkansas, Sis Hopkins, In Caliente* and *The Grand Ole Opry* (which was loosely connected to the radio show) were comic and not intended to be taken overly seriously, they presented an image, stereotyped but optimistic, of Southern and Western people as likeable, down-to-earth, folksy and, ultimately, more wholesome and sensible than their Northern, urban counterparts. The films proved durable, continuing through the 1940s and 1950s before eventually transferring to the small screen. However, it was for their promotion of the indigenous music of the South and West that the 'hillbilly films' were most significant, and their success illustrated the growing popularity of these forms of music across the wider country.[76]

Therefore, the culture of the 1930s fostered a tremendous thirst for knowledge about the South and West, and shed light on the poorer inhabitants, black and (particularly) white, of that region as never before. Now the American 'hinterland', in all its detail, was opened to the gaze of the North, albeit in a manner which served to romanticise and idealise these formerly despised elements of American society and render them, in many ways, 'noble savages'.

Folk revivalists would grow up with the images of the poor Southerners and Westerners captured by Dorothea Lange or Ben Shahn, and the music of performers such as the Carter family, in their psyches. They would experience the legacy of this Depression-era compulsion to locate and explore 'the true folk' of America, and it would shape their romanticised, but genuine, well-intentioned, respect for, and interest in, the music and culture of the people, black and white, of the South and the West – regions which seemed to them semi-factual and semi-mythical.[77]

Additionally, as Benjamin Filene has noted, it would be as a result, both of the work of Lomax and of this focus on the idea of 'the true folk', that the 'cult of authenticity' and the idea of the 'authentic' performer would emerge for subsequent generations – that is, the notion that a performer who embodies the heritage and culture of the music being performed is more genuine and worthy of note than an imitator.[78] This would become an all-important concern for the folk revival in the late 1950s and 1960s.

New Folk: Rediscovering Ethnic Cultures in Canada and America in the 1920s and 1930s

The focus of the folk music revival of the post-Second World War period upon the music of the West and Southern states remains so remarkable that its roots require thorough explanation. In singling out the foundations of interest in these regions, however, it is important not to forget certain other cultural changes which were instigated during the Depression and in the decades which surrounded it, changes which also played a significant role in shaping the scope of the folk revival: for example, another major development in the understanding of 'the folk' in both America and Canada was the

---

76   Wade Austin, 'The Real Beverley Hillbillies', *Southern Quarterly* 19 (1981): 83–94.

77   Fred Hobson, *Tell About the South: The Southern Rage to Explain* (Baton Rouge, LA and London, 1983).

78   Filene, *Romancing the Folk*, p. 49.

gradual acceptance of, and interest in, ethnic diversity and pluralism. As was the case with Lomax and the South, it appears that the 'discovery' of a greater diversity of folklore was principally the result of enterprising and committed individuals whose personal interests and visions came to attract others.

In Canada, John Murray Gibbon organised a series of concerts at the various railway hotels to demonstrate the great variety of Canadian culture; although the concerts often betrayed limited perspectives on the non-British ethnic groups in question, they were groundbreaking in their efforts to exhibit pride in multi-ethnicity during a period in which cultural intolerance of immigrants from non-British backgrounds was optimal. Marius Barbeau, a folklorist who collaborated with Gibbon on the Quebec 'railway concert', also possessed a wider vision of Canadian folklore and attempted to share this with the general public through his work at the National Museum in Ottawa.

Meanwhile, in the United States, insightful individuals working for the Federal Writers' Project fostered and promoted the exploration of ethnic culture as part of their exhaustive exploration of American culture. The work of Henry Alsberg, director of the Project, and Morton W. Royse, the Project's consultant for socio-ethnic studies, is particularly noteworthy in this respect, but the efforts of the charismatic Benjamin A. Botkin to popularise and showcase the tremendous ethnic diversity of American culture would reach the widest audiences, and would also directly inspire many future folk music revivalists. Nevertheless, while individuals such as Royse, Alsberg, Barbeau, Botkin and Gibbon were vital in the promotion of ethnic folklore, it could also be argued that, slowly, the cultural climates of both Canada and America were changing, and it was no longer appropriate for either country to cling to a vision of 'the folk' which denied the existence of diversity.

Railway Concerts: Immigrant 'Contributions' and the Expanding of 'the Folk'

During the late 1920s, a series of concerts was held at the various major 'railway hotels' across Canada. These concerts, organised by author and folklore enthusiast John Murray Gibbon, aimed to showcase the folk cultures of each Canadian province; they represented an optimistic and fairly lavish attempt to demonstrate that Canada's great diversity was indicative of its strength as a nation. According to scholar Janet McNaughton, some 14 concerts were organised at the railway hotels across the country between 1927 and 1930.[79] Those concerts which were held in Ontario and the Maritimes focused particularly on British cultures within Canada, while the Quebec concert, held at the Chateau Frontenac Hotel and presided over by the folklorist Marius Barbeau, presented *Quebecois* music and dance.[80] Most progressive were those concerts which were held in the western Canadian cities of Winnipeg, Edmonton, Regina and Calgary. According to McNaughton, Gibbon departed from conventional cultural philosophies by presenting at these concerts a

79 Janet McNaughton, 'John Murray Gibbon and the Inter-War Folk Festivals', *Canadian Folklore Canadien*, 3/1 (1981): 67–73.

80 This concert is discussed in Lawrence Nowry, *Man of Mana: Marius Barbeau* (Toronto, 1995), pp.283–90.

sampling of the cultures of the many Central and Eastern European peoples who had settled on the prairies. At a time when many middle-class Canadians of British and French origin believed that people of other ethnic backgrounds should be forced to assimilate into the dominant cultures, the presentation of the folk music and dances of Scandinavian, German, Ukrainian, Hungarian, Polish, Italian and Dutch settlers, among others, at these venues seemed considerably 'progressive and open-minded'.[81]

However, Gibbon and his colleagues were no radicals, and it appears that the concerts were in some ways as problematic as they were positive, at least with hindsight. For example, neither Asian nor Native Canadian cultures were featured at the concerts. Furthermore, as McNaughton points out, the concerts, though progressive in their decision to celebrate such a variety of ethnic groups, did little more than emphasise, through traditional folksong and dance, 'the picturesque aspects of peasant culture' to members of the audience.[82] They were not reflective of the daily lives or ordinary realities of the groups in question, and, hence, the concerts may have done little more than emphasise stereotypes and, even if some audience members may have gained a more favourable impression of these nationalities through the concerts, ultimately the ethnic groups appeared more quaint or primitive than realistic. Nevertheless, considering the staunchly Protestant and British character of Canadian society in the early twentieth century, the concerts were innovative and daring. They pointed to a new vision of Canada in which many cultures were brought together as a mosaic, a vision which, though in some ways ahead of its time, would eventually be promoted and enhanced by the folk revival movement of the 1950s and 1960s.

A key figure in the festival which was held at the Chateau Frontenac in Quebec City was Marius Barbeau. Barbeau was, at this time, emerging as a significant specialist in the folklore both of his native Quebec and of Native Canadian tribes, in particular the Wyandots, the Hurons, and the Tsimshian (Totem Pole) people of British Columbia. Barbeau was a charismatic and innovative individual whose approach to folklore was neither the romanticised one of Creighton nor the strictly anthropological one of Native specialists such as Franz Boas. One of Barbeau's particular interests was the linkage of 'high' and folk art. He deplored the snobbish attitude which many scholars of the arts held towards the work of 'ordinary' people, advocating that artists and writers turn back to the 'unexplored poetic or melodic riches of the people' of their native land for inspiration. 'Certain of our men of letters would gain the palm that eludes them if they would consider without prejudice the varied themes offered by their own country, instead of falling back on universal platitudes,' he declared in the 1920s.[83] While this reverence for the 'unspoiled folk' is reminiscent of the romanticised ideals of the Southern Writers' Project or Helen Creighton, Barbeau's interpretation of folk culture was in many respects forward-thinking, and far from purely limited or conservative.

---

81 McNaughton, 'John Murray Gibbon', p. 73.
82 Ibid., p. 71.
83 Quoted in Nowry, *Man of Mana*, p. 187.

Barbeau's relationship to, and views on, native culture are worth exploring in more detail. Native people, in fact, were scarcely included in any narratives of North American folklore during this period, although this would be rectified somewhat in the 1960s. In the early portion of the century, Native peoples and their cultures were usually considered to be subjects for anthropological, rather than folklore, study, in both Canada and America. Barbeau, it is true, moved beyond simply viewing Native culture as anthropology; his interest in folklore as art led him to invite Canadian artist A.Y. Jackson on his 1915 expedition to British Columbia, because he wished to hear the painter's view on totem poles as artistic expressions.[84] According to his biographer Laurence Nowry, Barbeau was also known as a champion of Native rights.[85] However, in correspondence and studies, Barbeau, according to Nowry, was given to using the term 'half-breed', a problematic and offensive term which, for Nowry, calls into question the true sentiments of Barbeau with regard to Native culture.[86] Whatever Barbeau's feelings towards Native peoples, he was, at this juncture, one of the few folklorists to work extensively with aboriginal cultures utilising a non-anthropological approach. This is significant, as, until the 1960s, few folklorists in either Canada or America were inclined to consider Native culture as 'folk culture'.

Barbeau remained, in many respects, a pioneer in his comparatively expansive attitude towards Canadian folklore. In a CBC interview given in 1965, Barbeau declared that, when thinking of folklore, it was not merely traditional materials but 'the talents, the ability to think or feel, inherited in each household, is of very considerable importance. It will be the wealth of the country. They (*sic*) are indispensable if Canada is to survive!'[87] In other words, for Barbeau, folklore was not merely something that should be preserved, but something which remained vibrant, dynamic and subject to change and refashioning.

Ethnic Folk Culture Discovered: Benjamin Botkin and the Federal Writers' Project

Many of those who worked for the Federal Writers' Project during the Depression in America shared Barbeau's dynamic and elastic definition of folklore. They were also, like Gibbon, interested in the many ethnic cultures which were so much in evidence, and yet so under-valued, in their country. Both Jerre Mangione and Jerrold Hirsch have discussed the role of the Federal Writers' Project in the 'discovery' of ethnic America. As Mangione notes, the board of the Project, under the direction of Henry Alsberg, was anxious to leave no 'gaps in the portrait' of America which it was so carefully and lovingly creating, and by 1938, the Federal Writers' Project began to produce ethnic studies.[88] Some of these studies were conducted at a

---

84   CBC interview with Barbeau from 1965, reprinted on the website of the Canadian Museum of Civilisation. <http://www.civilation.ca/academ/barbeau/basteng.html> (accessed 14 March 2004).

85   Nowry, *Man of Mana*, p. 108.

86   Ibid., p. 108.

87   From the CBC interview, 1965.

88   Mangione, *The Dream and the Deal*, p. 277.

localised level, while others represented efforts to document the experiences of certain ethnic groups on a national scale.[89] Local studies such as *The Italians of New York*, *Jewish Landsmanschaften of New York* and *The Armenians of Massachusetts* were produced in the late 1930s.[90] Morton Royse, the FWP's national consultant for socio-ethnic studies, subsequently conceived of a plan to undertake a comprehensive study of ethnic cultures in the United States, which would be provisionally entitled *Composite America*. Although Royse had been trained in the sciences, he was anxious now to portray the subjects of his study 'from the human angle' rather than using sociological methods.[91] While this study never fully came to fruition, the intentions which underlay it demonstrate both the extent of interest of the Project in ethnicity, and the desire of the writers to portray their subjects as human beings rather than as quasi-laboratory specimens.

In spite of the failure of the large-scale study of ethnic groups, a number of projects in ethnic folklore and culture were successfully completed. For example, both *The Albanian Struggle in the Old World and the New*, published in 1939, and *Copper Camp: Stories of the World's Greatest Mining Town, Butte* (1943), a study of a multi-ethnic mining community, were met with critical acclaim and a measure of popular success.[92] In tandem with such initiatives were the ethnomusicology projects of the WPA, which recorded a wealth of ethnic and folk cultures from various states, in particular Florida and California.[93]

Jerrold Hirsch also notes the detailed work which the Federal Writers' Project carried out in the field of African-American folklore. In spite of the demeaning portrayals of black people which were to be found in some of the Southern State Guides, Royse, Alsberg and the Negro Affairs editor of the FWP, an African-American named Sterling Brown, took pains to ensure that African-Americans were included in the project. The major accomplishment of the FWP in this respect was the extensive series of slave narratives which were recorded and anthologised in the 1930s and 1940s.[94]

Working alongside Alsberg and Royse was Benjamin Botkin, a folklore specialist who succeeded John Lomax as the Folklore Editor of the Federal Writers' Project from 1938–39. Botkin shared with his colleagues a dynamic and pluralistic

---

89   Hirsch, *Portrait of America*, p. 131.
90   Mangione, *The Dream and the Deal*, p. 277.
91   Ibid.
92   Ibid., pp. 277–85.
93   Sound recordings and documents appertaining to the California and Florida Ethnomusicology Projects are in the Archives of the American Folklife Center. They are now accessible on-line at <http://www.memory.loc.gov/ammem/afcchtml/cowhome.html> and <http://www.memory.loc.gov/ammem/flwpahtml/flwpahome.html> (accessed 14 March 2004).
94   'Slave narratives' were the products of extensive interviews with former slaves who were still alive in the 1930s. See, for example, Alan Brown and David Taylor, *Gabr'l Blow Sof': Sumter County, Alabama Slave Narratives* (Livingston, AL, 1997); George E. Lankford, *Bearing Witness: Memories of Arkansas Slavery – Narratives from the 1930s WPA Collections* (Fayetteville, AR, 2003); and Lindsay T. Baker, *The WPA Oklahoma Slave Narratives* (Norman, OK, 1996).

view of American culture, and he fully endorsed, and helped to shape, the FWP's embracing of ethnic studies in the late 1930s. However, Benjamin Botkin, more than any other figure at the FWP, brought the pluralistic, dynamic and vibrant vision of folklore into the public realm via his many popular and engaging anthologies of American folklore. Botkin began these anthologies in the late 1930s, and would publish them in the 1940s, beginning with *Treasury of American Folklore* in 1944, and followed by, among others, *Treasury of Western Folklore*, *Railroad Folklore* and, most interestingly, considering erstwhile, and continuing, assumptions that the 'real folk' were rural, *Sidewalks of America*, an anthology of city folkways.[95] These anthologies, which were essentially rather chaotic compendia of stories, games and song-lyrics, were multi-regional, multi-ethnic and all-inclusive, and proved highly popular.[96] As Jerre Mangione states, the *Treasury of American Folklore*, Botkin's first anthology, 'became a liberating force, rescuing folklore from the academically embalmed atmosphere in which it had long been contained and bringing it to a large audience that was hungry for the kind of Americana which reflected the nation's varied personality'.[97]

Botkin's light-hearted and exuberantly eclectic approach to folklore did not meet with universal approval. Of particular significance was the opposition to his methodology which was articulated by a fellow folklorist, Richard Dorson. Dorson himself would prove to be a pivotal figure in the development of folklore studies in America; as Simon Bronner and Benjamin Filene have shown, Dorson helped to professionalise folklore studies in the United States, and shared, in essence, the views of the FWP writers that American folklore should be distinctive and reflective of the unique origins and composition of the country. However, in viewing folklore as 'an academic specialty open to highly qualified experts', he was scathing of those who failed to maintain his high standards for folklore scholarship.[98] Botkin, who had ceased to work officially within the academy in 1939, was criticised severely by Dorson. After the publication of *Treasury of American Folklore* in 1944, Dorson condemned the 'scrap book' approach taken by Botkin. He derided the work as being 'in the most literal sense a scissors and paste job, with no philosophic unity and a wide discrepancy of sources', and he was appalled at its immediate success with critics and public alike. Dorson believed that Botkin's work served 'seriously to injure the cause of the mature study of American folklore'; he accused Botkin of sloppy research which only served to furnish 'the masses' with erroneous ideas as to what constituted folklore. His firm beliefs in educating the public correctly with regards to American folklore led to a controversial article, published in 1950, in

---

95 Benjamin A. Botkin, *A Treasury of American Folklore: Stories, Ballads, and Traditions of the People* (New York, 1944); Botkin, *A Treasury of Railroad Folklore: The Stories, Tall Tales, Traditions, Ballads, and Songs of the American Railroad Man* (New York, 1953); Botkin, *Western Folklore* (New York, 1964), and Botkin, *Sidewalks of America: Folklore, Legends, Sagas, Traditions, Customs, Songs, Stories and Sayings of City Folk* (Westport, CT, 1954).

96 *Sidewalks of America*, for examples, contains stories and lore from cities of every state, including, among others, items from Native, Hispanic, Irish and Jewish communities.

97 Mangione, *The Dream and the Deal*, p. 277.

98 Bronner, *Following Tradition,* p. 350. See also Filene, pp. 168–73.

which he outlined in no uncertain terms the differences between folklore and what he memorably dubbed 'fake lore', namely, the dilution and bastardisation of folklore by the forces of commercialism.[99]

Botkin's approach to his subjects proved commercially viable and highly appealing. As Jerrold Hirsch has stated, in a brief article on Botkin produced for the American Folklife Center, Botkin rejected what he terms 'the science of folklore', the approach adopted by Dorson and his supporters which valued 'the lore over the folk, the past over the present, the rural over the urban, the agrarian over the industrial, survivals over revivals, older *genres* over newer, emergent forms, oral transmission over technological media, homogeneous groups over heterogeneous groups'.[100] For this fluidity and acceptance of contradiction and multiplicity within folklore, the future folk revivalists of the 1960s – among them Kenneth Goldstein, Roger Abrahams, Ellen Stekert, Bruce Jackson and Archie Green – would come to value the attitudes of Benjamin Botkin more than those of Dorson.[101]

In fact, the embracing of ethnic and regional cultures which was pioneered by the FWP and Botkin would prove to be one of the crucial ideological foundations of the post-war folk revival. Jerrold Hirsch, in his study of the Federal Writers' Project, has articulated insightfully the philosophy of American culture which was held by the writers. In his view, the FWP, and individuals such as Botkin, Alberg and Royse, were 'romantic nationalists' with a 'mythic' view of their nation, rather than ideologues who sought only to work with socio-economic facts and statistics. 'There was,' states Hirsch, 'an inherently paradoxical attempt to both preserve and celebrate differences while seeking to transcend them in a sense of shared nationality.'[102]

At times, Botkin, Royse and colleagues found it difficult to rationalise precisely the position of the immigrant cultures in their society. Should they approach them from a 'melting pot' perspective, stating that their distinctiveness was slowly vanishing, or view instead their 'contributions' to American culture? Hirsch shows that both approaches were adopted by the Federal Writers – while many believed assimilation to be imminent, others, such as the authors of the Pennsylvania, New York and Massachusetts State Guides, depicted their subjects as cosmopolitan and diverse societies with multiple cultural influences.[103] Ultimately, Botkin, Royse and Alberg, 'thought', perhaps optimistically and romantically, 'that American diversity meant that America was always in the process of becoming.'[104] It was, in other words, an unfinished work, impossible to encapsulate precisely and always changing. Such a broad and dynamic vision of America would, some thirty years subsequently,

---

99   Quotes from Richard Dorson, *American Folklore and the Historian* (London and Chicago, IL, 1971), pp. 5–7

100 Jerrold Hirsch, 'Benjamin Botkin's Legacy-in-the-Making', reproduced online by the Folklife Center. See <http://www.loc.gov/folklife/botkin/hirsch.html>. See also 'Folklore in the Making: B.A. Botkin', *Journal of American Folklore*, 100 (1987): 3–38, by the same author.

101 Ibid.

102 Hirsch, *Portrait of America*, p. 96.

103 Ibid., p. 131–4.

104 Ibid., p. 138.

excite, intrigue and inspire the young people who flocked to form part of the folk music revival movement.

There were, however, problematic aspects to this romantic vision of America, and these problems would also be inherited by, and reflected in, the folk music revival of the post-war era. As Hirsch states, the view of nation held by the FWP writers was 'mythic' and not rooted in ideology. For this reason, the FWP remained ever-positive and inclusive in its approach, but did not examine, or even acknowledge, the presence of conflicts and problems within American culture.[105] For instance, in attempting to treat African-Americans with fairness, the FWP acted positively by incorporating slave narratives and black lore and culture into its work.[106] It did not, however, acknowledge or express the obstacles which continued, some seventy years after abolition, to dog the progress of African-Americans in society. While it is perhaps unfair to expect such inclusiveness and foresight from the FWP, there is no doubt that this aspect of the approach of the organisation would be inherited by the optimistic generation of the 1960s, and would be in evidence in the folk music revival. During the era of Civil Rights, integration and non-violence, positive affirmations of optimism for the future were preferable to angry detractions of society and its injustice. This optimistic approach would, however, prove incompatible with ever-changing 1960s culture. Nevertheless, the idealism of the folk revival in the late 1950s and early 1960s certainly owed much to the romantic, eclectic and inclusive approach adopted by the Federal Writers' Project, and by its leaders Benjamin Botkin, Henry Alberg and Morton Royse.

While Botkin and Royse in America, and Gibbon and Barbeau in Canada, were remarkable in shaping the viewpoint of the public with regard to ethnic cultures, it is also true to state that, in both countries, societal attitudes were slowly changing: cultural norms were haltingly, but tangibly, transforming in both Canada and America. In America, immigrant groups were slowly gaining in confidence, and were less reticent about showcasing their beliefs in the public sphere. This was evidenced by large folk festivals such as the Minnesota Festival of Nations, begun in 1932, which featured European, Asian and Indian cultures. The tradition of the ethnic festival continued into the 1940s, when, according to Richard Polenberg, it became 'something of a ritual' in large, ethnically diverse cities.[107] While Canada remained in the thrall of Britain and its culture, the old guard of the country was gradually becoming more tolerant of its minority groups. Norman Knowles substantiates this in his description of the 150th anniversary of the Loyalist landings in 1934. While, as was demonstrated, the 1884 pageantry was founded upon unquestioning British-Canadian patriotism and belief in the greatness of the British Empire, by 1934 such an approach to the festivities was no longer appropriate. As Knowles remarks, by this time, '[t]he Anglophilia and racial assumptions of many Loyalist promoters alienated large elements within Canada's increasingly diverse and multi-ethnic population.'[108]

105 Ibid., p. 96.

106 Ibid.

107 Richard Polenberg, *One Nation Divisible: Class, Race and Ethnicity in the United States Since 1938* (New York, 1980), p. 54.

108 Knowles, *Inventing the Loyalists,* p. 168.

Therefore, the UELA, which had formerly cherished a vision of the Loyalists as an educated elite, reinvented the forebears of its members as quintessential 'pioneers', with a new emphasis on their status as 'folk'. This, according to Knowles, was a sign of changing times. He notes that during the 1930s there was 'a growing interest in Upper Canadian antiques and in traditional handicrafts. Displays of Loyalist artefacts and pioneer crafts became a regular feature at meetings of the United Empire Loyalist Association and local history societies.' Knowles links this new focus on handcrafts and folk history to the trauma of the Depression, which affected Canada as gravely as it affected America; in his view, the new interest reflected 'a desire for stability and rootedness at a time of tremendous social upheaval and dislocation'.[109] Although Canada did not respond to the Depression with a comparable equivalent to the WPA Arts Projects, it is clear that, partly as a result of economic and social difficulties, and also as a result of general socio-cultural change, Canada, like America, was gradually altering the traditional narrative of its history, its people, its culture and its folklore.

Radicalising the Regional Folk: The Popular Front and the Origins of the Folk Revival

It is clear that 'the folk' was a crucial concept during the 1930s, and this was recognised by the coalition of left-wing groups and parties which came together in the mid-1930s to form the 'Popular Front'. It would be individuals and bodies associated with this coalition group that would imbue folk music with radical significance, reinventing 'the folk' of the American regions (especially the South and the South-west) as impoverished and victimised, but, ultimately, strong and staunch fighters against the forces of injustice. This radicalised notion of the folk would find its ideological home in the urban North, where the leftists were congregating, above all in New York City. As leftist political ideals merged with increasing admiration for the music and culture of the American downtrodden and the poor of the (non-northern) regions, the seeds of what would eventually become the folk music revival movement were firmly sown.

American Left-Wing Culture and the Rise of the Popular Front

The social and cultural turmoil caused by the Great Depression helped to create a climate of considerable tolerance to left-wing thinking; although leftist politics were far from being actively promoted, they was neither strongly discouraged nor persecuted, as they would be after the Second World War. However, before proceeding any further in a discussion of the American 'left' at this time, it is necessary to define what, precisely, constitutes a 'leftist' at this point in American history. The 'black and white' thinking of the House Un-American Activities Committee and the McCarthy 'witch hunts' of the post-Second World War period would create the

---

109 Ibid., p. 169. Ian McKay also discusses the arts and crafts revival of Nova Scotia in Chapter 3 of *The Quest of the Folk*.

erroneous but enduring assumption that, in America, one could either be, or not be, a fully-fledged Communist, and that there could be no middle ground or degrees of leftist opinion.[110] In reality, as Michael Denning has shown, the American 'Popular Front' of the 1930s was a loose coalition of individuals, parties and interest-groups, some of which were staunchly far Left in their philosophies, and others of which were socialists or those cast in the New Deal liberal mould. In contesting the notion that the Popular Front was essentially a Communist movement with a sympathetic periphery of non-Communist 'fellow travellers' who were basically liberal, Denning states that

> [A]ny examination of the Popular Front ... [suggests that] the rank and file of the Popular Front were the fellow travelers, the large periphery. But even this terminology is misleading; the periphery was in many cases the centre, the "fellow travelers" *were* the Popular Front. It is mistaken to see the Popular Front as a marriage of Communists and liberals. The heart of the Popular Front as a social movement lay among those who were non-Communist socialists and independent leftists, working with Communists and with liberals, but marking out a culture that was neither a Party nor a liberal New Deal culture.[111]

Thus, Denning illustrates the importance of viewing the leftist element of the Popular Front as varied and multi-faceted, rather than being considered uniform in opinion, beliefs and outlook.[112]

When the Popular Front was created in 1935, one of its major departures from the thinking of previous left-wing groups, such as the Industrial Workers of the World (IWW or 'Wobblies'), was its acceptance and endorsement of arts and culture, particularly those of the 'ordinary people'. Of great concern to the Popular Front was the war against fascism, which was escalating in influence in Germany, Italy and Spain, and so the organisation believed that culture might be 'a force for fostering community and revealing people's shared humanity', a weapon against racism and hatred.[113] Whereas previous left-wing groups had tended to see the culture of the workers as a meaningless, counter-productive escape from harsh reality, now the Popular Front aimed to understand popular tastes. As Benjamin Filene has argued, the Front 'became fascinated with music that seemed to speak in the voice of the people'.[114] For these reasons, the American Left of the 1930s developed an interest in folk music. In conjunction with this new focus on working-class culture, the Popular

110 See Denning, *The Cultural Front*, p. 5.

111 Ibid.

112 Warren Susman articulated similar ideas in his earlier examination of the 1930s; he warned historians against the tendency to view a stark contrast between 'the apolitical Twenties' and 'the political Thirties', and suggested that, in fact, during the 1930s, 'commitment to ideology' was far less strong than was often assumed. See *Culture as History*, pp. 151–2 and 183.

113 Filene, p. 70. It is also important to note the pioneering efforts of the NAACP in fostering the culture and artistic expressions of African-Americans in the 1920s, creating, in effect, the Harlem Renaissance. This grassroots movement preceded the Popular Front policy.

114 Ibid.

Front was also desirous to become more 'American' in its focus, considering that this would make it more relevant to its members and would broaden its appeal domestically. Hence, above all, the folk music in which the Front displayed particular interest was that of the United States. Thus, the first flush of interest in American folk music occurred from the midst of the Depression until, roughly, the middle of the 1940s. R. Serge Denisoff has called this period 'the proletarian renaissance', noting the increasing use by workers' newsletters and meetings of folksongs and performers, and he claims that this period effectively marked the beginning of the revival movement.[115]

'Folk Heroes' of Regional America and the Urban Left

Left-wing activity in inter-war America was guided by the Northern cities, particularly New York. However, the focus of the Left on folk culture led, inevitably, to a perusal of the cultures of the more rural regions of the country where the 'folk' were supposed to be – above all, the South, and the West and Midwest. Another important reason for this renewed focus on these regions was the fact that people in these parts of the country had suffered particularly devastatingly as a consequence of the Depression. However, while other folklore experts and Depression-era documenters such as Walker Evans and James Agee had tended to see the poor of these areas as pitiful and ultimately passive, if 'noble' amid their suffering, the left-wing admirers of the culture of the regions sought folk heroes. They searched for musicians and singers who were grassroots activists, strong figures who refused to accept the manipulative greed of their bosses, and whose work seemed to depict in a straightforward and honest manner the lives and sufferings of their communities. Among those upon whom they came to focus were 'Aunt' Molly Jackson of Kentucky, Ella May Wiggins of Gastonia, North Carolina, and, above all, the Oklahoma-born singer-songwriter Woody Guthrie.

'Aunt' Molly Jackson was the widow of a Kentucky miner who composed her own songs 'to pass [her] sorrows away'.[116] She had, indeed, endured a tremendous amount of suffering and hardship in her life; as well as losing her husband, son and brother in mining disasters, she herself was crippled in an accident, and had constantly to battle against starvation and debilitating poverty. In spite of this, however, she remained a relentless campaigner for the rights of miners and their families, especially during the Depression, which had a devastating effect on the Kentucky mining communities. She was a formidable advocate for, and organiser of, workers' unions, risking imprisonment and serious injury to confront the pit operators. 'I have often wondered why they have not killed me – they have beat me and tear-gassed me and had me thrown in jail,' she declared. 'Ah, yes, they tried to

---

115 R. Serge Denisoff, *Great Day Coming: Folk Music and the American Left* (Urbana, IL and Chicago, IL; London, 1971) p. 68.

116 Quoted in John Greenway, *American Folksongs of Protest* (New York, 1970), p. 252.

get rid of me but somehow they failed.'[117] Jackson also made several visits to New York to campaign for the establishment of workers' unions.

The major weapons of Molly Jackson's unionising campaigns were her self-composed songs, which were often narratives of specific tragedies or incidents within the mining communities, or reflections of the injustices faced by the workers. Her songs were composed in a traditional 'folk' style – simple and artless, with multiple verses, often with repeated lines, and uncomplicated melodies with basic guitar chord changes (sometimes borrowing from blues structures). 'Hard Times in Colman's Mines', 'Dreadful Memories' and 'Poor Miner's Farewell' depicted the struggles of the miners, while 'Hungry Ragged Blues' highlighted the sufferings of their starving wives and families. 'I am a Union Woman' was the rallying song, with which she always began her campaigning speeches, and 'Lonesome Jailhouse Blues' described one of the many times in which she was thrown into jail.[118] Jackson was the prototype of the protest songwriter; her music was of a functional nature, utterly fused with her message. She denied affiliation with the Communists, and disliked outsiders misinterpreting her music and its purpose, but, because of her militancy, set in a rural, regional context, she would become a heroine to her contemporaries, and to folk music enthusiasts of subsequent decades.

Various other working-class radical songwriters from the Western and Southern regions of America would become crucial to the Popular Front folk music advocates, including brother and sister Jim Garland and Sarah Ogan Gunning, both of whom were staunch union advocates (Gunning was also the half-sister of Molly Jackson). Ella May Wiggins was another female songwriter whose career was admired by the left-wing groups of the inter-war period; she had died in 1929, but the circumstances of her untimely, tragic death made her both martyr and heroine. A textile worker from Gastonia, North Carolina, Wiggins was, by the late 1920s, the young widowed mother of nine children.[119] After joining the National Textile Workers' Union, she began to compose songs such as 'The Big Fat Boss and the Workers' and 'The Mill Mother's Lament', which reflected the struggles of her fellow workers. Like those of Jackson, the songs composed by Wiggins were written in a simple, narrative, folkloric style; indeed, Wiggins often set her words to popular folk tunes rather than compose her own melodies. Because of her bold highlighting of societal injustice, Wiggins was considered notorious by her employers, and, when she was shot dead during unrest at a strike held in Gastonia Mill, many believed that she had been deliberately targeted. Although she did not live to see her fame spread to the North, Ella May Wiggins, like Molly Jackson, served as an inspiration for left-wing activists; her grassroots sense of justice and her uncompromising songs provided yet another 'regional heroine' for the politically active enthusiasts of folk music.[120]

---

117 Ibid, p. 259.

118 For music and lyrics for these and more of Molly Jackson's songs, see ibid., pp. 252–75.

119 As a textile worker, Wiggins represented a 'different' South – that of the exploited industrial workers rather than that of the stereotypical rural people.

120 Ella May Wiggins is also discussed in Jacquelyn Dowd Hall et al., *Like a Family*, pp. 214–5, 226–8.

However, in many ways the epitome of the political folk poet during this period was Woody Guthrie, a native of Oklahoma who proved himself particularly proficient, through his songs and poetry, at bridging the gap between his roots and the more sophisticated urban audiences among which he found himself in the 1930s and 1940s. Guthrie grew up in Okemah, Oklahoma, and by his teens he was 'a virtual orphan', his mother having been admitted to a mental asylum and his father having moved away to Texas after the failure of his land speculation ventures.[121] After a series of menial jobs in various parts of the country, Guthrie learned to play the guitar and fiddle, and eventually found regular work as a singer on Los Angeles radio station KFVD, entertaining the migratory workers. A staunch advocate for the rights of the working class, Guthrie's self-penned songs were largely works of protest, and, when he moved to New York, he found acceptance among the left-wing thinkers there. Both his two records of 'Dust Bowl Ballads', recorded for Victor records at the end of the 1930s and reflecting his Oklahoma heritage, and his autobiography *Bound for Glory* (1943), which recounted his travels and the deprivation he had witnessed in his native land, would become the stuff of legend for the folk revivalists of the 'boom' period.[122] Meanwhile, his many songs, including the cutting protest songs 'Plane Wreck at Los Gatos', 'Dead from the Dust' and 'Tom Joad', and the compositions which merged his knowledge of the great diversity of the United States with his left-wing ethos, such as 'Pastures of Plenty' and 'This Land is Your Land', would become synonymous with the folk revival from the 1950s onwards. Like Molly Jackson, Guthrie would compose protest songs in reflexive response to incidences of injustice, and his canon was both large and rich in its diversity.

Woody Guthrie seemed to embody all that the Popular Front sought to find in folk culture and song – he was, it appeared, an 'illiterate or semiliterate folk poet' who merged genuine proficiency as a songwriter with homespun wisdom, a semi-rural, regional heritage and, above all, a staunch left-wing sensibility.[123] Nevertheless, Guthrie's folksy persona was in many respects more of an invention than it was a reality; his Midwestern dialect and his scruffy appearance were, if not affected, certainly exaggerated for the benefit of his audiences in the urban North. Furthermore, it should be emphasised that Guthrie's career as a singer coincided only briefly with the development of the folk revival. By the early 1950s, his health was rapidly deteriorating as he fell victim to the hereditary wasting disease Huntingdon's Chorea. By the time that the 'great boom' in folk music was occurring in the early 1960s, Guthrie was unable to move or to communicate. Thus, as the revival of folk music developed over the 1950s and 1960s, Guthrie became less of a living reality and more of a legend, and, although his reputation had been forged to a great extent because of his skill as a songwriter, a certain mystique began to surround the facts of his life as the younger revivalists turned him into a political and cultural hero, imbuing him with the folk 'authenticity' that they so craved. However, contrary to such legends, Guthrie was a man who managed to embrace aspects of both the rural world of the folk and the urban intellectual milieu. He was extremely well-read, and

---

121 John Greenway, p. 278.
122 Woody Guthrie, *Bound for Glory* (New York, 1983, original edn 1943).
123 Denisoff, *Great Day Coming*, p. 136.

his autobiography, *Bound for Glory*, was written in a literary style far removed from the dialectical English which he adopted in his speech.[124] Therefore, Guthrie was able, in his career, to straddle the worlds of the intellectuals and the folk, and for this reason, and as a result of his retirement due to illness, which served in many ways to enhance his mystique, Guthrie was considered, from the late 1930s until long after his career was over, the ultimate regional folk hero, and, as Ronald Cohen has stated, he became 'the spiritual and musical godfather of the budding [folk] revival'.[125]

Expanding the Movement: Pete Seeger, People's Artists and the Folk Revival from 1945 to 1957

While it could be stated that Woody Guthrie served as a spiritual godfather to the folk revival, it was really one of his close friends, the ex-Harvard student Pete Seeger, who laid many of the actual foundations of the movement. Like Guthrie, Seeger had insight into several different worlds; as a result of his own education and the careers of his parents (musicologist Charles Seeger and concert violinist Constance Seeger), he had considerable understanding of the academic approach to folk music and folksong collection. Indeed, his father, Charles, had written extensively on American folk music and encouraged a greater respect for its diverse traditions. His son took up the cause wholeheartedly, but chose to take action rather than simply write; travelling around the South and the West to perform at workers' rallies with Woody Guthrie, and absorbing the music of performers such as Leadbelly, Seeger gained a sense of affinity with the 'ordinary' American people, and a desire to keep their cultures and songs alive through performance. Benjamin Filene considers Seeger's career as a performer 'an extension of [Alan] Lomax's career as a collector and promoter'. Like his father, Alan Lomax considered American folk music to be vibrant and part of the present, rather than the past; Seeger would become the living proof of this as he developed his remarkably eclectic repertoire of folk songs from around the United States and beyond, songs which he would perform in his own style and then teach to his audiences in order to demonstrate that folk music was something fluid, malleable and, above all, alive.[126] Seeger was not a traditional performer in that he could stake no claim to a regional or worker's heritage; however, his deep understanding of many cultures made him an ideal ambassador of folk music to younger audiences. He bridged the cultural and class gaps between the rural performers and their urban audiences perhaps even more deftly, and certainly more enduringly, than Guthrie had done, and, in his work, it could be argued that he became almost a living embodiment of the multi-ethnic ideals and work of Benjamin Botkin.

Pete Seeger was also a sympathiser with left-wing causes; his eventual investigation by the House Un-American Activities Committee, and the suspicion which surrounded him during the McCarthy era, led to his being inaccurately considered socialist or communist in his outlook. However, as with many of the Popular Front members, Seeger held beliefs which were staunchly worker-orientated

---

124 See ibid., pp. 136–7.
125 Cohen, *Rainbow Quest*, p. 106.
126 Filene, *Romancing the Folk,* p. 190.

and which heavily favoured the rights of labourers to unionising and fair working conditions, but which were not centred around any specific political ideology. Israel Young, a New Yorker who was active in folk music from the 1940s onwards, and who would become a central figure in the New York, and wider, folk revival, summarised Seeger's often ambiguous political position in an interview of 1965. 'Pete Seeger is really more of an idealist than a Communist or a left-winger or anything like that,' he declared. 'He really is like a knight on a white horse.'[127] Nevertheless, Seeger spent most of the 1940s performing with the Almanac Singers, a loose confederation of politically active musicians whose membership included, at different times, Woody Guthrie, Sonny Terry and Brownie McGhee, and African-American singer Josh White. More consistent members were Millard Lampell, Bess Lomax Hawes, Agnes 'Sis' Cunningham and Seeger. The Almanacs, an acoustic-style band, performed at trade union meetings and workers' rallies, anti-fascist organisation meetings, and made appearances at the participatory folk music concerts, now called 'hootenannies', which had begun in New York City during the 1940s.

The Almanac Singers were eventually forced to disband after Pete Seeger was drafted into the Forces in 1943. However, when the Second World War was over, folk music showed no sign of losing popularity, and, in 1946, Seeger was one of the founders of a new artistic organisation called People's Songs Incorporated (PSI). Based in New York, and co-founded by, among others, Lee Hays, Irwin Silber and Oscar Brand, PSI was intended as a means of promoting socially conscious music for the benefit of the workers, through organising concerts, and through promoting the compositions of songwriters whose music would not be deemed compatible with the demands of 'mainstream' entertainment. PSI was also greatly responsible for continuing and further promoting the interest of folk music enthusiasts in the music styles of the American regions. 'Hoots' were now regular occurrences among those in New York City who called themselves 'left-of-liberal', and, as Irwin Silber stated, the ultimate aim of these participatory folk music concerts was to promote 'music, ideas and a sense of the real America'. The 'hoots' were to promote a 'variety of form', not confining themselves to one type of music, and they were also intended to provide a sympathetic environment for 'new and young artists' as well as more seasoned performers.[128] The emphasis on variety promoted by the 'hoots' would remain constant throughout the folk revival, and were fundamental to the eclectic outlook of the revival of the 'boom' period.

A sister organisation of PSI, People's Artists Inc., was also created in 1946 as a source of fundraising and management for socially conscious performers. Its quarterly bulletin was initially created for the purpose of printing and disseminating 'songs of labor and the American people'; it also offered to publish songbooks for unions, and even write special union songs to order.[129] *People's Songs* was unabashedly political in its outlook, but, within its limited boundaries, it, too, promoted eclecticism. It published songs from a wide variety of cultural backgrounds; for example, in the

---

127 Israel Young, 1965. Interview by Richard Reuss. Tape-recording, 8 July. Box 1, Tape AFS 19,800. American Folklife Center, Library of Congress, Washington, DC.

128 Denisoff, *Great Day Coming*, p. 114.

129 *People's Songs*, Vol. 1 No. 1 (February 1964), front page.

issue of June 1947, Italian, French, Irish, Chinese and Jewish songs were featured.[130] Furthermore, perhaps because of its clearly stated and narrow agenda, *People's Songs* reflected few of the prejudices about folk music that would plague the movement in the late 1950s and early 1960s.[131] Notions of what precisely constituted 'authentic' folk music were absent from the magazine. In one issue, composer Elie Siegmeister contributed a piece on the natural symbiosis of classical and folk music, and another issue (one of the first in which the magazine was renamed *Sing Out!*) even featured a song for 'pop [music] fans' entitled 'Peace Hop'![132] Slowly, as the folk revival itself changed in character and scope, the magazine would change – renamed *Sing Out!* in 1949, by Irwin Silber, who would remain editor of the magazine until the mid-1960s, the periodical remained a bastion of the folk revival movement as it unfolded.

Folk Dance in the New York Scene: A Forgotten Tradition

One key aspect of the 1940s folk revival that is often overlooked is the ways in which folk dance societies both served to promote diversity further in the movement, and to bring young people to folk music. Of particular significance was the American Square Dance Group, operated by Margot Mayo in New York during the early 1940s. The group, which ran its own bulletin, *Promenade*, and which attracted some 100–150 members, is frequently omitted from narratives of folk revival history. Nevertheless, in the eyes of Israel Young, an active founder member of the Square Dance Group, Margot Mayo was a crucial force in bringing folk music, particularly Southern folk music, to curious young people.[133] Although he recalled that Mayo was a known Communist, he stated that he did not remember her ever singing or teaching topical songs in the Square Dance Group, and that her vision of folksong was 'pure', consisting mostly of Southern mountain music.[134] The folk dances she taught included Civil War quadrilles, morris dancing and traditional Southern square dancing, and her society became a place for social interaction as well as for learning about folk culture. In an interview with folklore student Richard Reuss in 1965, Israel Young stated that, in his view, Mayo had been one of the true founders of folk music activity in New York, and that People's Artists' claim to centrality had overshadowed her efforts. Staunchly apolitical in his outlook, Israel Young stated that he had felt great resentment when the left-wing folk singers adopted square dancing in their hoots and transformed them into political entities by singing dance instructions such as 'swing your union maid around'![135] However, regardless of the

---

130 *People's Songs*, Vol. 2 No. 5 (June 1947).

131 These will be discussed at length in Chapter 2.

132 Elie Siegmeister, 'Folk Song and Symphony', *People's Songs* Vol. 3 No. 5 (June 1948); 'Peace Hop', *Sing Out!* Vol. 1 No. 5 (September 1950).

133 Israel Young, 1965. Interview by Richard Reuss. Tape-recording, 8 July. The estimate of 100–150 members is Young's. *Promenade*, printed by the American Square Dance Group, ran for several years in the early 1940s. The American Folklife Center in the Library of Congress holds copies of issues from 1940–early 1942.

134 Ibid.

135 Ibid.

conflicting visions of Margot Mayo's group and the People's Artists activities, it is important to include Mayo's group in the history of the revival's development, and to give it its place in the story of the New York revival.[136]

By the early 1950s, the roots of the eclectic folk revival of the 'boom' period were clearly in evidence. Pete Seeger's artistic approach was nurturing a sense of eclecticism and a sense of place which the presence of regional performers such as Woody Guthrie and Molly Jackson had originally exhibited. The New York 'hoots' were also allowing for a wide variety of music styles, and, in the neighbourhood of Greenwich Village, enthusiasts of bluegrass music were, by the early 1950s, beginning to gather in Washington Square on Sunday afternoons to listen to Roger Sprung 'picking' on his banjo and George Margolin leading a wide variety of folk songs.[137] Israel Young, devotee of square dances and, though not a musician, a keen observer and theoriser on the subject of folk music and the revival, opened his Folklore Center, an establishment of central importance to the revival both in New York and in general, in Greenwich Village in 1957. From the first, therefore, variety characterised the folk revival, and an appreciation for the eclecticism and diversity of American culture seemed integral to those who embraced folk music through political conviction. The eclectic nature of the revival, as the next chapter will demonstrate, would be greatly enhanced during the 'boom' period of the late 1950s and early 1960s.

Secular Jewish Culture in North America and the Folk Revival

While it is true that the roots of the folk revival were largely a consequence of American cultural developments and conditions, the popularity of revival-style folk music was beginning to spread beyond the United States borders even prior to the 'great boom' of the post-war era. One vital factor in the 'North Americanisation' of the early folk revival was the increasing interest of both Canadian and American Jewish communities in folk song and folk culture. In the American context, the 'Jewish factor' in the folk revival of the Depression era onwards has been much remarked upon, although little studied. Many of the most significant and pivotal figures in the American folk revival were Jewish – not merely well-known performers such as Bob Dylan, Jack Elliott and John Cohen, but also some of the most important organisational figures such as Moses Asch (founder of Folkways records), Kenneth Goldstein, Ruth Rubin, Irwin Silber, Israel Young, Manny Greenhill and many others.

Secular Jewish culture was represented in the folk revival from the early period, with the Israeli-born Theodore Bikel as its most prominent representative. However, other early folk revivalists desired to further understanding of Jewish music and

---

136 Although Mayo's group was not a professional company of dancers, its activities are not unrelated to those described in Ellen Graff's *Stepping Left*. (Graff, in dealing with trained modern dancers, does not discuss or mention Mayo.)

137 The first Washington Square 'picking sessions' were held in the summer of 1946, but grew significantly in strength in the 1950s. See George Margolin's account of the early sessions, 'Sidewalk Hootenanny', *People's Songs* Vol. 2 Nos. 1 & 2 (February/March 1947).

culture. In 1951, a Jewish Folk Lab was formed by Miriam Rappaport, in which enthusiasts could attend workshops and forums on Yiddish songs and culture.[138] Ruth Rubin, a specialist in Yiddish song, was also prominent in the early revival, and her translations of Yiddish left-wing songs often appeared in *People's Songs*.[139] Rubin also lectured on, and performed, Jewish songs in New York from the 1940s onwards. Her interpretation of Jewish culture was, however, very much in a secular, left-wing vein. According to Israel Young, Rubin presented a biased vision of Jewish-American music which excluded altogether the religious music of the *Hassidim* because she considered religious Jews to have been excessively passive and apolitical. Young also criticised Rubin for insisting upon performing material herself, rather than introducing traditional performers who would bring insights 'from [their] lives' into her lectures – thereby, in his view, maintaining complete control of the material and how she believed it should be interpreted. According to Young, Ruth Rubin was the most significant and prolific figure in Jewish-American folk music at this time.[140] Whether his criticisms of her are just or not, it is clear that the left-wing, secular elements of Jewish culture were prominent in the folk revival as it unfolded. Left-wing sentiment had been carried by the Jewish immigrants from their villages in Eastern Europe to the tenements and sweatshops of the North American cities, and in the context of the new world, it represented a means by which Jewish North Americans could form strong bonds with one another and also reach out to the wider, non-Jewish community.[141]

A significant amount of early folk revival activity in Canada stemmed from the Jewish community. One of the crucial centres for early Jewish-Canadian folk music was a summer camp for Jewish families named Camp Naivelt. Situated several miles from Toronto, Camp Naivelt was founded by the Jewish Women's Labour League as a children's summer retreat, and, like the many similar Jewish camps in the United States, subsequently grew to become a popular destination for working-class, urban Jews.[142] According to former camp-goers, Camp Naivelt, besides fostering strong ethnic and community ties, also helped to promote the humanitarian ideals which

---

138 'Jewish Folk Lab Gets Yiddish Songs', *Sing Out!* Vol. 1 No. 6, 1951.

139 For example, her version of 'Hey Zhukoye', a Soviet Jewish song, was reprinted in *People's Songs* Vol. 2 Nos. 6&7 (August 1947). Rubin's importance was also articulated by Happy Traum in my interview with him of 7 December 2002. See also Ruth Rubin, *Voices of a People: The Story of Yiddish Folksong* (New York, 1973).

140 Israel Young, 1965. Interview by Richard Reuss Tape recording. 26 July. Tape 19,801, Box 1. American Folklife Center, Library of Congress, Washington, DC.

141 Folksinger Happy Traum articulated such ideas in my interview with him of 7 December 2002, and Judith Cohen provided some reminiscences by e-mail in 2003. Ronald Cohen also discusses Jewish involvement in the folk revival in his introduction to *Wasn't That a Time*, p. 8. For a good account of left-wing Jewish activism in Toronto at the turn of the century, see Ruth A. Frager, *Sweatshop Strife: Class, Ethnicity and Gender in the Jewish Labour Movement of Toronto, 1900-1939* (Toronto; Buffalo; London, 1992).

142 The left-wing Jewish camps in America are discussed in Paul C. Mishler, *Raising Reds: The Young Pioneers, Radical Summer Camps and Communist Political Culture in the United States* (New York, 1999) and Judy Kaplan and Linn Shapiro, *Red Diapers: Growing Up in the Communist Left* (Urbana, 1998).

would lead many young Jewish people into the student movement and the folk revival in the 1960s. As Canadian historian Ester Reiter expressed it, the camp helped to reinforce the belief that 'to be Jewish is to care about issues beyond [one]self.'[143]

As a result of this dual focus upon the Jewish community and the wider society, the folk songs performed by campers at Naivelt constituted a mixture of ethnic labour songs and the 'heroic union songs' of contemporary, non-Jewish performers such as Pete Seeger or Woody Guthrie.[144] The camp was visited by Seeger, Paul Robeson and other leading leftist folk performers, who provided inspiration and encouragement to the budding musicians of Camp Naivelt. Their visits coincided with the McCarthy Communist trials, and, according to former camper David Lewis Stein, Seeger declared that Canadian musicians had a particularly significant role now that folk music activity in America was under threat.[145] Certainly, Camp Naivelt nurtured the talents of some significant Canadian revival performers, including future Yorkville-goers Sharon (Trostin) Hampson and Zal Yanovsky, and, particularly, the Travellers, who would become a commercially successful group heavily influenced by The Weavers.[146]

Camp Naivelt and the Toronto Jewish community were instrumental in promoting folk music in Canada; this early, pre-1960s folk music movement represents an early instance of the trans-border appeal of the genre. It is vital to acknowledge the central role played by Jewish North Americans in the folk revival, from the earliest stages; their impact on the unfolding movement shall be discussed intermittently throughout the work.

Towards 'the Great Boom': The Weavers

From the late 1940s onwards, folk musicians with left-wing sympathies came under increasing attack from a government obsessed with the belief that Communists were infiltrating the United States. In the early 1950s, however, the brief career of a group of People's Artists performers calling themselves The Weavers would provide an important link between the strongly political revival of the late 1940s and the folk music boom of the late 1950s which, despite retaining a strong political tone, was also, perhaps inevitably, entangled with the forces of mass culture and

---

143 Quoted in Carolyn Blackman, 'Camp Naivelt Celebrates 75 Years', *Canadian Jewish News*, 20 July 2000.

144 David Lewis Stein, 'Lazy Days of Communist Camping in Brampton', *Toronto Star*, 10 August 2000.

145 Ibid.

146 Nicholas Jennings mentions the protégés of Camp Naivelt on p. 37 of *Before the Gold Rush: Flashbacks to the Dawn of the Canadian Sound* (Toronto and New York: Penguin, 1997). The camp is also mentioned (under its initial name of Camp Kinderland) in Morris Biderman's autobiographical *A Life on the Jewish Left: An Immigrant's Experience* (Toronto, 2000), and on 5 May 2000, when the camp celebrated its 75th anniversary, CBC aired the programme 'Lost and Found Sound' (*Moments in History*) which featured a recently recovered concert held at Naivelt in 1960.

commercialism.[147] Although the members of The Weavers – Pete Seeger, Lee Hays, Ronnie Gilbert and Fred Hellerman – had emerged from the left-wing culture of New York, and although their career as a group would be cut short in the early 1950s by the McCarthy 'red scare', they presented an image and a sound which proved to be highly viable commercially. They were entertainers as much as they were ideologues. Their songs, including a sanitised version of Leadbelly's 'Goodnight, Irene', 'Kisses Sweeter than Wine', 'Tsena' (an arrangement of an Israeli folksong), 'On Top of Old Smoky' and the Seeger-arranged African chant 'Wimoweh', were crisply arranged and sung with the mellifluous polish usually associated with a 1950s pop balladeer. Their style certainly marked a dramatic contrast to the rougher sounds of Woody Guthrie's solo performances. It was estimated that, in 1952 alone (the last year of their career together), The Weavers sold some four million records.[148] Their folk-based style proved utterly compatible with the demands of the popular market. Folksinger Oscar Brand, who observed The Weavers' career, remarked that none of the members of the group had anticipated, or indeed sought, such tremendous popularity; he stated that, when The Weavers were 'finally struck down in full flight' by the governmental investigations, and the subsequent blacklisting of the group and its members by the mainstream entertainment industry, 'they may even have been a little relieved.'[149] The tensions between commercial success and political conviction would prove to be an enduring theme in the folk revival movement. However, nonplussed by the stance of the government, Pete Seeger would continue, throughout the 1950s, to act as the ambassador of folk music to the public, performing throughout the United States and beyond, and opening up the rich and eclectic world of the folk to a new sector of the population – namely, the students of Berkeley, Yale, Cornell and numerous other institutions. If Seeger did not succeed to raise the awareness of folk music of all young Americans – at least those who were white and middle class – then, by 1958, with the release of The Kingston Trio's single 'Tom Dooley', virtually every member of the 'baby boom' generation would be equipped to enter the mysterious world of the folk.

Conclusion

Throughout the twentieth century, in both Canada and America, the definition of 'the folk' altered considerably. Initially, in both countries there existed a strong belief that the only folklore worthy of consideration was that which had emanated from the British Isles. Such a belief was a consequence of strongly Anglo-centric attitudes at the turn of the century. By the inter-war period of the twentieth century, however, the narrow definition of 'the folk' began to expand, and, gradually, folklorists, writers and folklore collectors began to promote the view that the North American continent was a place of great regional and ethnic diversity. John Lomax forcefully challenged

---

147 See Chapter 2. Ronald Cohen has provided an insightful chapter on the brief but fruitful career of The Weavers in *Rainbow Quest*, pp. 67–93.

148 Denisoff, *Great Day Coming*, p. 146.

149 Oscar Brand, *The Ballad Mongers: Rise of the Modern Folk Song* (Westport, CT, 1962), p. 121.

the notion that only British-American folklore was worthwhile by demonstrating the centrality and the unique worth of African-American folklore. Both Lomax and writer Carl Sandburg also revealed the richness of white American folklore and culture in the Southern states and in the Western states of America. This focus on the South and West would be continued during the 1930s, when the Federal Arts Projects and the documentary photographers of the Depression era brought these regions to the forefront of the beleaguered American consciousness.

During the 1920s and 1930s, in both Canada and America, the notion of 'the folk' was also being expanded to include those who came from non-British white backgrounds. The railway concerts of John Murray Gibbon in Canada, and the work of the Federal Writers' Projects in the United States, brought immigrants and non-British white ethnic groups into the narrative of American and Canadian folklore for the first time.

The left-wing Popular Front movement of the 1930s, from which the original urban folksong revival sprang, inherited and promoted this expanded view of North American folk culture, and, in their desire to represent the ordinary people, they continued to place a strong focus on the great cultural and ethnic diversity of North America. In discussions of 'the true folk', Southern and Western American groups still held a position of particular importance, as did the music of African-Americans. Advocates for these cultures, particularly Pete Seeger, promoted their music and brought it to increasingly large audiences.

Although the original urban folk music movement of the 1940s and early 1950s was curtailed by the McCarthy inquisitions, there was no doubt that folk music had entered the public consciousness quite considerably during this period. By the late 1950s, folk music would experience an unprecedented 'boom' in popularity, and the revival, essentially, entered a second phase. In this phase, it became far wider in scope and membership, as it intersected with the culture of a young and quite unique generation. This generation was privileged and idealistic, and ready to promote, to a far greater extent, the dream of a 'rainbow-patterned', diverse North America.

Chapter 2

Visions of Diversity: Cultural Pluralism and the 'Great Boom' of the Folk Revival, 1958–1965

Introduction

Although the folk revival had its roots in the urban culture of left-wing intellectuals, by the end of the 1950s, folk music was beginning to intersect with the ever-growing youth culture. Groups such as The Weavers and The Kingston Trio were attaining 'Top Ten' hit records, and the readership of formerly small publications such as *Sing Out!* was increasing steadily. The revival found audiences in America, Western Europe (particularly the United Kingdom), and also in Canada.

The proximity of Canada to the United States, and the strong influence of American culture on the country, meant that, while geographical distance and longer national histories enabled Western European revivals to emerge from the shadow of the American revival to be considered 'authentic', separate movements in their own right, the 'uniqueness' of the Canadian folk revival was not always so apparent. Indeed, it could be argued that, when the folk revival became a movement of increasing popularity in the late 1950s, its presence in Canada simply represented another instance of American cultural domination. However, to assert this is to oversimplify the nature of the movement. The revival of the late 1950s and early 1960s was, indeed, American in origins and, despite its roots in the dissenting left-wing movements of the inter-war period, it remained, ultimately, idealistic about the role and democratic practices of the United States.

Nonetheless, concerns of nationalism or national identity in the revival of the early 1960s were secondary to a more dominant focus on cultural diversity and pluralism. The revival in both America and Canada celebrated the North American continent as a place of infinite variety and eclecticism; it revelled in the obscure and the detailed, and possessed a vision of 'unity in diversity'. This vision was not, of course, purely the invention of the 'great boom' of the revival. It was, partially, at least, inherited from the 'first wave' of the revival in the 1940s and early 1950s, and from the cultural movements which had originally informed this initial revival – most notably, the activities of early folklore collectors, and the inclusive, folk-cultural spirit of the Great Depression era.[1] However, the revivalists of the late 1950s and early 1960s would enhance the attempts at cultural pluralism and diversity of the earlier revival, and would, as a result, create a movement with far wider boundaries.

---

1   See Chapter 1.

The 'apparatus' of the 1960s folk revival served to enhance the eclecticism of the movement. An examination of some of the major venues of folk revival music – especially coffee-houses and folk festivals – and of the major periodicals of the folk revival demonstrates that the movement was extremely multi-faceted and proud of its great diversity. It accommodated the music of many cultures, musicians and fans of all levels of ability and understanding, and a wide spectrum of opinions regarding the true nature and purpose of folk music. While the many elements gathered beneath the broad 'umbrella' of the revival did not always co-exist easily, they were, ultimately, tolerant of one another. The folk revival movement of the late 1950s and early 1960s did, indeed, present a view of North America as a 'rainbow-patterned' continent.[2]

In attempting to assess why the folk revival of the 'boom' period possessed such a diverse view of North American folk culture, it is possible to uncover several explanations. The Sixties generation (or 'baby boom' generation) which participated in the folk revival was a generation which grew up amidst comparative social and economic security. Despite this, the post-war world of suburban housing, mass culture and conformist values instilled in many of these young people a sense of cultural disorientation and barrenness, for which the revival of folk music constituted part of the remedy. It is significant that those who gravitated towards folk music were white, largely urban or suburban, middle-class youth, estranged by privilege from the immigrant roots of parents and grandparents. Many had grown up in a culture which valued standardisation of culture and values, and which downplayed any sense of diversity or tradition. Thus, many young people would seek to recapture, in the revival, a sense of cultural belonging, whether the desired cultural group was their own or one to which they were outsiders. Immersing oneself in the music of an ethnic or cultural group which at least appeared to possess 'authenticity' and cohesion was a compulsion of the revivalists, and, while such an activity presented problems, both for the movement and for those of the cultural groups in question, it also serves to explain the fascination with diversity exhibited by folk music enthusiasts during this time.

The eclectic character of the folk revival was also closely related to the political stance of many of these same 'baby boomers'. Folk music, during the early 1960s, continued to go hand-in-hand with political activism, and thus many of those who loved folk music also participated in civil right struggles and in the budding student movement. These white, middle-class student revivalists during the early decade at least, still maintained faith in the government to bring about political and social change for the better, and believed that the democratic system would triumph in attaining equality for all social and racial groups. The achievement of unity in diversity was a major goal for the student movement of the early 1960s, and the revival reflected and promoted this aspiration. Such a goal was not without its shortcomings. It would prove itself to be unrealistic by the mid-1960s, and would raise difficult issues about cultural ownership and authenticity, and about the imposition of dominant culture values upon groups of differing ethnic, class and racial origin. Nevertheless, it was

---

2   This quote comes from Pete Seeger, from the introduction to Jean Ritchie (ed.), *The Newport Folk Festival Song Book* (New York, 1964), p. 4.

an aspiration which appeared desirable and applicable to the young people of both Canada and America, who shared a broadly liberal outlook during this time in which a sense of international generational solidarity among the young of the Western world was paramount, cutting across national boundaries. Revivalists in America, thus, believed that to be a true 'American', one had to embrace all the cultures of one's country, understand its variety, and, as Guthrie had advocated, love and respect the land. To be a young left-wing activist at this time was not to turn against one's country, but to remake it according the spirit of its great, egalitarian leaders and render it true to its democratic founding principles.

Canadian revivalists, young, largely white, and liberal like their American counterparts, sympathised with this and could see much that was relevant to them. As North Americans, they, too, could appreciate the music and culture of the regions of their continent. They also sympathised with many of the motives and viewpoints of the American student movement, sensing a generational affinity with its members; Canadian student organisations with similar goals and objectives were formed during this period. They could also, in turn, celebrate and 'rediscover' Canadian traditions; attempts to 'Canadianise' the revival did not so much represent cultural chauvinism or anti-Americanism as they demonstrated a natural extension of the revival's spirit of inclusion, diversity and love of cultural detail.

Involvement in the revival also carried connotations of exclusivity during the early 1960s, something that was extremely important to many young people at this time. If folk music was not entirely a commercial fad, then it was certainly a cult movement which possessed an 'in-crowd' mystique. Involvement in the folk revival was, in the early 1960s, an indication that one aspired to be intellectual and rebellious, something which seemed incongruous to many older traditional musicians, but which was partially inherited from the beatnik movement of the 1950s, and which would later leave its imprint on the late 1960s rock music culture. In an effort to maintain integrity within the revival, commentators often noted that young participants would compete with each other with a mentality which was jokingly termed 'folkier than thou'; in their efforts to demonstrate that they were devotees only of the 'purest' folk music, these revivalists would involve themselves in increasingly obscure forms and styles of music, thus inadvertently increasing the eclectic scope of the movement. Therefore, for various reasons the folk revival of the early 1960s was a movement of diversity in which the continent of North America became an 'imagined community' which was defined in terms of cultural variety, community and the spirit of 'ordinary people'.[3] Young, largely white North American revivalists embraced ambitious, universalistic goals, and satisfied their yearnings for authentic cultural experiences, by celebrating and constructing their continent as a patchwork quilt of cultures, peoples and societies, a phenomenon of infinite variety. Narrower issues of national identity, in the meantime, were placed in a secondary position, and would not rise to the surface in either country until the middle years of the decade.

---

3   Benedict Anderson, *Imagined Communities: Reflections on the Origins and Spread of Nationalism* (London and New York, 1991).

From 'People's Songs' to Commercial Success: The Expansion of the Folk Revival in the Late 1950s

By the early 1950s, groups such as The Weavers had begun to attain notable success with their polished performances of folk songs, and it was becoming clear that folk music (as defined by People's Songs Incorporated and their associates and followers) possessed considerable potential for commercial success.[4] This success had been difficult for The Weavers to justify, in the light of their political ideals, but perhaps naturally, their achievements encouraged other enterprising folk musicians to experiment with more 'mainstream' audiences. Singers such as Burl Ives, a jovial performer who sang traditional material in a stylised and accessible manner, and Harry Belafonte, who helped to increase the popularity of calypso music in the mid-1950s, successfully penetrated a more popular market. Folk music, therefore, had begun to move beyond its role as the weapon of 'the people', and professional performers such as The Weavers, Ives and Belafonte brought it to a larger audience which sought entertainment rather than political instruction.

While it is clear that commercialisation and popularisation were occurring gradually throughout the 1950s, revival historians such as Robert Cantwell maintain that the major catalyst for the 'great boom' of the folk revival was the 1958 release of 'Tom Dooley', a hit single by a young vocal group called The Kingston Trio. The song was an adaptation of a traditional Appalachian ballad describing the murder of a young woman by a mountain man named Tom Dooley. It was unique and novel in its arrangement, blending the exquisite harmonies of young white male vocalists with a calypso beat, and – most curiously – it had a banjo figuring centrally in the instrumentation. For young listeners, at whom the song was aimed, this was, at once, recognisable popular music and something quite new and distinctive. As Robert Cantwell has remarked, the Trio's version of the traditional song was as much a 'new twist' on contemporary popular music as it was a departure from other popular styles of the era. In his words, 'Tom Dooley' represented 'an unexpected departure from, and at the same time an ingenious sublimation, almost a reinterpretation, of what was, at that point, one of the most remarkable entrepreneurial successes in the youth market, rock-and-roll music'.[5] As Cantwell explains, the song, with its dark themes of murder, retribution and execution, removed the young listeners from their environment of 'high school corridors and sock hops' and transported them to the world of Southern mountain culture, albeit a somewhat clichéd view of that culture.

Simultaneously, The Kingston Trio's performance of 'Tom Dooley', however singular, could also be located firmly within the context of contemporary popular music. As Cantwell remarks, the trio, 'with their colorful short-sleeve Ivy League

---

4   See Chapter 1 for a detailed discussion of the career of The Weavers and its significance.

5   Robert Cantwell, 'When We were Good: Class and Culture in the Folk Revival', in Neil Rosenberg (ed.), *Transforming Tradition: Folk Music Revivals Examined* (Urbana, IL and Chicago, IL, 1993), p. 42. Cantwell also discusses this song in the Prologue to his monograph, *When We Were Good: The Folk Revival* (London and Cambridge, MA, 1996), pp. 1–10.

shirts, close-cropped hair, their easy drollery and unambiguous enthusiasm', was 'manifestly collegiate', and it was evident that the group was also rooted in the environment with which the audience of the song was more familiar.[6] Their version of 'Tom Dooley' also exhibited many of the stylistic aspects of the commercial pop music of the period. Their vocals were tuneful and harmonised with flawless accuracy, in the style of contemporary (white) popular singers such as The Crew Cuts or Frankie Avalon; their music had been arranged with slick professionalism, and the rhythm of their version of the song was redolent of that of calypso music, which was at that time a style of music very much in vogue. Robert Cantwell has also pointed out that the lyrics of the Trio's version of the song omitted much of the graphic detail of the young woman's murder which was found in older, more 'traditional' renderings.[7] The Kingston Trio was, thus, a polished, accessible and audience-friendly group whose music represented a peculiar mixture of the exotic and the familiar/popular, and their tremendous success helped to redefine the place of folk revival music in the North American consciousness.

The success of The Kingston Trio was controversial, especially among 'first wave' revivalists whose political convictions led them to deplore the commercial success of 'Tom Dooley'.[8] Others found the record trite and excessively mannered, and considered it to be a threat to traditional musicians who played in a more naturalistic and untutored style. These disagreements regarding what precisely constituted true, or 'authentic', folk music (present in folklore discourse since the days of Francis James Child) would become central to the 'great boom'.[9] However, it is evident that music which possessed folk roots (whether an arrangement of a traditional song, or a song which utilised folk instruments such as guitar or banjo) was, by the eve of the 1960s, accessible to an ever-widening, and, most importantly, an ever more youthful, audience.

It could be argued, therefore, that the folk revival's boom period was brought about, to a considerable extent, by the forces of commercialism. The intersection between the commercial mainstream and folk music would continue, and increase, throughout the 1960s. Some groups – for example, The Brothers Four and The Limeliters of the very early '60s – were highly imitative of The Kingston Trio in sound and style, and presented sanitised and stylised folk music to a mainstream, popular audience. Other groups and individuals were more ambivalent towards popular success, but they discovered, nonetheless, that their music was commercially viable. Peter, Paul and Mary, a New York trio which had been active in the folk revival since

---

6   Cantwell, 'When We Were Good', pp. 44–5.

7   Ibid., pp. 40–41.

8   As discussed in Chapter 1, revivalists of the 'People's Songs' era appeared to value political message over concerns of what constituted 'authentic' folk music, and so editions of *People's Songs Bulletin* would contain folk songs in a popular style, classically arranged folk music, and other hybrid forms. However, the 'first wave' revivalists deplored the idea of performing music for commercial gain, and thus were critical of the Trio.

9   For an early discussion on the merits or otherwise of commercial music, see Robert Coulson, 'Commercialism in Folk Music', *Caravan*, October 1957. (*Caravan* was a very small-scale folk music publication which began in 1957 and ran until the mid-1960s. It possessed a faithful readership and, while it lasted, was highly regarded by folk enthusiasts.)

the 1950s, attained a 'top ten' hit with Pete Seeger's 'Hammer Song' in 1963. Seeger, himself, was successful as a solo artist, and younger revival performers such as Bob Dylan and Joan Baez found considerable commercial success in the early 1960s. These commercially successful musicians would become the public face of the folk revival, possibly leading many to conclude that they were especially representative of its scope and outlook.[10] Some of the 'first wave', politically inclined revivalists, such as *Sing Out!* editor Irwin Silber, were perpetually troubled by the extent of commercialism in a movement which had begun as a left-wing reaction to American capitalism.[11]

However, the entanglement of the folk revival movement with popular culture was, perhaps, inevitable. As the revival historian Daniel Gonczy has suggested, it was virtually impossible for the movement, however unique it considered itself, to avoid being infiltrated by mainstream culture once its popularity began to grow. Mass sales of records by The Kingston Trio, Pete Seeger, The Weavers, Joan Baez, Peter, Paul and Mary, and Bob Dylan; a 'star system' which ranked musicians in a hierarchy of popularity; and the creation of a banal but popular ABC television show, *Hootenanny*, in 1963 – the ultimate commercialising and sanitising of the revival – were all factors which were, in Gonczy's view, unavoidable, being 'such a natural part of American cultural values'.[12] Therefore, commercialism was visible within the revival from the late 1950s onwards, and its presence grew stronger as the 1960s proceeded. Those who wished to keep all commercial interests out of the revival were fighting a losing battle. With the increasing commercialising and mainstreaming of folk music, culminating in advent of folk-rock music in the mid-1960s, came the final demise of the original dream of a communal, non-profit, political 'people's music', as envisaged by Irwin Silber, Pete Seeger and the other creators of People's Songs Incorporated.

It is particularly important to discuss the role of commercialism of the 'great boom', prior to discussing the many other facets and aspects of the diverse movement, because newspaper columnists and commentators of the 1960s in Canada were inclined to think that the popularity of folk music in their country was merely another transplanted American 'fad'– further evidence of the stranglehold of American popular culture upon Canadian culture. Such an explanation of the origins of the Canadian folk revival is worth investigating.

The Growth of the Folk Revival in Canada: A Derivative Movement?

Canadian culture was becoming increasingly influenced by the United States throughout the twentieth century, and, by the post-war period, this was manifesting itself in ways that were quite blatant, as American television, American radio, and American fast food and cinema permeated the culture of many parts of Canada. This

---

10   See, for example, *Time* magazine's pieces on the folk revival in the early 1960s.

11   Eventually, in 1967, Silber would resign from *Sing Out!*, after several years of disputation with other members of the editorial board.

12   Daniel J. Gonczy, 'The Folk Music Movement of the 1960s: Its Rise and Fall', *Popular Music and Society* 10/1 (1985), p. 28.

was particularly true in Southern Ontario, and in other well-populated portions of the country which were in close proximity to the American border.

Styles of American popular music were equally prominent in Canada, and had been since the turn of the century. Again, this was the case in Southern Ontario especially, where, in the post-war era, Canadian residents could tune into American radio stations such as WLAC and WSM Nashville, and listen to popular music shows such as *The Grand Ole Opry* or barn dance music programmes.[13]

As Leslie Bell, Canadian journalist, teacher and musician, remarked in 1955, prior to the ascendance of rock 'n' roll, 'the advent of the modern gramophone and of sound film, radio and television during the last thirty-five years has resulted in this country's being flooded with the popular songs of the United States.' He described the Canadian tastes for American dance band music and jazz; he also exhibited awareness of the long-standing curse of the Canadian music scene – namely, the exodus of talented musical individuals to the United States in pursuit of more lucrative careers. Although Bell maintained that Canadian tastes were not exactly identical to those of their neighbours to the south – he insisted that 'Canadians ... are not as immediately attracted by novelty tunes and frivolous lyrics as are Americans and show a greater preference for pleasant melody', and he also noted Canadian preferences for British styles, such as music-hall songs – he regretfully found himself forced to emphasise 'the role of the United States in the story of Canadian popular music'.[14]

During the 1950s, Canadians were swamped with American rock 'n' roll, and exhibited intense pride in Canadian 'equivalents' to American teen idols, such as Bobby Curtola, a 'Canadian Fabian', and the Ottawa-born teenager Paul Anka, who gained a number one hit with his song "Diana" in 1957. Extraneous musical trends would, likewise, be rigorously embraced in Canada during the 1960s – imitators of American rhythm and blues bands and 'British invasion' style bands proliferated throughout the early and mid-1960s in cities and towns across Canada.[15] Thus, there is no doubt that Canada was profoundly influenced by American cultural and musical trends by the mid-twentieth century.

Nonetheless, it is erroneous to assume that America dominated utterly a helpless Canadian music industry. As has been stated, the influence of American music depended, to a great extent, upon the geographical location of Canadians; those in southern parts of the provinces, particularly Ontario, received a considerable

---

13 Both Rick Danko and Garth Hudson, who would later join the backing band of American singer Ronnie Hawkins prior to becoming members of influential group The Band, mentioned listening intently to music on American radio stations as children. See Steve Caraway, 'Robbie Robertson/Rick Danko: Heart and Soul of the Band', *Guitar Player* December 1976, and Garth Hudson's comments in the piece on The Band featured in Irwin Stambler, *Encyclopedia of Rock, Pop and Soul* (New York, 1989, rev. edn), p. 30.

14 Leslie Bell, 'Popular Music', in Ernest MacMillan (ed.), *Music in Canada* (Toronto, 1955), pp. 208–15.

15 For instance, The Lords of London and The Sparrow in Toronto, and The Guess Who of Winnipeg, who were particularly influenced by The Beatles. Further information about such influences on Canadian music may be found in popular publications such as John Einarson, *Shakin' All Over: The Winnipeg Sixties Rock Scene* (Winnipeg, 1987) and Brian Kendall, *Our Hearts Went Boom: The Beatles' Invasion of Canada* (Toronto, 1997).

amount of American programming. Any discussion of post-war Canadian popular culture should, thus, consider the many voices which were raised in concern over the potential Americanisation of Canadian media – in particular, the members of the Massey Commission, a body which pressed for an independent and meaningful Canadian culture. Much of the programming on CBC television after 1945 aimed to promote Canadian content and culture.[16] A protective 'Canadian content' regulation for television was also introduced in the early 1950s.

Furthermore, despite the strong influence of American culture, distinctive Canadian musical voices were to be heard on the airwaves in the post-war era. The Maritime fiddler Don Messer presented a weekly programme entitled *Don Messer's Jubilee*, which boasted an avid national audience, and which presented a vision of Canada reflective of the regional culture of the Maritimes, rather than the dominant Southern Ontario culture.[17] The music of Don Messer was also part of a strong tradition of distinctively Canadian country music, a genre which continued to attract many listeners. Neil Rosenberg has shown that, although American country music was popular in Canada, the country music which was to be found in the Maritimes was a distinctive regional variant of the genre which incorporated a number of influences from British music hall and vaudeville to Celtic folk music.[18] Robert Klymasz has also contributed to this field of study with his work on Ukrainian-Canadian country music in the Prairie Provinces.[19] Therefore, in post-war Canada, 'popular music' was much more than merely American music transplanted.

In spite of such manifestations of musical autonomy, it is possible to view the movement's spread to Canada as being, largely, a result of the influence of American popular culture on the country. Key figures of the folk revival, from Joan Baez to Simon and Garfunkel, were eagerly welcomed by urban Canadian audiences when they toured north of the American border in the early 1960s, and, when Canadian folk music acts such as Gordon Lightfoot and Ian and Sylvia Tyson began to find success, the Canadian press framed their good fortune in terms of their American counterparts, describing them in such terms as 'Canada's answer to Bob Dylan' or 'the Canadian version of Peter, Paul and Mary'.[20] Canadian observers, in the press, certainly appeared to view the folk revival of their country as another passing American fad, and were often inclined to view it somewhat scathingly. A short piece in the Toronto *Star* in August 1963 on 'The Folk Song Syndrome' amusedly discussed 'the apparent taste of the young for union protest songs, dustbowl blues, slave laments, and love ballads that tell of murder or suicide or both' and viewed the movement as essentially nothing more than another 'entertainment business

---

16   Paul Rutherford, *When Television Was Young: Primetime Canada, 1952–1967* (Toronto; Buffalo, NY; London, 1990), p. 14.

17   For a celebratory tribute to Messer, see Lester B. Sellick, *Canada's Don Messer* (Kentville, Nova Scotia, 1969).

18   Neil Rosenberg, *Country Music in the Maritimes: Two Studies* (Memorial University Dept. of Folklore Reprint Series No. 2, 1976).

19   Robert Klymasz, "Sounds You Never Heard Before': Ukrainian Country Music in Western Canada', *Ethnomusicology*, 16 (1972): 372–80.

20   See, for example, Marvin Schiff, 'Modern Writers Blowing Cobwebs from an Old Idea', Toronto *Globe*, 17 April 1965, an interview with Ian Tyson and Gordon Lightfoot.

bonanza'.[21] Generally, the press tended to focus on folk music concerts and events which were poorly organised and mediocre, such as the Maple Leaf Gardens' 'Harvest Hootenanny' in October 1963 (described by *Globe and Mail* columnist Marvin Schiff as 'a night of tedium unrelieved'), or on the more overtly commercial events, such as the 'Folkathon' (folksinging marathon) held for charity in the Shoppers' World Plaza in Toronto in June 1963, a phenomenon denounced by Schiff as '[one] of the worst excesses of folk music faddism'.[22] For the press, at least in Toronto, which became, as will be made apparent, the ostensible centre of the Canadian revival, the movement was little more than another forgettable popular culture trend which would be bound, ultimately, to go the way of other such passing phases. Hence, it would be relatively easy to portray the folk revival in Canada as a direct imitation of a movement originating in America, a youth culture trend which was transient and essentially replaceable.

While arguments of American cultural imperialism may, perhaps, be considered most applicable to English-speaking Canada, considering the geographical proximity and the many similarities of origin, economy and language of the two nations, they are, as usual, too simplistic and extreme. Those who participated in the Canadian folk revival during the 1960s certainly do not deny the tremendous influence of American music and politics upon the Canadian movement, but they would never simply describe themselves as having been passive receptors of an extraneous tradition which seemed more appealing and interesting than their own. One former participant, when asked if he considered the Canadian revival to have been a copy of the American movement, or something quite distinct, replied: 'well, copy and distinct aren't the only alternatives'.[23] Former revivalist musicians in Canada are frequently, and justifiably, baffled, even irritated, by the contention that they were victims of cultural imperialism; they will often respond to the effect that, although the music they played was, indeed, American in origin, they did not see it that way – it was 'just music', not to be dissected or separated so arbitrarily.[24] As folk revival participant Brian Walsh remarked, when asked if there was a 'distinctly Canadian' quality to the music of Canadian folk musicians, responded that he preferred to consider music as 'the individual artist's own voice. And I think that's the way to put it – it's the individual artist's own voice. It's not like the Group of Seven. The Group of Seven tried to have the Canadian artistic voice in the early part of the century; now these folks weren't doing that. They were just doing their thing.'[25]

---

21 Barrie Hale, 'The Folksong Syndrome', *Toronto Star*, 10 August 1963.

22 Marvin Schiff, 'A Night of Tedium Unrelieved', *Globe and Mail*, 19 October 1963; and 'A Blaring Bandwagon Rolls Towards Obscurity', *Globe and Mail*, 25 April 1964.

23 Brian Walsh, in discussion with the author, Toronto, 8 October 2002. The Group of Seven was an artistic movement of the early twentieth century, comprised of seven painters who specialised in naturalistic and singular depictions of the Canadian landscape.

24 Many of those whom I have interviewed expressed such a viewpoint – including Richard Flohil, Ken Whiteley and Michael Van Dusen.

25 Brian Walsh, discussion. The Group of Seven were Canadian artists whose depictions of the landscapes of their country were considered unique and were lauded by nationalists for their 'Canadian' qualities.

Theories of cultural appropriation clash, therefore, with the pervasive and widespread belief that music is 'a universal … language which touches a common chord across humanity and which transcends cultural differences'.[26] Beliefs of such an intuitive and emotional nature, although they may be easily dismissed as 'constructions' in the academic sphere, can never be destroyed, and attempting to take issue with them may prove futile.

As far as the folk revival in Canada is concerned, although its American origins and influence must be taken into account, to attempt to explain it entirely as an instance of another American popular culture 'fad' in translation is to misunderstand the complexity of the movement. Commercialism was, in reality, merely one aspect of a movement which was, until the mid-1960s at least, intensely multi-faceted. The 'great boom' was not simply a consequence of young people buying more folk music records. Commercial successes brought folk music to larger audience, but the movement, even in the height of its popularity, still owed much to local 'scenes' and to the efforts of particular key groups, organisations and individuals. These 'revival makers' were diverse in age, viewpoints and interests, and, partially as a result of this, they helped to create and sustain a movement which was intensely diverse and pluralistic in its scope. Partially as a result of the complex interplay of local, regional and national folk 'scenes', and of the varied interests of the revival makers, the 'great boom' was a movement of tremendous diversity. Like the original revival of the immediate post-Second World War era, the folk movement of the early 1960s promoted the view that folk music was, in the words of Neil Rosenberg, 'a broad texture, a mosaic, that included many different facets'.[27] An examination of three of the major types of forum for folk music revival activity – namely, coffee-houses, folk festivals and revival magazines – as well as of those who organised and helped to shape these forums, illustrates the ways in which the revival reflected and promoted its vision of a 'rainbow-patterned' North America.

Making an Eclectic Revival: Coffee-houses, Folk Festivals, Folk Magazines and the Promotion of Musical Diversity

The mosaic-like character which the revival possessed was both reflected in, and promoted by, the nature of those *locales* which served as its major venues during this period; namely, urban coffee-houses and folk festivals. Both the coffee-house and the folk festival were venues in which a diverse group of people might, in addition to hearing the featured 'star' performers, perform their own particular material, listen to one another, and discuss music and ideas.

Coffee-houses had, by the early 1960s, become vital gathering-places for young folk musicians across the North American continent. The epicentre of the coffee-house scene was in New York City, and particularly in the Greenwich Village area. Italian residents of this neighbourhood owned and operated coffee-houses which were intended principally for their own community members, but which came to be

---

26   Keith Negus, *Popular Music in Theory* (Cambridge, 1996), p. 177.

27   Neil Rosenberg, 'Overview', in Ronald D. Cohen (ed.), *Wasn't That a Time! First-Hand Accounts of the Folk Music Revival*, (Metuchen, NJ, 1993), p. 72.

frequented by the artists, writers and bohemian thinkers who had been congregating in the district since the turn of the twentieth century.[28] By the 1950s, many coffee-houses, some of which were Italian, and others which had been opened by enterprising businesspeople, began to include entertainers.[29] Responding to the tastes and bohemianism of many of their clients, coffee-house owners often booked jazz artists, and Chet Baker, Charles Mingus and John Coltrane made regular appearances around the village. By the early 1960s, as folk music became increasingly popular among young intellectuals of the neighbourhood, coffee-house owners responded by promoting their premises as folk music venues where well-known musicians could perform, and where budding talents could experiment. In Greenwich Village, by the early 1960s, folk music could be heard at, among other places, the Café Wha?, the Village Vanguard, Gerde's Folk City, and the Gaslight.

Coffee-house 'culture' spread throughout North America, as young folk music enthusiasts sought suitable venues in their local area, and as entrepreneurs recognised the commercial potential of folk music. Chicago, Boston and San Francisco, as well as Montreal and Toronto, also boasted particularly active coffee-house 'scenes' in which folk music was central, but coffee-houses of a similar nature could be found in smaller cities and towns across the continent.[30] Radio programmes devoted to folk music – such as Studs Terkel's *Almanac* radio show in Chicago, Oscar Brand's *Folk Song Festival* in New York, and the work of Ed McCurdy on CBC radio, among others – enthusiastically promoted the local scenes and their musicians.[31] The coffee-houses across the country were local manifestations of an international movement, and, as such, they helped to promote and encourage the diversity of the movement, through the presentation of a wide range of musical acts, and through the promotion and showcasing of all levels of talent.

In major folk music neighbourhoods such as Greenwich Village and Yorkville in Toronto, amateur performers would be provided with the opportunity to showcase their material during 'open stage' nights. In Toronto, for example 'hoot nights' were held, first at the Bohemian Embassy coffee-house, and then at the Riverboat each Monday evening throughout the early and mid-1960s. These evenings were organised

---

28   For a more detailed discussion of the development of the coffee-house 'scene' in Greenwich Village, see Chapter 3.

29   For an interesting contemporary account of the Greenwich Village 'scene', see Thomas J. Fleming, 'Greenwich Village: The Search for Identity', *Cosmopolitan*, December 1963. See also Chapter 3 of this study.

30   An interesting 1966 publication by the Denver Folklore Center provides a list of coffee-houses in each major American city. See Harry M. Tuft, *The Denver Folklore Center Catalogue and Almanac of Folk Music Supplies and Information for the Fiscal Year 1966* (Denver, CO, 1966), pp. 195–8 (from the collection of the American Folklife Center, Library of Congress, Washington, DC).The importance of Boston's celebrated Club 47 is mentioned in Jim Rooney and Eric Von Schmidt, *Baby Let Me Follow You Down: The Illustrated History of the Cambridge Folk Years* (Garden City, NY, 1979), p. 91, and references to the club are featured throughout the memoir.

31   See Ronald Cohen, *Rainbow Quest: The Folk Music Revival and American Society, 1940–1970* (Amherst, MA and Boston, MA, 2002), pp. 39 and 115–16. Cohen's detailed book provides in-depth accounts of the developments of many of the local folk scenes.

by the Toronto Folk Guild, a small, loose affiliation of folk music enthusiasts who first gathered together in the late 1950s, and who would come to play an important role in the development of folk music in the city, and in Ontario at large. According to Toronto folk musician Ken Whiteley, Estelle Klein, who was the head of the Folk Guild and the organiser of the 'hoots', wished to promote as diverse a vision of folk music as possible, and everything from traditional singing to jug band and skiffle music was present on these occasions.[32] This diversity was evident in the other folk music venues around Yorkville, in which the blues of the legendary Muddy Waters or Lonnie Johnson, the more commercial sounds of local groups such as The Dirty Shames, the original songs of budding composers such as Joni Anderson or Bruce Cockburn, and even jazz and poetry, could all be experienced at the various coffee-houses and clubs in any one evening.

As significant as the diversity of music presented was the fact that these revival venues were welcoming and encouraging to amateurs as well as famous professional performers. Indeed, amateurs had a whole range of potential venues to choose from; in Greenwich Village, many of the 'unknown' folk music performers would congregate in clubs and coffee-houses known as 'baskethouses' where they might perform short sets and subsequently obtain payment by passing a hat around the audience, while scores of amateur enthusiasts of all levels of ability would join in the weekly sessions in Washington Square simply for enjoyment.[33]

'Coffee-houses' *per se* were not the only venues to promote such inclusiveness and diversity. Indeed, the title of 'coffee-house' was often applied liberally to any venue, or even event, at which folk music was played and coffee was provided. For instance, urban High Schools and Colleges held 'coffee-house' evenings regularly, and Ken Whiteley recalls that 'coffee-houses' hosted in churches were a magnet for inexperienced, fledgling performers.[34] Other establishments played key roles in encouraging the diversity of the folk revival in particular cities. For example, Israel Young's Folklore Center, which opened in Greenwich Village in 1957, was a vital place of congregation for folk music enthusiasts in New York; Young, a gregarious personality and a passionate observer of, and commentator on, the folk music scene, encouraged and enjoyed the discussion of folk music in the store.[35] Young also organised concerts for budding performers, thus providing venues for local, as well as nationally known, talent. The Old Town School of Folk Music, also established in 1957, played a comparable role within the Chicago folk music scene. Founded by Win Stracke and Frank Hamilton, the School, which provided instrumental instruction, lecture series and a forum for discussion for young folk music enthusiasts, aimed to promote and encourage local talent, and to foster a view of folk music which was diverse and all-embracing, with emphasis placed on 'social'

---

32 Ken Whiteley, in discussion with the author, Toronto, 13 January 2003.

33 The origins of the Washington Square sessions are discussed in Chapter 1. The sessions will be further discussed in Chapter 3.

34 Ibid.

35 John Cohen (II), in Cohen (ed.), *Wasn't That a Time*, p. 180. Young's was not the only folklore centre in existence – as Neil Rosenberg pointed out to me, similar, if less prominent, institutions also existed in Denver, Ottawa and Toronto, among other cities.

learning, rather than rigorous, 'classical' training.[36] Coffee-houses, and other, similar venues, were clearly crucial to the promotion of diversity within the folk revival of the late 1950s and early '60s. They provided a local 'framework' for a movement which had grown to national proportions; they promoted all levels of talent; and they encouraged a diversity of musical styles.

Folk music festivals also helped to promote the diverse character of the folk revival during the late 1950s and early 1960s. Folk festivals were not innovations of this era – festivals of Southern US music styles, such as the National Folk Festival held in the 1930s, and festivals which celebrated cultural diversity in a broader sense, such as John Murray Gibbon's 'Railway Concerts' of the late 1920s, had been successful and influential.[37] As folk music grew in popularity in urban circles during the 1940s, the 'People's Songs' revivalists began to organise some small-scale folk music festivals, such as the 'Sing Out, America' Festival, held in Chicago in October 1947.[38]

The folk festival which became particularly central to the 'great boom' of the 1960s was the Newport Folk Festival, held in Newport, Rhode Island. The first Newport Festival was held in 1959, and was organised by George Wein, who had been encouraged by the success of the Newport Jazz Festivals, held at the same site some years earlier. From relatively small beginnings, the Newport Folk Festival became an event of great importance to the revival of the 1960s. It was also a vital forum for the great diversity of music styles which formed part of the folk revival, particularly after 1963, when festival organisers began to emphasise the inclusion of traditional musicians as well as revivalists.[39] Thereafter, Newport featured a tremendous variety of acts; for example, in 1964, according to *Sing Out!*, the festival showcased 'a melange of "big names" coupled with lesser-known traditional talent and up-and-coming city artists'.[40] Peter, Paul and Mary, The Clancy Brothers, Dylan, Baez, Seeger, Judy Collins and several other distinguished musicians shared the stage with traditional singers such as blues artists Mississippi John Hurt and Elisabeth Cotton, country and bluegrass performers such as Hobart Smith, Doc Watson and Ralph Stanley, a sacred harp group and a Cajun band, among many others. Southern and Western American music styles were presented, as was the music of other ethnic and cultural groups within America. Folk revival participants often sought to be informed as well as to be entertained, and, thus, academic perspectives on folk music were provided at the 1964 festival by distinguished folklorists such as D.K. Wilgus and Alan Lomax.[41]

---

36   Frank Hamilton, in ibid, pp. 156–7. See also a Letter Excerpt from Frank Hamilton regarding the progress of the school, printed in the folk music magazine *Caravan*, March 1958.

37   For more details on these festivals, see Chapter 1.

38   Advertised in *People's Songs*, Vol. 2 No. 8, September 1947.

39   See Cohen, *Rainbow Quest*, pp. 208–209.

40   Paul Nelson, 'Newport: The Folk Spectacle Comes of Age', *Sing Out!* 14/5 (November 1964), p. 8. The American Folklife Center of the Library of Congress, Washington, DC, has a collection of Newport Folk Festival Programmes from 1959–69.

41   Ibid., pp. 6–11.

The Mariposa Folk Festival emerged in 1961 as a Canadian parallel to the Newport Festival. The initial festival was organised by Ruth Jones, Crawford Jones and Pete McGarvey, and was held in Orillia, a small town some miles north of Toronto.[42] The original festival was a very small-scale affair, but, gradually, it grew in strength, and began to feature a diversity of performers – a mixture of the traditional and the neo-traditional, the popular folk 'stars', the commercial and the unusual, from Canada, America and beyond. The 1966 festival, for example, featured, among others, blues performers Sunnyland Slim and Big Walter Horton, gospel singers The Staples, The Canadian Indian Dancers, traditional Ontario singers Tom Brandon and LaRena Clark, local bluegrass band The Gangrene Boys, commercial Yorkville folk group The Stormy Clovers, as well as famous performers such as Pete Seeger, Gordon Lightfoot, Tom Paxton and Ian Tyson. The festival programmes were comprised of short biographies of the performers as well as educational articles and essays on specific folk music styles; folklorist Edith Fowke contributed a piece on Ontario folk music and Leigh Cline wrote an article on Old-Time music.[43]

Newport and Mariposa were both, thus, highly eclectic festivals, and many former participants saw no need to interpret their agendas as having been anything other than a desire to represent as many styles of folk music as possible. Nevertheless, Newport was the larger gathering, and it pre-dated the Canadian festival by a year; it may, therefore, be worthwhile to consider the extent to which the Mariposa organisers were concerned with creating a festival which was not 'in the shadow' of Newport, and whether or not issues of Canadian identity or nationalism played any part in their agenda. Once again, it is impossible to formulate a simplistic answer to such a question. Evidence does exist which suggests that some organisers and commentators did think that Mariposa should be a 'Canadian' festival; considerable attention was given to this issue in the editorial of a 1963 edition of *Hoot* magazine, a Canadian revival periodical. Ed Cowan, publicity director for Mariposa in 1963, suggested that the creation of a nationally focused perspective had been a crucial issue for the festival:

> For the past two years the hottest single issue at the festival has been the 'truly Canadian sound' … Is there a Canadian tradition and if there is, why don't we hear more about it? The arguments were strong and sometimes bitter … Collectors argued that performers ignored the many thousands of songs that were purely Canadian. They also berated Canadian performers for not having the courage of their so-called convictions by getting out and collecting some Canadian material.[44]

Jack Wall, director of the festival that year, concurred with this by stating that it was his aim to make Mariposa 'a truly Canadian event', one which might even make a contribution to the celebration of the Confederation Centennial of 1967. Neither

---

42   Canadian writer Stephen Leacock, who had been born in Orillia, had written a number of 'sketches' in which he gave his hometown the fictitious name of 'Mariposa' – hence the name of the Festival.

43   Programme for the Mariposa Folk Festival, held at Innis Lake, Ontario, 5–7 August 1966 (Toronto Public Library, Central Branch, Vertical Files).

44   *Hoot* , Issue 1, August 1963.

contributor explained in detail what constituted a 'a truly Canadian sound' – that is, whether Canadian music was simply a form of folk music which originated in Canada, or whether its 'Canadian' quality was something less evident which had to be discerned by intuition. However, the brief pieces in this edition of *Hoot* certainly seem to suggest that discourse on the folk revival and its relationship to Canadian identity was both prolific and significant. Halifax-born singer Denny Doherty would confirm this notion in his interview with Nicholas Jennings, when he claimed that his group, The Halifax Three, were turned away by the Mariposa Folk Festival committee in 1962 because, as recorded artists who performed in bars, '[they] were way too successful for [anti-commercial revivalists] … Plus, [they] weren't performing Canadian folk songs, which was a huge faux pas …'[45]

It is arguable that those who wished to 'Canadianise' the Mariposa festival in this way were not the representative majority, but merely a small faction within the organising committee and audience. The folklorist Edith Fowke helped to promote a 'Canadian' focus at Mariposa. Fowke, who contributed a great deal to workshops and programmes at the Mariposa Festival, frequently emphasised the virtues of Canadian traditional songs (especially those originating in Ontario) because of her strong belief in the particular purity and integrity of music passed down through oral traditions. Ruth Jones, one of the original founders of Mariposa, was also, apparently, concerned with preserving the 'Canadian' qualities of the festival.[46] Their viewpoints were, however, in considerable contrast to that of Estelle Klein, another profoundly influential organiser of Mariposa, who would direct the Festival throughout the late 1960s until 1980. Ken Whiteley perceived Estelle Klein to be most broad-minded in her definition of folk music and in her view of what the Mariposa Festival should represent:

I can't understate the importance of Estelle Klein's vision … and what she did with Mariposa was … a huge influence. [*sic*] She had a very broad taste, and she recognised that world music, folk and blues … [there was] no distinction really there. She had no problem with electric instruments versus acoustic instruments or any of those kinds of issues. And she had this very broad interest … and at the same time, she was interested in having people make connections … and to recognise that the Stormy Clovers or … these different folk-rock bands … were part of a continuum.[47]

Estelle Klein, who had first become interested in folk music through friends who were involved with labour movements, was greatly influenced by the eclectic nature of the Newport Folk Festival, and hoped to create, in Mariposa, a festival of a similar breadth and diversity. She was not overly concerned with the creation of a 'Canadian' festival, although fellow organisers continued to believe that this was a priority. Feeling the necessity to provide for young folk music enthusiasts 'a breadth of knowledge' of their subject of interest, she set about bringing in as great

---

45   Quoted in Nicholas Jennings, *Before the Gold Rush*, p. 46.

46   Estelle Klein, telephone conversation with the author, 1 April 2004. Ken Whiteley discussed the careers of both Estelle Klein and Edith Fowke during my interview with him on 13 January 2003.

47   Whiteley, discussion.

a diversity of musicians as possible.[48] By the early 1970s, she had established, at Mariposa, workshops for Native culture and for Francophone folklore and culture, and she would attend small festivals organised by particular ethnic groups and invite some of their participants to appear at Mariposa.[49] For Klein, therefore, the idea that the Mariposa Festival should be recognisably 'Canadian' was not as significant as the drive to make the Festival as eclectic and varied as possible.

Richard Flohil, who was active in music promotion in Toronto from the late 1950s onwards, suggests that, although Canadian material was showcased at Mariposa, these performances were not motivated by chauvinistic nationalism. Flohil remarked that, in his view, 'it was natural that when a folk event was in Canada, they were obviously going to look at Canadian folklorists for guidance. That was just natural; it wasn't about not doing American stuff.'[50]

Thus, it is fair to conclude that, while some participants and organisers of Mariposa concerned themselves with the creation of a 'Canadian' festival, whatever that might signify, others held broader views which, similar to those of Newport organisers, focused on the celebration of place, whether that place was one's own region or town or one far away, both geographically and culturally. Just as Newport featured a *mélange* of traditional musicians, from near and far, and newcomer revival performers, so too, did Mariposa celebrate eclecticism in a manner which was partially similar to, and partially in contrast to, the Newport Festival.

Folk festivals such as Newport and Mariposa were memorable to participants, not merely for the events on the main stages, but also for the sharing of songs and musical ideas via the organised 'workshops' or merely while sitting in the audience. Folk musician Michael Van Dusen's main recollection of the Mariposa Folk Festival was of 'people … sitting around everywhere with autoharps, guitars and banjos – any number of instruments … Sitting around in absolutely bucolic settings … under willow trees … groups of people, unamplified, sitting around and jamming'.[51] Just as the coffee-houses had been important centres for amateur music-sharing and 'jamming', so too were the folk festivals important forums for the sharing of ideas and the interactions among members of the audience.[52]

Newport and Mariposa, and other, subsequent festivals, clearly helped to shape the tastes of folk music enthusiasts by offering a tremendously diverse programme of musicians. Every category of folk musicians identified by Ellen Stekert – from traditional musicians and their imitators to 'new aesthetic' singer-songwriters – was represented at the major folk festivals.[53] Later festivals, such as the gatherings in Philadelphia and Edmonton, Alberta, would, likewise, showcase a wide range of

---

48   Estelle Klein, telephone conversation.

49   For example, Klein met a troupe of Portuguese 'stick dancers' at a Portuguese festival in Toronto, and invited them to appear at Mariposa in the early 1970s.

50   Richard Flohil, in discussion with the author, Toronto, 6 May 2003.

51   Michael Van Dusen, in discussion with the author, Toronto, 27 November 2002.

52   Neil Rosenberg discusses the participatory nature of the 'workshops' at folk festivals in *Bluegrass: A History* (Urbana, IL and Chicago, IL, 1985), p. 150.

53   Ellen Stekert's classifications of the different kinds of folk music in the revival are outlined in the Introduction.

musical styles while maintaining a certain measure of uniqueness in their characters.[54] Overall, therefore, the folk festivals were instrumental in encouraging and promoting the regional, eclectic vision of the revival of the early 1960s.

The magazines of the revival also served to promote and encourage further this fascination with musical diversity. *Sing Out!,* which had begun in 1946 as the left-wing *People's Songs Bulletin* had, by the early 1960s, become a widely-read and widely-available publication.[55] Although it retained much of its political character (largely due to the editorial influence of Irwin Silber, whose left-wing views were well-known and who had been involved with *People's Songs* since its origins), the magazine was, by the early 1960s, a compendium of brief, varied articles on multifarious styles of music. Articles written by freelance journalists and the editorial team (which included, by the early 1960s, John Cohen, Israel Young, and Pete Seeger) presented a wide range of opinions and, indeed, definitions of folk music. For instance, one edition from late 1964 contained pieces on Mississippi John Hurt, Tom Paxton, calypso music, British whaling songs and country musicians Sam and Kirk McGee.[56]

Of all the regular contributors to *Sing Out!*, Pete Seeger was the most encouraging of this diverse perspective on the music of the United States. As a political campaigner and enthusiastic folksong collector, he had spent his life travelling around the country and beyond, and in each edition of the magazine, in his 'Johnny Appleseed Jr.' column, he would recount tales of his musical and cultural discoveries. Benjamin Filene has argued that Pete Seeger had a particular appeal for many young revivalists because his background as a middle-class, former Harvard student was most similar to theirs; he revealed to them, through his experiences, that the workaday world of 'the folk' might be accessible to them.[57] Hence, his columns for the magazine, collected in edited form in his autobiographical work *The Incompleat Folksinger*, helped to form, in the minds of his younger followers, impressions of a world of cultural richness and infinite diversity, a world in which they might have a share, whatever their cultural background – or perceived lack thereof. As he admitted:

> I am several generations away from whatever folk traditions my great-grandparents had. Now, suddenly I come along and realize my paucity and try and recapture a few traditions … My own solution has been to try and learn from other people. I have learned from Negro people, from Jewish people, from Ukrainian people and many others.[58]

---

54   For a popular overview of the history of the Edmonton Folk Festival, see Rod Campbell, *Playing the Field: The Story of the Edmonton Folk Music Festival* (Edmonton, 1994).

55   See Chapter 1 for more detail on *People's Songs Bulletin* and the early days of *Sing Out!*. The magazine was renamed in 1949.

56   Ibid.

57   Benjamin Filene, *Romancing the Folk: Public Memory and American Roots Music* (Chapel Hill, NC and London, 2000), p. 204.

58   Pete Seeger, *The Incompleat Folksinger,* edited by Jo Metcalf Schwartz (New York, 1972), p. 544.

Seeger, thus, was particularly instrumental in shaping the eclectic dynamic of the revival, particularly through his writings in *Sing Out!*

Sing Out! was, arguably, one of the most catholic of the folk revival periodicals, catering to the broad spectrum of folk music fans (with the possible exception of those who loved the more 'commercial' types of folk music) and attempting to reach and respond to as wide a range of readers as possible. However, other major folk music magazines of the 'boom' period were more specialised and specific in their outlook and intentions. These served, arguably, to complement the broader perspective of *Sing Out!* and to respond to, and shape, the interests of those readers who had more particular opinions on what folk music should be. For example, *Broadside* magazine was begun in the early 1960s by Agnes 'Sis' Cunningham, a former member of the left-wing Almanac Singers.[59] This magazine contained virtually no editorials or articles; it was a compilation of music and lyrics for new and old topical (social or political) songs from all over the world. This emphasised and reflected the interests of those revival participants who believed that folk music should continue to be an instrument of social protest, as well as encouraging young people to become more involved in the folk music movement by learning to sing and play these songs for themselves. The magazine was also an important vehicle for new songwriters – the songs of Bob Dylan and Phil Ochs, among others, were first published in *Broadside*.

Equally important to the promotion of diversity in the revival, however, were the small-scale, individualistic, and often eccentric, periodicals known as 'fanzines'. Among such publications were *Gardyloo*, which existed for a short time during the late 1950s, and *Caravan*, begun by Lee Shaw in 1957, and in existence until the early 1960s.[60] Perhaps the most unique, and significant, of such 'fanzines' was *The Little Sandy Review*. Begun in 1959 by Paul Nelson and Jon Pankake, two devotees of folk music, the small, cheaply produced magazine was comprised solely of reviews of folk records, concerts and festivals, and was available purely by subscription. The original edition of the magazine contained a revealing statement from the editors concerning their outlook and purpose: 'Our creed is a very simple one. We are two people who love folk music very much and want to do all we can to help the good in it grow, and the bad in it perish. After reading this issue, it should be very apparent to anyone who we think is good and who we think is bad and why.'[61]

Such blissful subjectivity was, as Jon Pankake would state in 1991, a vital facet of the magazine's status as part of a 'subjournalistic tradition [known as the] fanzine'.[62] As Pankake explained, 'fanzines' like *The Little Sandy Review* were intended for a select audience, and were thoroughly and wilfully biased; there was no room for

---

59   The origins of *Broadside* are briefly discussed in Cohen, *Rainbow Quest*, pp. 179–83.

60   Copies of *Caravan* from No. 1 (August 1957) to No. 14 (December–January 1959–60) are held in the American Folklife Center, Library of Congress, Washington, DC. The Folklife Center holds two or three editions of *Gardyloo* from the late 1950s.

61   *Little Sandy Review*, No. 1 (1959). See also Ronald Cohen's brief discussion of the magazine in *Rainbow Quest*, pp. 164–68.

62   Jon Pankake in Cohen (ed.), *Wasn't That a Time,* pp. 105.

any opinions other than those of the editors and the magazine's small but faithful fan-base.[63] Between 1959 and 1965, *The Little Sandy Review* would devote itself to the elevation and promotion of 'good' folk music, and the merciless condemnation of 'bad' folk music. Its notion of what was 'good' basically included all traditional musicians and those who appeared, in their view, respectful of tradition. Musicians from 'authentically' traditional backgrounds such as The Clancy Brothers, Bill Monroe, The Stanley Brothers and Almeda Riddle were always praised. Also into the 'good' category fell performers such as singer-songwriter Malvina Reynolds, and husband and wife Ewan McColl and Peggy Seeger. Pseudo-traditionalists such as The New Lost City Ramblers were also lauded repeatedly. 'Everything they touch turns to gold,' enthused Nelson and Pankake.[64] Those musicians and performers whom they deemed 'bad' were, conversely, mocked quite unmercifully; anything commercial in orientation was dismissed as 'folkum' (a purist word for 'phony' folk music), while the efforts of popular and widely acclaimed 'boom' performers such as Joan Baez, Judy Collins and Bob Dylan seldom met with approval.[65] *The Little Sandy Review* was also, interestingly, highly sceptical about the authenticity of the relationship between political songs and folk music. In an article entitled 'P for Protest' in the edition of October 1964, the editors declared that they found the proliferation of political folk songs 'distasteful and silly':

> Although we may feel as strongly about the problems of the day as the most dedicated crusader, we also feel that the basic nature of folk song and folk-type songs, with their simplicity, intimacy and immediacy, is more potentially suited to the more personal problems of mankind, to the interior ethos rather than the great social and political movements of the macrocosm.[66]

This particular viewpoint was especially controversial, and incurred the anger of, among others, *Broadside* editor Sis Cunningham.[67] However, the opinions of the *Little Sandy* editors as to what constituted 'good' folk music were, clearly, firm and highly specific, and grounded in a sense of traditionalist music.

While Pankake seemed, retrospectively, to consider his 'fanzine' to have been of limited interest and significance, Israel Young, who, as owner of the Greenwich Village Folklore Center, was very much at the heart of the folk revival in New York

---

63 Ibid. One example of this extreme bias occurred in No. 6 (mid-1960), when Manny Solomon wrote into the magazine to criticise its 'freewheeling iconoclasm'; the editorial of that month's edition made it evident that Nelson and Pankake were not prepared to receive criticism of any kind!

64 Ibid., No. 11 (c.early 1961 – many issues were not dated). John Cohen wrote to thank Nelson and Pankake for their support in late 1960, and the letter was published in *LSR* Vol. 1 No. 10. Cohen also began to contribute a column to the magazine in the early 1960s.

65 The term 'folkum' was defined as 'phony' folk music in the first edition of the magazine in 1959. In No. 14, (c.1961) Judy Collins was described as 'Elektra's contribution to the urban folk music revival's burgeoning Petticoat Brigade', while, in No. 27 (December 1963), Dylan's *Freewheeling Bob Dylan* was described as 'a flat tire'. Both Dylan and Baez were criticised in No. 29 (early 1964).

66 *Little Sandy Review*, No. 25 (October 1963)

67 Ibid.

and, indeed, beyond, disagreed. In his opinion, the '*LSR*' 'had an influence way beyond its readers'.[68] For all those who desired to be in the 'inner circle' of the folk revival world, the magazine's editors were nothing less than arbiters of good taste. While, initially, the readership of the magazine was little more than 300 or 400, by 1965, '*LSR*' could claim around 2000 readers.[69] Significantly, the magazine was, also, well-written, containing articles which, though highly biased, were articulate, often witty, and sound in structure. Jon Pankake revealed later that he and Nelson were attempting to emulate the witty, erudite style of *New York Times* film and book reviewers.[70] In this respect, the magazine could almost be considered a precursor of the articulate, skilful (and highly opinionated and elitist) rock music journalism which would emerge as a veritable literary form in the late 1960s.[71]

Eventually, Nelson and Pankake were unable to cope with the demand for their magazine, and, in 1965, they sold it to Irwin Silber, editor of *Sing Out!*, the editorial staff of which Nelson subsequently joined. However, while it was in existence, *The Little Sandy Review* was the voice of the self-styled 'experts' on folk music – those who were disdainful of commercial music and who wished to gain knowledge of specific, particularly traditional, folk genres and performers. Its eccentricity and uniqueness of approach, thus, helped to enhance the diversity of opinions, and the awareness of different styles of music, within the folk revival.

Owing undoubtedly to its smaller population and folk scene, Canada had fewer domestically produced folk music magazines. *Sing Out!* was the preferred periodical of Canadians, and from around 1964 onwards it contained a column on Canadian singers and events, focusing particularly on Toronto. For a brief period of time, however, a magazine entitled *Hoot!* was produced by the Toronto Folk Guild; with smaller circulation and a very limited budget, production of this magazine was irregular, and its issues were not punctuated by vigorous debates over commercialism versus purism or authenticity versus imitation as were those of *Sing Out!*. In general, the editors of *Hoot!* were more open-minded in their dealings with such issues; for example, while *Sing Out!* was expressing its revulsion to the folk-rock experiments of Bob Dylan, *Hoot!* was more inclined to see the 'fallen idol' of the revival as an artist experiencing new growth. *Hoot!*, however, did share with its American counterparts a vision of the revival as the showcase for a plethora of music styles. One edition contained items on, among other things, Old-Time Southern music, jug bands, black Canadian singer Jackie Washington, autoharp music, ragtime, the music of Bulgaria, Mike Seeger, and Marie Hare, a Canadian singer.[72] The magazine contained pieces on Canadian music, contributed by Helen Creighton, Edith Fowke and Estelle Klein, but not disproportionately so; as with the other periodicals of the revival and the music festivals, it reflected the desire of folk music enthusiasts to be knowledgeable about, and experience first-hand, as diverse a range of musical

---

68   Israel Young, 1965. Interview by Richard Reuss. Tape-recording, 26 July. Box 1, Tape AFS 19,800. American Folklife Center, Library of Congress, Washington, DC.

69   These statistics are Israel Young's, from his interview of 26 July 1965.

70   Pankake, in Cohen (ed.), *Wasn't That a Time*, p. 113.

71   Rock journalism will be discussed in more detail in Chapter 4.

72   *Hoot* magazine, Volume II No. 1, January 1966.

styles, particularly from the North American continent, as possible; apparently, the more obscure and 'rare' these styles were seen to be, the more they were valued by the revivalists.

Politics, Cultural Dislocation and the 'Exclusive Factor': Explaining the Eclecticism of the Folk Revival

Why did the folk revival adopt this inclusive, idealistic and pluralistic character? In attempting to answer this question, it is perhaps useful to begin with the nature of the world in which the young American and Canadian folk revival participants grew up.

Historians have made much of the affluence and economic security into which the post-war generation of North Americans was born, a factor that distinguished the 'baby boomers' from previous generations born and brought up in the comparatively uncertain, hard times of the First World War or, more especially, the Great Depression.[73] The Second World War had not only boosted the ailing economy and brought an end to the Depression that had blighted North America throughout the 1930s and early 1940s, but it had also left Canada and, particularly, America considerably wealthier than the rest of the world. Unlike mainland Europe, Britain and Japan, North America had not experienced the devastation of war on the home front, so that, while the military casualties of both Canada and America were high, neither country had been plundered and bombed as had the other nations involved in the war. This situation left Canada and, especially, America at a considerable economic advantage in 1945.

The United States government was determined to use this new-found prosperity to support the large numbers of soldiers who were returning home, and ease their transition into civilian society; the governments feared that mismanagement of such a period of upheaval and transition might bring about another collapse in the economy. In America, with the passage of the Servicemen's Readjustment Act, otherwise known as 'the GI Bill of Rights', in 1944, money became available to the eight million ex-soldiers and their families for various purposes – they might seek and use funds for buying a house, returning to college or university, or starting a business. The impact of this upon American society, as documented by historians such as James Gilbert, William R. Chafe and Michael J. Bennett, was profound indeed, as a

---

73   See, for example, the following overviews of the period: James Gilbert, *Another Chance: Postwar America, 1945–1968* (Philadelphia, PA, 1981); William H. Chafe, *The Unfinished Journey: America Since World War II* (New York and Oxford, 1995); James T. Patterson, *Grand Expectations: America, 1945–1974* (New York and Oxford, 1996). Discussion of the post-war economy in Canada is included in Donald Creighton, *The Forked Road: Canada 1939–1957* (Toronto, 1976) and Robert Bothwell, Ian Drummond and John English, *Canada Since 1945: Power, Politics and Provincialism* (Toronto; Buffalo, NY; London, 1989).

new generation of Americans gained access to private housing, university education and greater economic prosperity.[74]

The 'baby boom' children of the United States, who would become the backbone of the folk revival movement in the late 1950s and early 1960s, reaped the full benefit of the rewards which the government had bestowed on their parents. Considerably more economically and socially secure than the generation of their parents, they cultivated a distinctive identity, and brought about the growth of a unique new culture of independent young adulthood. James Gilbert has outlined the nature of this new culture. As he demonstrates, white American teenagers of the 'new' middle class could now have their own income, whether they received pocket money from parents, or held down part-time jobs. They were also able to stay at school longer, and as a result created their own 'high school culture' and made the school environment more their own.[75] Because they had never experienced serious economic hardship, they were often perceived to be self-confident, having been afforded the luxury of celebrating their youth rather than seeing it as an obstacle to economic or social advancement. The booming, post-war consumerist world took note of this, and marketed cars and clothing especially for teenagers. Teen magazines and teen movies began to appear. And, of course, the record industry began to recognise the power that rock 'n' roll music held for white teenagers with money to spare. Such economic and social autonomy would play a foundational role in the development of the culture of 1960s youth, the group that would embrace the folk revival in such large numbers. Even though many folk revival participants would condemn the materialism of the world into which they had been born, the economic security of their backgrounds enabled them to pursue opportunities and goals that had been denied to their parents' generation.

In many crucial respects, the situation of post-war Canada mirrored that of the US. The Canadian government, concerned, as were the Americans, with the potential hazard of an economic crash following the return of the soldiers, issued extensive plans to boost social welfare. When the anticipated economic crisis failed to materialise, the Canadian economy was left in a stable state and, like their American counterparts, Canadians could easily obtain loans for mortgages through the Canadian Mortgage and Housing Corporation, formed in 1945.[76] Donald Creighton has also demonstrated that, although no precise equivalent to the GI Bill of Rights existed in Canada, 'preferential treatment' was shown to war veterans for the purposes of finding jobs and re-establishing themselves as civilians. As in the United States, the Canadian veterans were anxious to complete or to further their education, and the

---

74   Gilbert, *Another Chance*; Chafe, *The Unfinished Journey*. (Both books devote considerable attention to the discussion of the GI Bill of Rights and its impact.) See also Michael J. Bennett, *When Dreams Come True: The GI Bill of Rights and the Making of Modern America* (Washington, DC and London, 1996).

75   James Gilbert, *Cycle of Outrage: America's Reaction to the Juvenile Delinquent of the 1950s* (New York, 1986), pp. 15–23.

76   Doug Owram, *Born at the Right Time* (Toronto; Buffalo, NY; London, 1996), p. 56.

Department of Veteran Affairs furnished some fifty thousand former soldiers with sufficient funding to return to school or university.[77]

In comparing the economic and social conditions of post-war Canada and America, the world in which the folk revivalists of the 'boom' period grew to maturity, it is important not to over-generalise. It is certainly true that the economic situation of post-war Canada was stable, and that, for many (in particular Canadians of British origin), the promise of a better life was fulfilled. Suburbs sprang up rapidly in Canada, as they had done in America, particularly around the larger cities such as Montreal, Toronto and Vancouver. Some suburbs, such as Don Mills, on the outskirts of Toronto, were predominantly white and Anglo in character, and appeared to mirror the archetypical (or stereotypical) American suburb.

Despite this, historian Valerie Korinek has challenged the enduring myth that 'endless affluence and good times' prevailed in the Canadian suburbs after the war.[78] Korinek disagrees with the claims of Doug Owram that Canada was as prosperous as America following the war; on the contrary, she cites statistics of the period which illustrate that the overall standard of living in Canada was, in fact, lower than that of the United States.[79] She also draws attention to the fact that, in Canada, a 'suburb' did not automatically connote a middle-class housing area, but could also, depending on one's location, refer to a working-class area populated by a diversity of peoples. A Winnipeg suburb might not necessarily be socially or ethnically parallel to a suburb of Halifax or of Toronto.[80] This point is further emphasised by the work of Veronica Strong-Boag on women in the Canadian suburbs. Her study demonstrates that, in the post-war period, the suburbs of major Canadian cities were often heavily populated by Southern and Eastern European immigrants, many of whom were refugees or displaced persons. For the immigrant women of Strong-Boag's study, the suburbs were places of intense hardship, isolation and cultural alienation, and were far from being the idyllic dream-locations of popular American myth.[81]

Nevertheless, Korinek does state that many suburbanites in Canada, despite living on a smaller budget than their average American counterparts, did participate in a culture of material abundance and consumerism. If they did not possess the money to buy certain goods, then they purchased on credit. 'A modest level of affluence' was to be found in many of the Canadian suburbs, and advertisements, catalogues and technological revolutions reminded consumers that there was always the prospect of more.[82] While suburbs in Canada may have been more varied in socio-economic terms than those of the United States, there is no doubt that, in general, many of the young, largely white people who were attracted to folk music in the 1950s and 1960s

---

77   Creighton, *The Forked Road*, p. 116.

78   Valerie J. Korinek, *Roughing It in the Suburbs: Reading Chatelaine Magazine in the Fifties and Sixties* (Toronto; Buffalo, NY; London, 2000), pp. 6–7.

79   Ibid., p. 6. The statistics come from a study by John Porter entitled *The Vertical Mosaic: An Analysis of Social Class and Power in Canada* (Toronto: University of Toronto Press, 1965).

80   Ibid., p. 19.

81   Veronica Strong-Boag, 'Home Dreams: Women and the Suburban Experiment in Canada', *Canadian Historical Review*, 72/4 (1991): 471–504.

82   Korinek, *Roughing It in the Suburbs*, p. 7.

were rebelling against a 'middle-class' culture which they perceived to be restrictive and homogeneous. Their rebellions led them towards folk music as a meaningful alternative to the conformity of their surroundings.

The sense of restrictiveness and stifling conformity was not merely sensed by young people of the 1950s. Despite the greater degree of wealth enjoyed by white North Americans during this time, historians have been swift to point out a darker picture lurking beneath the serene image of domestic contentment which often appears to characterise the 1950s. Instead, they have described this decade as a period of intense conformity and social restriction – or, as Todd Gitlin has expressed it, 'an extreme and wrenching tension between the assumption of affluence and its opposite, a terror of loss, destruction and failure'.[83] The involvement of America in the Cold War, fear of nuclear annihilation, and the repressive anti-Communist domestic crusades of Senator Joseph McCarthy, led to an intense and widespread suspicion of anyone who seemed 'different'. Elaine Tyler May has described a society in which suburb-dwellers monitored each other's behaviour and exhibited a profound, paranoid suspicion of all non-conformists, particularly homosexuals and women who worked. May and James Gilbert have also written at length on societal fears surrounding juvenile delinquents, whose rebellious activities were often blamed on mothers who had 'neglected' their children while working in the wartime industries.[84] Gender roles were now to be strictly defined, and a happy, traditional family life was considered the ultimate attainment. May has argued that mass culture and consumerism served as panaceas for social malaise brought about by such restriction and suspicion and by the ever-present threat of nuclear holocaust.[85] Canadian historian Mona Gleason has demonstrated that many of these fears – fears of 'rising divorce rates, juvenile delinquency, increases in the number of married women in the workforce, and general anxiety about the threat of communism and nuclear annihilation as the Cold War loomed' – were also present in post-war Canada.[86]

Intellectuals of the era deplored such a defensive and limiting outlook and warned that it would bring only misery. Contemporary critics of 1950s society included David Riesman, whose book *The Lonely Crowd* depicted a society of lacklustre sterility in which the individual was utterly alienated in the desperate struggle to conform. John Keats's *The Crack in the Picture Window* was similarly scathing towards the 'mass society' of unoriginal automatons created by 1950s culture, while Betty Friedan's *The Feminine Mystique* described the misery and depression faced by suburban housewives who were doomed to an unfulfilling life of banal domesticity.[87]

---

83   Todd Gitlin, *The Sixties: Years of Hope, Days of Rage* (Toronto; New York; London: Sydney; Auckland, 1987), p. 12.

84   Gilbert, *Cycle of Outrage* Chapter 1; and May, *Homeward Bound*.

85   See also Stephen J. Whitefield, *The Culture of the Cold War* (Baltimore, MD and London, 1991) and the chapter on the 1950s in Arlene Skolnick, *Embattled Paradise: The American Family in an Age of Uncertainty* (HarperCollins, 1991).

86   Mona Gleason, 'Psychology and the Construction of the 'Normal' Family in Postwar Canada, 1945–60', *Canadian Historical Review*, 78/3 (September 1997), p. 443.

87   David Riesman with Reuel Denney and Nathan Glazer, *The Lonely Crowd: A Study of the Changing American Character* (New Haven, CT, 1950); John Keats, *The Crack in*

It is, perhaps, easy to over-simplify the extent of cultural conformity and paranoia during the 1950s; revisionist scholars such as Joanne Meyerowitz have challenged the assumptions of Betty Friedan et al. by suggesting that, in fact, the popular media was more supportive and admiring of working women than is first apparent.[88] Dominick Cavallo has suggested that the apparent self-confidence of the baby boom generation was less the result of rebellion against the conformity of the parental generation than it was a consequence of the child-centric outlook of the white middle-class family of the 1950s. He argues that smaller families, greater prosperity and more attention from parents instilled in baby boomers a strong self-confidence, capabilities for self-expression and a potent sense of 'autonomy, self-esteem and competitiveness'.[89] In the Canadian context, Valerie Korinek's study of *Chatelaine* magazine has shown, like the work of Meyerowitz, that not all women's magazines of the era were content simply to promote an image of domesticity or conformity.[90] Whether the rebellious tendencies of young white middle-class people in the 1950s developed as a result, or in spite, of their upbringings, it is clear that, while they may have shared in the economic benefits of the mass society, many of them appeared to desire none of its cultural implications. Shunning the atmosphere of their neighbourhoods and the more rigid lives of their parents, middle-class teenagers of the 1950s devoured the works of 'beat' writers Jack Kerouac and Allen Ginsberg and hankered after the ideal of utter freedom which was exhibited in these works. They listened to the wild rock 'n' roll music of Chuck Berry, Elvis Presley and Jerry Lee Lewis, music which to their parents was the very essence of profanity and anarchy, and they idolised screen rebels such as Marlon Brando and James Dean, whose angst embodied their own latent discontent with their sterile cultural surroundings.

Significantly, the majority of these teenagers were not, themselves, overtly rebellious in general, but they had a profound admiration for those who were, just as they lionised poor black musicians and young rebels for actualising their dreams of liberty.[91] The admiration, even envy, of the 'other', and the bestowing of the 'other' with desirably rebellious cultural and social values, would play a large part in the baby boom generation's involvement in the folk revival.

---

the Picture Window (New York, 1962); Betty Friedan, *The Feminine Mystique* (New York, 1963).

88   Joanne Meyerowitz, 'Beyond the Feminine Mystique: A Reassessment of Postwar Mass Culture, 1946–1958', *Journal of American History*, 79/4, (1993): 1455–82.

89   Dominick Cavallo, 'Middle-Class Child Rearing' from *A Fiction of the Past: The Sixties in American History* (New York, 1999), p. 58. It is also important to mention Peter J. Kuznick and James Gilbert (eds), *Rethinking Cold War Culture* (Washington, DC and London, 2001), a volume of revisionist essays which challenges many of the scholarly preconceptions of the era, such as the prevalence of anti-Communist paranoia (Peter Filene) and 1950s cultural homogeneity (Alan Brinkley). Another significant collection of essays which deal with the underlying complexities of the 1950s is Joel Foreman (ed.), *The Other Fifties: Interrogating Midcentury American Icons* (Urbana, IL and Chicago, IL, 1997).

90   Korinek, *Roughing It in the Suburbs*.

91   In his study *Cycle of Outrage*, James Gilbert has, in fact, shown that the fear of juvenile delinquency was greater than actual incidents of rebellion or crime.

To a great extent, then, the involvement of youth in the folk revival during the 1960s was a symptom and a symbol of cultural dislocation in the post-war era of comparative abundance. It is plausible to argue that the love of cultural specificity and diverse music styles experienced by young people in both Canada and America was due, in part, to their loss of identification with any culture of their own. Thus, it is possible to look at the revival as an attempt by young people to regain some kind of ethnic and social identity for themselves. Many revival participants were second- and third-generation Europeans; their parents and grandparents had fought hard against prejudice and poverty to assimilate into North American society, and in the climate of post-war affluence their offspring were finally reaping the benefits of their efforts. Yet the baby boomers felt cut off from their heritage in a culture which they perceived to value only homogeneity, conformity, materialism and corporate uniformity at the expense of diversity.[92] A sense of cultural and ethnic identity, thus, became central to the revivalists. The Old Town School of Folk Music in Chicago, for instance, aimed to encourage young performers to seek out and identify 'their musical genealogy' so that they might understand themselves and celebrate their origins. As Frank Hamilton, one of the founders of the enduring institution, recalled, 'we had students research their own lives and the folk music in their families. We said, "Go back to your parents, your grandparents, and their ancestors. Do your musical genealogy. Learn those songs."'[93]

Despite the fact that many of the young revivalists were the descendants of 'ethnic' North Americans – Irish, Italian, and, particularly, Jewish – one of the remarkable aspects of the revival of the early decade was the fact that the 'identity' sought by revivalists was, frequently, not that of their own present or ancestral communities. Rather, the music of other cultures seemed to possess greater mystique; above all, the music of the Western and Southern states of America – that is, the regions in which 'the folk' were said to reside.[94] By this time, the revivalists were often far removed from the immigrant backgrounds of their forebears; while their grandparents had struggled hard to conceal their origins in order to assimilate into North American society, their grandchildren perceived their often urban upbringings, in which ethnicity was at times downplayed, as bland and without cultural distinction.

Indeed, in the case of the young Jewish revival participants, it has been suggested by some commentators that many were drawn to embrace political radicalism and the revival as a reaction against their ethnic identity. According to Lewis Feuer, many Jewish baby boomers were frustrated by the perceived passivity of their ancestors during the Holocaust, to the extent that some wished to disassociate themselves from what they considered to be 'victim' status, and even 'obliterate [their] Jewish

---

92   Robert Cantwell speaks eloquently about this aspect of the movement in 'When We Were Good', his contribution to Rosenberg (ed.), *Transforming Tradition*.

93   Quoted in Cohen (ed.), *Wasn't That a Time*, p. 157.

94   This process of cultural adoption is in some ways similar to the 'dynamic of love and theft' described by Eric Lott in *Love and Theft: Blackface Minstrelsy and the American Working Class* (New York, 1993).

derivation'.[95] While the relationship of Jewish revivalists to their identity remained complex and multi-dimensional, rather than simply constituting outright rejection, it is clear that many were seeking to assume a different identity to compensate for what seemed to be lacking in their own ethnic background. The revivalists, Jewish and otherwise, searched for cultures that, in their eyes, possessed history and validity; as Oscar Brand noted, 'meaningful' was an adjective frequently employed by young folk revivalists in regard to their choice of music.[96] New York folksinger Happy Traum, who would subsequently become editor of *Sing Out!*, recalled this intense hunger of his generation for music that was 'meaningful'. He recalled, that, as the folk revival intensified,

> Suddenly we had these songs that were about something. Even if they were about hoeing corn or ... you know, things that we didn't have any clue about, really ... you know, like digging coal in the mines ... In reality we knew nothing about that; we were just New York, middle-class kids. But it gave us a sense of singing about something real, whether it was farmers, labourers, unions, miners, anything.[97]

Ellen Stekert wrote in 1966 that 'the cultural expressions which seem to be most popular with the imitative group are the Southern Mountain instrumental tradition ... and the Negro blues.'[98] Stekert found it absurd that these imitators were from 'the middle-class, educated, white city' but did not attempt to explain the particular appeal of the American, working-class music styles to the revivalists.

However, I. Sheldon Posen, a revivalist from Toronto, suggested that this focus on the cultures of others came about because

> People were shopping for alternatives to what was offered them either by the marketplace or by their culture. Many were looking to give their lives new or expanded meaning by adopting aspects of the lives of others. With varying degrees of sincerity and innocence, people became tourists – or pilgrims – traveling in someone else's culture. They made choices from a menu they saw offered them by the rest of North America and the world, of music to play, food to cook, clothing to wear. The feeling was, the more 'authentic' the item or emulation they found, the more valid their experience of it and the transformation it produced.[99]

The revivalists' perception of the cultural richness and purity of the nether regions of America thus led to the focus of the revivalists on folk groups as a source of 'valid cultural experience'. Prominent folklorists encouraged the young revivalists to imitate, and become 'advocates' for, the music of the American regions; Pete Seeger, who was an acknowledged traveller among various cultural and musical

---

95 Feuer's name is mentioned in Chaim L. Waxman, *Jewish Baby Boomers: A Communal Perspective* (New York, 2001), p. 5. (Quote is Waxman's).

96 Oscar Brand, *The Ballad Mongers: Rise of the Modern Folk Song,* (Westport, CT, 1962) p. 59.

97 Happy Traum, in discussion with the author, Woodstock, NY, 7 December 2002.

98 Stekert, 'Cents and Nonsense', p. 97.

99 I. Sheldon Posen, 'On Folk Festivals and Kitchens: Questions of Authenticity in the Folk Revival', in Rosenberg (ed.), *Transforming Tradition*, p. 128.

worlds, heartily encouraged such imitation and borrowing. In response to heavy criticisms of 'Rambling' Jack Elliott which had appeared in *Sing Out!* in early 1964, Seeger stated: 'My guess is that there will always be young people who for one reason or another will feel that they have to violently, radically re-form themselves. A personal revolution. They abandon the old like a hated mask and rebuild on new foundations.'[100]

In Seeger's view, thus, there was something intensely liberating about becoming an imitator and adopting a 'historically viable alternative culture'.[101] Groups such as The New Lost City Ramblers, an 'old-time' music group which devoted itself to the reproduction, or imitation, of traditional Southern songs and instrumental music, took their mission of promoting their chosen style of music very seriously, and were usually disdainful of the commercial folk performers. In turn, they were accused of being 'inauthentic', and were constantly being called upon to justify their appropriation of a musical culture that was not their own. Ellen Stekert was highly critical of this trend among the revivalists; she believed that their interest in traditional music arose from a political agenda far removed from the cultures they celebrated, and was thus misplaced and perhaps even exploitative. As she remarked rather sardonically, 'one may live the life of the traditional singer for a while with great ease if he knows that at the end of the trip there is a warm bath and lox and bagel.'[102] Arguments over the 'authenticity' of imitators versus traditional musicians abounded throughout the revival; imitators were never permitted to forget that, no matter how much they resembled the traditional performers, they would always be considered derivative by factions within the movement. As John Cohen of The New Lost City Ramblers recalled, revivalists of traditional music were often 'forced to examine their own criteria and validity in a way that border[ed] on self-hatred.'[103] At times there was a bitterness, almost a desperation, about this desire for authentic identity. As Oscar Brand remarked,

> many of the young singers cannot forgive fate for having started them off in urban environments. They want to *be* sharecroppers, they want to *be* dirt farmers, they want to *be* blind Negro street singers. Since this is denied them, their rage is boundless, and it is turned upon anyone who reminds them of their own roots in modern life.[104]

The concern with authenticity remained central for the revival, and it was a controversy that would never be resolved, since the quest for, and explanation of, personal and community identity was so vital to the movement. Folk revival scholars who were revival participants during the 1960s continue to search for new frameworks of understanding of the movement which do not entail merely

---

100 From Pete Seeger's column in *Sing Out!*, 14/1, February–March 1964, pp. 71–3.

101 Cantwell, *When We Were Good*, p. 355.

102 Stekert, 'Cents and Nonsense', p. 97. Her comment implies the Jewish origin of the folk musicians at whom her criticism is directed. However, she wrote an *addendum* to her original 1966 article in which she expressed regret for this comment. (See Rosenberg (ed.), *Transforming Tradition*, pp. 84–92.)

103 John Cohen, quoted in Cohen (ed.), *Wasn't That a Time*, p. 46.

104 Brand, *The Ballad Mongers*, p. 228.

accusations of cultural appropriation and 'inauthenticity'; folklorists such as Sheldon Posen and Neil Rosenberg, for example, have begun to argue that folk *revival* must be understood as something quite distinct from traditional folk music *per se* – revival entails a distinct understanding of music, a distinct repertoire, and involves a unique cross-section of people, and must thus be understood on its own terms, rather than via unfavourable and over-simplified comparisons with traditional folk music communities.[105] Certainly, however, the multi-cultural focus of the revival, and its love of the culturally specific, was partly as a result of the apparent identity crisis experienced by the post-war generation, a crisis which remains the focus of research and discussion.

The Folk Revival and the Politics of the Early 1960s

The fixation of the folk revival with cultural diversity and pluralism was also closely tied to the political activities of young people at this time. During the early 1960s, folk music became symbolically intertwined with the activities and ideals of the civil rights movement, the New Left, and student and youth protests against nuclear weaponry and American involvement in South East Asia, among other issues. Folk music, as 'experts' reminded their disciples during the revival, had been an instrument of social change for centuries, and had been widely used by founder figures of the folk revival such as Guthrie and Seeger. Building on this tradition, the 1960s folk revival intersected with current events; many student activists were revival participants, and often folk musicians were drawn into political activism by their revival activities, and vice versa. The protest songs of Dylan, Phil Ochs, Tom Paxton and the multifarious contributors to *Broadside* magazine remain the most direct, obvious link between the revival and 1960s politics, but the broader folk movement, with its musically open-minded perspective, and its particular love of the American 'folk', was inextricably connected to the political philosophies of young people in the early decade.

In the United States, college enrolment during the 1960s was more than four times what it had been in the 1940s, and by 1970, 50 per cent of the population sector aged 18–22 attended college. In Canada, by the mid-1960s, university enrolments had risen to one out of ten 18-year-olds, and by the early 1970s, one in six of this age-group attended university. The Canadian statistics were not as dramatic as those of America, but there was no doubt that the student population was increasing steadily.[106] Students were becoming a new and significant social group in North America at a time when political and social unrest was rapidly fermenting.

The student movement of the early 1960s in America was an expression of self-confidence and power by a uniquely privileged generation which was little affected

---

105 See Posen, 'On Folk Festivals and Kitchens', pp. 135–6, and Neil Rosenberg, 'Starvation, Serendipity, and the Ambivalence of Bluegrass Revivalism' from Rosenberg (ed.) *Transforming Tradition*, pp. 194–8.

106 Statistics from Wini Breines, 'The New Left and the Student Movement', in Alexander Bloom (ed.), *Long Time Gone: Sixties America Then and Now* (Oxford and New York, 2001), p. 24, and Owram, *Born at the Right Time*, pp. 180–81.

by poverty or deprivation, but militant in its desire to eradicate such evils on behalf of other sectors of society. In Canada, too, it appears that, overall, the student movement was largely comprised of young people from backgrounds of prosperity. As has been demonstrated, the percentage of young Canadians attending university in the 1960s was lower than that of the United States. Furthermore, a survey of 1965–66 indicated that, of all Canadian undergraduates, only 35 per cent were the children of 'blue collar' families. Indeed, another set of statistics suggested that, at the very most, only 20 out of 100 children of the poorer Canadian families were even attending high school.[107] Therefore, universities in Canada remained, in the early and middle 1960s at least, the domain of the middle class, and student activists themselves recognised this factor, often campaigning to force universities to adopt a 'quota' system for poorer and ethnic students in order to diversify the student body.[108]

By the late 1960s, the character of university education in Canada, as in the United States, would begin to alter considerably, as would the character of the student movement. Not only did 'the movement' widen and liaise with minority groups from Native and black communities, not to mention high school students from all walks of life, but experimental projects such as Rochdale College in Toronto would attempt to lift the traditional restrictions on university education.[109] However, in the early 1960s, the student movement itself, in both Canada and America, remained driven by young people who were, predominantly, white and middle class.

The left-of-centre stance of the North American student movement was grounded, not in the more traditional leftist political ideology of the inter-war American 'Old Left', but in a sense of social relevance and direct action. From the late 1950s onwards, leftist groups began to appear on North American campuses, formed in response to current political issues; early organisations, such as the inter-varsity Student Peace Union (SPU), formed in Chicago in 1959, and the Canadian Combined Universities Campaign for Nuclear Disarmament (CUCND) devoted themselves to the cause of nuclear disarmament. However, after the signing of the Test-Ban Treaty in 1963, student activists redirected their attentions to the many other growing concerns, in particular, civil rights in the Deep South and growing American involvement in South East Asia. In 1960, a more overarching and ambitious organisation replaced earlier student groups; Students for a Democratic Society (SDS) became the self-appointed new light of left-wing politics in America, and its ethos was reflected in the universities of Canada through such groups as the Student Union for Peace Action (SUPA), a broader and more community-focused organisation, which

---

107 These statistics are quoted in Julyan Reid, 'Some Canadian Issues' from Tim and Julyan Reid (eds), *Student Power and the Canadian Campus* (Toronto, 1969), pp. 6–11.

108 Ibid. The notion of university students being 'middle class' and 'privileged' is also reiterated by Philip Resnick in 'The New Left in Ontario', in Dimitrios J. Roussopoulos (ed.), *The New Left in Canada* (Montreal, 1970), pp. 92–100. Pieces in this book on the other provinces suggest a similar situation elsewhere.

109 Short pieces on a number of demonstrations and protests in Canadian high schools at the end of the 1960s are included in Tim and Julyan Reid (eds), *Student Power and the Canadian Campus*, pp. 177–192. These occurred on a national scale, but most remarked upon was the unrest which occurred in Forest Hills Collegiate Institute in Toronto, when a radical club named The Student Guard was banned by the Principal.

replaced the CUCND in 1964. The SDS was filled with youthful, perhaps brash, confidence that it would be the organisation which would successfully lead the country to seek and find, in the words of one member, 'radical alternatives to the inadequate society of today'.[110] Its manifesto, the Port Huron Statement, composed in 1962 by Tom Hayden, was considerably influenced by non-Marxist, humanitarian thinkers of the left such as Paul Goodman and, in particular, C. Wright Mills, the radical sociologist scholar from Columbia University. In 1960, Mills wrote a letter to the New Left, urging the movement to preoccupy itself first and foremost with the society in which it existed – it must be ever critical of that society and of its structure, and must never become complacent. He was not ashamed to call the New Left movement a 'utopian' phenomenon; for him, to be utopian was to concern oneself with community, with something beyond the immediate, self-focused world of the individual. Most significantly, Mills made a strong point of placing upon students, or the 'young intelligentsia' as he called them, the responsibility for the radical change of society.[111]

The Port Huron Statement was greatly inspired by the direct-action philosophies of Mills, and was filled with a confident, passionate sense of purpose and with a sense of the special mission of politically awakened youth. Members of the SDS devoted themselves to assisting the less privileged members of society, not with charity or condescension as in the past, but by exhibiting a true and earnest understanding of their circumstances and lives. They formed ERAP, the Economic Research and Action Project, whereby students moved into impoverished inner-city areas with the hope of building an 'interracial coalition of the poor' in which black and white residents could work together to build more prosperous communities.

In Canada, from 1965 onwards, members of SUPA established similar projects among the African-Canadians of Nova Scotia, the Native peoples of northern Saskatchewan and the impoverished communities of various urban areas in Francophone and Anglophone Canada.[112] Many of the SDS members also travelled south, participating in marches, voting drives and Freedom Rides. The students professed the utmost respect for those whom they aimed to assist, and willingly relinquished comfortable homes and lifestyles to live among the poor and work in often frighteningly alien cultural settings. However, the students were, in their

---

110 Historiography of the SDS and the student New Left in America is considerable in size and scope. Among the most significant studies of the movement are James Miller, *"Democracy is in the Streets": From Port Huron to the Siege of Chicago* (New York, 1987) and Terry H. Anderson, *The Movement and the Sixties* (New York and Oxford, 1995). Personal reminiscences form the basis of Todd Gitlin's *The Sixties: Years of Hope, Days of Rage* and Peter Collier and David Horowitz's highly critical work *Destructive Generation: Second Thoughts About the Sixties* (New York, 1989). Doug Rossinow's bibliographical essay 'The New Left: Democratic Reformers or left-Wing Revolutionaries?' from David Farber and Beth Bailey (eds), *The Columbia Guide to America in the 1960s* (New York, 2001) discusses these and other related works on the New Left.

111 C.Wright Mills, 'Letter to the New Left', in Alexander Bloom and Wini Breines, *Takin' It to the Streets: A Sixties Reader* (New York and Oxford, 2003, 2nd edn), pp. 61–6.

112 Dimitrios J. Roussopoulos, 'Introduction', in Dimitrios J. Roussopoulos (ed.), *The New Left in Canada* (Montreal, 1970), p. 10.

philosophies, self-consciously setting themselves apart from their beneficiaries, believing that they, 'the young intelligentsia', had a special mission and a unique ability to solve their difficulties.

It is clear that many of the key aspects of student protest were eagerly embraced by the young people of Canada, although determining just why the student movement was present in Canada at this time is not a straightforward question to answer. Some would argue, once again, that Canadians were simply aping an American movement, often with less commitment and a reduced sense of responsibility. Michael Van Dusen, born in Canada but educated and radicalised in the United States, suggested that, at least in the early 1960s, Canada was 'dreamy' in its attitude to political and social problems. Van Dusen felt that, throughout the '60s, protest in Canada was, for the young, more of a diversion than a necessity. He recalled that, when living in Toronto, '[he] would go to protests and [he would] think, "Well, it's a nice day for a parade." There wasn't that visceral sense of antagonism.'[113]

Michael Van Dusen's perspective on the student movement in Toronto, though valid, cannot serve as the only explanation for the presence and motivation of the movement in Canada as a whole. Even though it is true that Canadians found inspiration in, and direction from, the vocal and vibrant example of American student politics, their movement was no ineffectual imitation or a mere diversion for bored young people. Recent work by historians Ruth Frager and Carmela Patrias on the growth of human rights movements and campaigns in Ontario in the post-war period illustrates that the student movement, at least in that province, was not simply imitating the American example, but was building on a foundation laid by grass-roots community organisers and activists.[114] Frager and Patrias argue that, after the Second World War, Canadians began to acknowledge and recognise the existence in their country of prejudice and discrimination against religious, ethnic and racial minorities. The gradual move towards legislation to counteract such prejudice was the result of 'campaigns that were carefully and painstakingly orchestrated by small groups of Anglo-Canadians, and especially by key minority groups'.[115] Frager and Patrias note that, of all minorities in Ontario, it was African-Canadians, Japanese-Canadians, and, above all, Jewish Canadians who were most prominent in human and civil rights activities at this time.[116] Jewish people were, by the post-war era, 'integrated' into Canadian society to the extent that they could become 'influential and effective campaigners' against discrimination. Furthermore, because Jewish people could be found all across Ontario, even in the smaller towns (where they might run small businesses), a community 'network' existed which enabled anti-discrimination

---

113 Van Dusen, discussion.

114 Ruth A. Frager and Carmela Patrias, '"This Is Our Country, These Are Our Rights": Minorities and the Origins of Ontario's Human Rights Campaigns', *Canadian Historical Review*, 82/1 (March 2001): 1–35.

115 Ibid., pp. 2–3.

116 Ibid., p. 5. They argue that Chinese-Canadians, Catholics and Aboriginal Peoples were absent from the campaigns – the Chinese, perhaps, because they were still small in number in 1950s Ontario, Catholics because they distrusted interdenominational ventures, and Aboriginal Peoples because they did not believe that legislation was the most appropriate solution to their problems at that time.

campaigns to spread around the entire province.[117] As has been demonstrated in the previous chapter, the Communist Party was strongly represented in North American Jewish culture at this time, and left-wing organisations for working-class Jews such as the Jewish Labour Committee of Canada (working alongside the Canadian Jewish Congress, which was more general in its outlook) were active in the struggle for civil liberties.

In outlining the efforts of Jewish Canadians, and of African-Canadians and Japanese-Canadians, to put an end to racial discrimination in the workplace and in society at large, Frager and Patrias note the interaction between American and Canadian civil rights organisations. For example, the black US activist A. Philip Randolph travelled frequently to Ontario to address the African-Canadian community. The American Jewish Committee and the American Jewish Congress also corresponded and liaised closely with their Canadian counterparts. As a result of the many campaigns and protests of these groups, the first anti-discrimination acts were passed by the Ontario Parliament. As early as 1944, the Racial Discrimination Act, which prohibited public signs or notices expressing racist or discriminatory views, was passed, and in 1951, the Fair Employment Practices Act introduced preventive measures against discrimination in the workplace. Therefore, in tracing the origins of the student movement in Canada, it is important to remember the precedent which was set by the various minority groups in Ontario, and indeed beyond.

The increasingly global perspective of the student movement in the 1960s also serves to explain its strong presence in Canada.[118] The student movement of the 1960s was not confined to North America, but also thrived in other developed and far-flung countries such as Germany, Japan, France, Belgium and the United Kingdom. It seemed an internationalist phenomenon, to the point that some allegedly feared a mass conspiracy among the students of the world.[119] 'The movement' would increase in strength and size in all these countries, as the decade progressed, and as America's involvement in Vietnam was escalated; protests against the conflict were held on campuses across North America and Western Europe throughout 1968. The extent of anger at these demonstrations was considerable, but critics of the students, especially those at universities outside America, failed to understand their motivations. As Canadian student protester Julyan Reid stated: 'Critics ask Why? [*sic*] It's not your war, it's an American mistake, so why do *you* demonstrate? *You* don't fear the draft, and the demonstrations have gone far beyond sympathy demonstrations. The same criticism applies to students in England, Germany, France.'[120]

Reid's own answer to the queries of the critics was both thoughtful and useful in helping to understand some Canadian attitudes to radical politics. According to

117 Ibid., p. 17.

118 For a contemporary account of the global character of the movement, see Julian Nagel (ed.), *Student Power* (London, 1969).

119 According to Julyan Reid in 'Some Canadian Issues', p. 12. Steve Hewitt's interesting study of the RCMP secret activities on Canadian campuses, *Spying 101: The RCMP's Secret Activities at Canadian Universities, 1917–1997* (Toronto; Buffalo, NY; London, 2002) certainly reveals a deep-seated suspicion of all student-run societies of the 1960s, political and otherwise.

120 Julyan Reid, 'Some Canadian Issues', p. 12.

Julyan Reid, the international aspect of the protest was a consequence of 'the Third World War' – that is, a war that was 'third world' in the sense that it was waged against the Third World (South East Asia), and because it was the 'third total war in the average young person's memory span' – the other two being the Second World War and the Cold War.[121] Reid proceeded to explain the implications of this for students of the Western world:

> [The student protesters] are all part of an international industrial world[;] economically we are tied together by multiple international and individual trade agreements. We are tied militarily with NATO, NORAD, plus all the remnants of allied relationships, both formal and emotional. The whole of Western democracy forms a military-industrial complex and the network is such that no member could ever honestly say that they [*sic*] stand apart. The tie is cultural in the largest sense of the word. It is a military-industrial culture and the universities, although they may teach in different languages, are processing the students for the same purpose, to perpetuate and regenerate that culture.[122]

Turning to Canada, Reid concluded that: 'No Canadians fight in Vietnam, yet the students know and feel that they are part of the culture that is fighting; no amount of delicate extrication from various international military and trade agreements is really going to cancel this feeling.'[123]

Although this explanation appertains particularly to the latter half of the decade, when student involvement in Vietnam protest and counter-culture activity reached a peak, it is possible to use Reid's theory in the context of the early 1960s. Canadian student protesters who participated in SUPA, in civil rights and in other related humanitarian ventures were, it seems, driven by a sense of economic and social commonality with their American peers. Another former New Leftist from Canada articulated a view of his peers' involvement in the movement which addressed directly their class and social status, and which suggested that in these respects, the Canadian radicals resembled closely their American counterparts in background and attitude:

> Most of the people in the New Left that I knew, they were the sort of middle-class kids who'd been brought up to believe in decency, and they'd been brought up to believe in equality, and they'd been brought up to believe in all those ideas. They began to find that these ideas were being violated all around them, and this was wrong …[124]

However, there were many Canadian students for whom activism signified, above all else, a highly critical stance of the United States; these students often advocated that their fellow Canadians should take a nationalistic stand against 'imperialistic'

---

121 Ibid., p. 13.

122 Ibid.

123 Ibid.

124 Quoted in Cyril Levitt, *Children of Privilege: Student Revolt in the Sixties – A Study of the Student Movements in Canada, the United States, and West Germany* (Toronto; Buffalo, NY; London, 1984), p. 41.

America.[125] Between the two extremes were those who possessed attitudes which resembled, yet also differed from, those of their American counterparts. Their position on civil rights, for example, was often tempered by the feeling that, historically, racism in Canada had been less endemic than in the United States. Ken Whiteley, a Toronto musician who declared that it was, to a considerable extent, issues of social protest than motivated him to become part of the folk revival, believed that perspectives were different among Canadian youth 'perhaps because we were not living to the same extent with the same legacy of racism ... Not to say that Canada doesn't have its own legacy of racism, but a different one. Certainly much less pronounced.' [126]

This sense of Canadian racism – against black people and against Natives, in particular – having been widespread, but not as potent as in America, was pervasive, and this viewpoint continues, whether accurate or not, to be expressed; nonetheless, young Canadians who were sympathetic to civil rights did, to a great extent, consider the movement to be of relevance to them, and joined with their American counterparts in supporting, and drawing inspiration from, the black freedom fighters of the Southern states.

Accusations that the stance of the student movement was patronising and presumptuous would abound, and the ideals of the organisations frequently fell short of reality; the ERAP workers were faced with factionalism and difficulty, and the SDS involvement in civil rights provoked hostility among black Southerners which would prompt the Student Non-Violent Co-ordinating Committee to reject outright the assistance of white people in 1965. Not all SDS members were in agreement over their supposed status as ambassadors to the lower classes, and many would imbibe only selective ideals and beliefs of the organisation; others, still, did not affiliate themselves with the SDS, but shared in its sympathies for civil rights and social justice. Nonetheless, the naïve, perhaps presumptuous, attitude of white youth in the early 1960s that the world might quite easily become a place of diverse peoples in harmony, and their belief in what Daniel J. Gonczy calls the 'political and ideological mirage which eloquently bespeaks solidarity', serves to explain, in part, the appeal of folk music to socially conscious young people in the early 1960s, and the celebration of regional eclecticism which became so integral to the revival.[127] The interest of revival musicians in different musical cultures reflected both a sense of mutual commonality, utopian unity and respect, and a sense of the 'otherness', whether directly articulated or not, of the ethnic or regional group in question. Earnest in their desire to help the poor and the suffering, the left-wing youth of North America were, nonetheless, venturing into alien territory among people of whom they knew little; desperate to build bridges though they were, they were ultimately conditioned by their own beliefs and ideals; these ultimately simplistic, romantic ideals often

---

125 See, for example, the contribution of student protester Escott Reid in Tim and Julyan Reid (eds), *Student Power and the Canadian Campus*. Cyril Levitt also discusses the role of Canadian nationalism in the student movement in *Children of Privilege*, p. 161.

126 Whiteley, discussion. A similar opinion was expressed by Richard Flohil during my interview with him.

127 Gonczy, 'The Folk Music Movement of the 1960s', p. 23.

proved incompatible with the complex realities of society and life in the Southern
states or the Native reservations. The attitude of the folk revivalists towards cultural
'others' was, thus, frequently simplistic and romanticised; folk music provided a
rose-tinted lens through which to view political problems, transcending and blurring
complexities for good or ill.

While exhibiting interest in the music of people from all over the world, revival
performers, ultimately, turned to marginal American groups for their greatest
inspiration, following the legacy of the inter-war revival, and in correspondence with
current political events. In particular, black performers past and present were lionised
by the movement, reconstructed as raw but profoundly gifted musical masters. Jeff
Todd Titon, an historian of the blues revival of the 1960s, has suggested that '[t]he
blues revival was a white, middle class love affair with the music and lifestyle of
marginal blacks. The romantic strain projected a kind of primitivism on the blues
singer and located him in a culture of natural license.'[128] Richard Flohil, who was
instrumental in bringing blues musicians such as Big Bill Broonzy, Muddy Waters
and Mississippi John Hurt to Toronto in the early 1960s, has suggested that often
individual black musicians were automatically given the status of master musicians.
It is possible that revivalists, perhaps naively, assumed that a black performer must
be an expert musician.[129] The well-meaning white musicians elevated the black
performers to the status of master musicians, exhibiting an earnest desire to learn
from them while seemingly desperate to demonstrate their desire to right past
wrongs and prove themselves capable of understanding black life and culture. Young
white guitarists would embark on pilgrimages to Mississippi or to Chicago ghettoes
to visit blues 'legends', and, as Benjamin Filene has noted, it was considered a
victory if a white performer was accepted by black musicians.[130] Such performers
would often adopt a scathing attitude towards white popular and folk musicians,
condemning them for committing cultural theft from the black communities. Such
unquestioning adoration and envy was, in many ways, as problematic as the more
overtly patronising and paternalistic approach of earlier folklorists such as John
Lomax in his dealings with Leadbelly and Josh White, as documented by scholars
such as Jerrold Hirsch and Benjamin Filene.[131] Ultimately, the representation of
black culture, while positive and praising, at times to excess, was still on the terms
of the white revivalists. The African-American Julius Lester, writing for *Sing Out!* in
1964, expressed frustration with the white fixation with black culture, commenting
that white and black singers should cease desiring to exchange places and accept
themselves. 'What a crazy country we live in,' he stated. 'Young Negroes [*sic*] want
to be middle-class white Americans. Young whites want to be Negroes. Both mistake

128 Jeff Todd Titon, 'Reconstructing the Blues: Reflections on the 1960s Blues Revival',
in Rosenberg (ed.), *Transforming Tradition*, p. 225.

129 Richard Flohil, in discussion with the author, 6 May 2003.

130 Filene, *Romancing the Folk,* pp. 92–3.

131 Ibid., and Jerrold Hirsch, 'Modernity, Nostalgia, and Southern Folklore Studies: The
Case of John Lomax', *Journal of American Folklore*, 105 (1992): 183–207.

the shadow for the substance. Won't both be surprised when they find they've only swapped one horror for another?'[132]

In Canada, blues music found an eager and captive audience among folk revivalists and budding rock musicians alike. Among some of the Canadian folk performers, there existed the same tendency to elevate and worship the traditional 'old master' of the blues as a quasi-mystical figure.[133] For black Canadian-born folk musicians such as Torontonian Jackie Washington, this equation of black musicians with the blues often proved problematic. Washington, a 'new aesthetic' singer-songwriter, remarked in 1977, 'I know a lot of people figure because I'm black I have to sing blues. What do you do when you're born in Canada and you never been near the Delta? Only the Delta Theatre.'[134] For Washington, it seemed that the white revivalists' love of the blues created a racial stereotype which proved damaging to his individuality as an artist.

In spite of the excessive naivety of some of the white revivalists, a sense of confidence that the interracial gap might easily be bridged was integral to the civil rights movement of the early 1960s. Many white revivalists became personally involved in the civil rights struggle, exhibiting the same idealised and, at times, over-simplified understanding of the needs and politics of the Southern black communities. Folksinger Guy Carawan participated in the Freedom Rides and later published anthologies of civil rights songs.[135] Prominent folksingers such as Bob Dylan, Joan Baez, Pete Seeger and Peter, Paul and Mary were regularly present at protests and sit-ins, and the alliance between the civil rights cause and the folk revival arguably reached a climax at the March on Washington in 1963, a major

132 Julius Lester, 'The View from the Other Side of the Tracks', *Sing Out!*, 14/4 (September 1964), p. 39. Julius Lester was present during some of the Israel Young-Richard Reuss interviews, and made some significant remarks, including some observations about the lack of black readership for *Sing Out!* (Interview of 15 July 1965, Box 1). Israel Young himself, as owner of the Folklore Center, remarked that young black people did not frequent his store. Blues performer Taj Mahal, who had a positive experience of performing for white folk audiences at Newport, also noted that 'there weren't that many young black cats into the music.' (See Von Schmidt and Rooney, *Baby Let Me Follow You Down*, p. 218). There is much evidence to reinforce the idea that the revival was fundamentally a 'white' movement.

133 See, for example, white Canadian musician Colin Linden's description of a visit to blues musician Tampa Red in Chicago in Bill Usher and Linda Page Harpa, *For What Time I Am In This World: Stories from Mariposa* (Toronto, 1977), p. 23. Linden described the 'excitement in the air of a dingy side street in black Chicago which breathed life back into the juke joints, roadhouses and burnt-out barbe-que restaurants'.

134 Ibid., p. 113.

135 Guy and Candie Carawan, *We Shall Overcome! Songs of the Southern Freedom Movement* (New York, 1963) – compiled for SNCC. See also *Freedom is a Constant Struggle* (New York, 1968), by the same authors. These books were largely comprised of original songs, some of which were specially composed, and others which had been spontaneously 'created' during the marches and sit-ins. The Carawans reminisced about their career in folk music and their involvement in the Civil Rights movement in Matt Watroba, 'Guy and Candie Carawan: Keeping Their Eyes on the Prize', *Sing Out!*, Vol. 44 No. 3, Spring 2000.

civil rights rally at which numerous folksingers performed.[136] Folk songs possessed a power to unite and inspire crowds, but after some time the black communities, particularly in the North, would consider such a power to be superficial; by the mid-1960s, Black Power spokesmen would condemn the protest songs, and the integrationist civil rights movement in general, as having been falsely naïve and ignorant of the complex problems of Southern blacks.[137] Nonetheless, there was a crucial link between the idealistic politics of the civil rights movement and the fixation of the revivalists with the music of Southern blacks; their idealistic view of black musicians and their great interest in their work, though problematic in its implications, reflected the earnest optimism of the revivalists as they sought to bring about cultural harmony and unity. The music and culture of Southern and Western whites (or the white 'American folk') was treated with similar reverence by revivalists in the 1960s. Woody Guthrie, as a Midwesterner from Oklahoma, had perhaps been the initial inspiration for this interest, drawing attention as he did to the society, culture and problems of marginalised white Americans. Revivalists worshipped Guthrie, admiring his political ethos even if they could not act on it as he had done, and young male musicians such as Bob Dylan and 'Rambling' Jack Elliott, both born into middle-class Jewish families, emulated his sound and his lifestyle, and even invented similar cultural backgrounds for themselves. Presently, other Southern white musicians were adopted as heroes by the revivalists – bluegrass performers such as Earl Scruggs and Bill Monroe, traditional singers such as 'Aunt' Molly Jackson and Sarah Ogan Gunning and 'mountain' musician Roscoe Holcombe, were showcased by music festivals and revival magazines. The poverty of their backgrounds and the alleged homogeneity of their cultures were prized by revivalists with a social conscience and a tendency to romanticise the less fortunate whom they desired to befriend and assist; the tendency to 'confuse poverty with art' was once again paramount.[138] Aspiring fiddlers and banjo players from the urban North would, once again, make pilgrimages to the South to visit and learn from traditional musicians, and young Northern musicians, such as banjoists Mike Seeger and Eric Weissberg, protégés of the Washington Square 'picking sessions', attempted to assimilate into their culture by competing against Southern musicians in festivals and contests. The attitude of the revivalists towards white Southern musicians was also shaped by certain preconceptions and biases. For instance, they were disdainful of contemporary country music for its electric instrumentation and blatant commercialism, and considered only Bluegrass to be a viable genre because it employed acoustic instruments; according to Neil Rosenberg, Bluegrass was 'virtually the only form of contemporary country music acceptable to the folk boom of the late fifties and early sixties, where electric instruments were considered inauthentic and symbols of the alienation of mass culture'.[139]

---

136 Concise narratives of the involvement of folksingers in civil rights protest may be found in Cohen's *Rainbow Quest*, pp. 183–7, 204–8 and 230–3.

137 This will be discussed at length in Chapter 4.

138 Ellen Stekert, 'Cents and Nonsense', p. 94.

139 Neil Rosenberg, *Bluegrass: A History* (Urbana, IL and Chicago, IL, 1985), p. 6.

Rosenberg has also asserted that Bluegrass found acceptance with revival audiences because of the virtuosic standard of musicianship it required. He suggests that, although folk enthusiasts rejected the elitism of other genres such as classical and jazz, they also sought in folk music styles such as Bluegrass the aspects of those genres which they admired. 'Among people who performed music from their own oral traditions, the real folk,' states Rosenberg, 'revivalists looked for virtuosi – often inarticulate and untutored but able to make artful performances. These were perennial favourites, valued as classical or jazz musicians were for their artistic abilities.'[140]

Thus, Bluegrass and other Southern and Western music styles were as much idealised constructions of the revivalists as they were traditional music genres. The 'virtuosi' themselves were, equally, lauded as raw but authentic geniuses, proof of the beauty and worth of the 'ordinary', impoverished Americans from allegedly well-preserved ethnic cultures, but, once again, social and political reality fell short of the romanticised ideals of the urban 'folkniks'. Perhaps one of the greatest ironies of the Southern music revival was the fact that those musicians whom the leftist urbanites admired were frequently living embodiments of the reactionary conservatism abhorred by the movement; Jon Pankake, editor of *The Little Sandy Review,* described this as one of the innate 'absurdities' of the movement.[141] There were also some aspects of their performances which the self-styled sophisticates of the revival found embarrassing – according to Rosenberg, college audiences would cringe at the simplistic comedy routines and evangelical piety of imported Bluegrass players.[142]

Therefore, the elevation of Southern black and white musicians during the revival was very much a product of the political ideals of the student left. In particular, the lionisation of black musicians was closely linked to the optimistic character of the early civil rights movement, which believed in the co-existence of black and white. Revivalists lauded the blues musicians as folk heroes, treating them as saints in an effort to build new bridges with the black community. White Southerners were, equally, and rather ironically, admired for their ethnic and cultural 'authenticity' as untutored musical virtuosi; in this can be seen the left-wing sympathy for the workers, and the students' idealisation of the poor people they desired to help. Unintentionally, the attitude of the revivalists proved patronising and reductive for both musical cultures, imposing on them values and status that had not been of their creation. Nonetheless, it is important to note that the folk revival proved beneficial, at least in some respects, for many 'traditional' musicians. Bluegrass musicians such as Bill Monroe and blues artists such as Muddy Waters and Lonnie Johnson were drawn back from increasing obscurity by the movement; as a result of the folk revival, they found themselves at the centre of a new narrative of their respective histories, and while this may not always have been financially viable, it proved soothing to their egos and ensured that their music would survive in public memory and on record.

---

140 Ibid., p. 171.
141 From Cohen (ed.), *Wasn't That a Time*, p. 113.
142 Ibid., p. 154.

Canadian revivalists were enamoured of Bluegrass and Appalachian music insofar as they represented aspects of the eclectic regionalism of the early movement; it would, perhaps, be excessive to suggest that the political and cultural significance of these genres for Americans was present in Canada to a similar extent. As has been stated, the concern of Canadian youth for issues which were fundamentally American, such as the civil rights movement of the Southern states, and the Vietnam conflict, was often tempered by a sense of difference and detachment, and, thus, their enthusiasm for Southern music, though great, possessed the same qualities.

Canadians were as concerned as Americans with locating 'authentic' musicians, and this was not devoid of political meaning for them; although Canadians had not experienced the same racial division as had the Americans, they had mistreated and deprived Native people economically and culturally (albeit, in their view, not to the same extent as Americans) and the Canadian folk revival was eager to provide a platform for Native performers, just as the SUPA members had been anxious to help deprived Native communities across the country. Prominent singer-songwriters such as the Canadian-born Buffy Sainte-Marie drew attention to the issues of Native communities, and the Mariposa Folk Festival would provide a platform for many Native performers throughout the 1960s and 1970s, including Alanis Obomsawin, Francis Aterondiatakon Boots, Bobby Woods and Winston Wuttunee. However, once again the revivalists possessed certain expectations of the 'ethnic' performers, and were bewildered if these failed to be met; one Native group, The Canadian Indian Dancers, a pan-tribal group of men and women who performed dances from their various cultures, appeared at Mariposa in 1966 and were berated by the reviewers of *Hoot* for allegedly failing to take themselves seriously and for appearing 'sarcastic', 'bitter' and 'self-parodying'.[143] Revivalists, earnest and serious in their approach to tradition as they conceived of it, often disliked anything which deviated from their expectations.[144]

It is important to note, however, that, after the establishment of the Native culture workshops at Mariposa in the early 1970s, many Native performers were featured at the festivals, some of whom addressed their largely white audiences quite forcefully on matters of cultural difference and tolerance.[145] Francis Aterondiatakon Boots, Bobby Woods and Winston Wuttunee illustrated the differing world views

---

143 *Hoot!*, Volume 2 No. 5, September 1966. A description of The Canadian Indian Dancers appears in the Mariposa Festival Programme of 1966, p. 15. The group consisted of three women and four men who came from the Ottawa, Ojibway, Cree and Squamish tribes. They performed various dances, including, according to the programme, an eagle dance, a hoop dance and a gift dance.

144 Much literature has been produced on the cultural implications of the 'performance' of Native peoples for the entertainment of whites, in both the Canadian and American contexts. For Canada, see, in particular, Veronica Strong-Boag and Carole Gerson, *Paddling Her Own Canoe: The Life and Texts of E. Pauline Johnson (Tekahionwake)* (Toronto; Buffalo, NY; London, 2000). In the American context, see the various essays in S. Elizabeth Bird (ed.), *Dressing in Feathers: The Construction of the Indian in American Popular Culture* (Boulder, CO, 1996).

145 Valerie Korinek notes that, by the late 1960s, more white Canadians were becoming aware of the problems facing many Native communities, owing to the rise of Red Power

of Native and white Canadians. Meanwhile, Native singer and storyteller Alanis Obomsawin, who would co-ordinate Native and Inuit workshops at Mariposa in the mid-1970s, berated non-Native Canadians for their intolerance towards Native speech patterns and perceived 'misuse' of English words. 'I want you to listen to us, to the way we speak,' she urged the audience. 'Don't make us speak like you. Just listen!'[146] Whether or not their audiences did listen, Native Canadians did at least have some opportunity to voice their concerns and to shatter stereotypes before the predominantly white audiences at Mariposa.

The political goals and ideals of the folk boom generation thus clearly served to enhance the pluralistic nature of the movement. Believing that racial integration, peace and the co-operation of peoples were valid and attainable goals, the folk revival of the 1960s optimistically constructed the continent around it as a diverse, but ultimately unified, land.

The Folk Revival and the 'Cult of Exclusivity'

A third possible explanation for the diversity of the folk revival lies with the exclusive connotations of the movement in the late 1950s and early 1960s. Like other movements which appealed to youth, the folk revival had a particular mystique and its own 'in-crowd' mentality. The revival emerged, in part, from the beatnik culture of the 1950s, and attracted many of the same aspiring young intellectuals; folksinger Roy Berkeley recalled that he had found folk music 'not only naive but also embarrassing' until he went to Greenwich Village to meet the intellectuals of whose circle he longed to be part. 'They were intellectuals, thinkers, questioners. And what kind of music did they like? Folk music! I began to look at folk music with a different eye,' he recalled.[147] Thus, for a brief period, folk music was the music of young people who considered themselves discerning and sophisticated.

The eclectic nature of the folk revival enabled enthusiasts effectively to 'progress' from accessible and popular styles of music to the more rare and specialist genres. As Oscar Brand, another performer and commentator on the revival, noted,

> Experts aver that many folk fans took up the art in order to be different from the average American. As more people became aficionados, the early adherents were forced to espouse more esoteric forms of folk music – turning from Burl Ives to Bascom Lamar Lunsford, from Lunsford to Pete Steele, and from Pete Steele to whichever backwoods minstrel was

---

in North America generally, and to the inclusion of editorials on Native peoples featured in magazines such as *Chatelaine* (*Roughing It in the Suburbs*, pp. 344–5).

146 These performers are featured in Usher and Page-Harpa, *For What Time I Am In This World*. Obomsawin and Boots are on pp. 71–2 and Woods and Wuttunee on pp. 84–5. Alanis Obomsawin later became a film-maker, and was awarded the Order of Canada in 1983 for her contribution to cinema. Among her most recent projects was a four-part documentary series on the Oka Crisis (a struggle between Native communities and the government and police) of 1990. (See Matthew Hays, 'Oka Crisis: Worst Moment Revisited', *Globe & Mail*, 21 June 2000).

147 Roy Berkeley, quoted in Cohen (ed.), *Wasn't That a Time*, p. 188.

as yet undiscovered by the masses. That this group does not represent the majority ... is self-evident. [148]

Thus, according to Brand, the more popular folk music became in the mainstream sector, the more obscure and specific the interests of the revivalists. Once again, the 'apparatus' of the folk revival served to encourage, and mould the views of, those with special interests or strong opinions on folk music. The workshops held at the major folk festivals encouraged discourse and discussion on very particular forms of folk music, be it Bluegrass or traditional Ontario song. Magazines such as *The Little Sandy Review* catered especially for those who held particular views on folk music, and who wanted to broaden their tastes or enter the self-styled 'inner circle' of folk music 'experts'. *Sing Out!*, in accommodating the views of all parties, ensured that such 'experts' could both make their opinions known and argue with those who disagreed with them. Frank Hamilton of the Old Town School of Folk Music in Chicago disliked the existence of snobbery in the movement; he recalled that, among his students, '[t]here were Frankenstein monsters, instant authorities on folk music.' The School, through its programmes for the students, tried to 'diffuse' such attitudes.[149] However, ultimately, the presence of those 'experts' who valued the most 'rare' or 'authentic' folk music, whatever the shortcomings of their attitudes, served also to promote the revival's eclecticism, and ensured that its enquiring spirit and love of detail was kept alive.

Conclusion

The folk revival of the early 1960s in America and Canada was a movement which promoted a vision of the North American continent as a vast patchwork of societies and cultures. Such a vision was furthered by the structure of the movement; its emphasis on coffee-house performances, periodicals and folk festivals enhanced the celebration of diversity. Although the political motives for such a vision were not necessarily shared by Canadians and Americans to the same extent, the young people in both countries felt a sense of cultural dislocation and alienation which led them to explore and embrace the music of many groups of people, but particularly the 'American folk' of the South and West. Many were also led to such explorations by the sense that folk music was something exclusive and select, something quite separate from the mundane world of mainstream pop music. During the early decade, thus, there was little emphasis on nationalism for either the Canadian or the American revival. A sense of Canadian difference was felt in the early movement, but was never outlined in a coherent manner; rather, the American movement appealed, at this time, to Americans who sought a new identity, and to Canadians for whom the North American, regional focus of the movement seemed perfectly relevant.

Gradually, this would change. The idealistic outlook of youth in the early 1960s would become soured by events in Vietnam and by the proven naivety and impracticality of its political movements. As American youth became disillusioned

---

148 Brand, *The Ballad Mongers*, p. 55.
149 Frank Hamilton in Cohen (ed.), *Wasn't That a Time*, p. 157.

with their country, celebrations of the forthcoming Canadian Centennial were encouraging Canadians to consider themselves proud to be separate from the United States, and to celebrate their 'identity', whatever that might be. Simultaneously, events at the 1965 Newport Folk Festival brought the halcyon days of the folk revival to an end; folk music was changing, as was the continent of North America. The relationship between folk music and national identity in both Canada and America would alter accordingly.

Chapter 3

Folk Music and Community in 'The Village': Greenwich Village and Yorkville in the 1960s

Introduction

The urban character of the post-war folk revival has been widely discussed, and, despite the fixation of many revivalists with the regional cultures and music of America and Canada, such an interest sprang, to a great extent, from an invented, celebratory, artist's 'sense of place'. This 'sense of place' both transcended and blurred the more problematic, empirical reality of region as geography, with all its implications of cultural, political and social complexity. Reasons for the urban nature of the movement have hitherto been suggested or implied – the movement had, in its inter-war, formative years, sprung from the left-wing intellectual subculture of the urban North, and particularly of New York City; other socio-cultural explanations include the often-discussed middle-class demographic of the revival and the fact that so many revivalists were students attending universities and colleges in major cities.

The coffee-house districts of the North American cities both served to promote, and develop further as a result of, the urban nature of folk music culture. As growing numbers of young aspiring folk musicians made their way to the cities where they might find both fellow enthusiasts and venues in which to perform, local entrepreneurs, motivated by a mixture of cultural and economic interests, began to feature and encourage folk music acts in their restaurants and cafés. Presently, coffee-houses featuring folk music began to proliferate, above all in New York City and in Toronto, two cities which became major magnets for hopeful folk musicians from across the continent. New York was the centre of the urban revival in America, and, essentially, in North America; although it is important to note the presence of other vital 'scenes' in the United States, especially in San Francisco and in Chicago, where the influential Old Town School of Folk Music was situated, the prime significance of Greenwich Village as a folk music neighbourhood is difficult to dispute.[1] It was situated in the heart of the city in which the urban folksong revival essentially began, and its vibrant, unique culture had provided ideal conditions for the nurturing of the movement. Greenwich Village, as a long-established bohemian enclave, was

---

1   Neil Rosenberg talks about the need for more detailed studies of folk music outside New York in his contribution to Ronald Cohen (ed.), *Wasn't That a Time!: First Hand Accounts of the Folk Music Revival* (Metuchen, NJ, 1991).

perhaps a natural haven for the folk music movement, but Toronto's Yorkville district, which became the Canadian equivalent of Greenwich Village, was less of an obvious location for the development of folk music. The 'bohemianisation' of this once-prosperous former village, which had been incorporated into the city during the latter years of the nineteenth century, seemed more of an incidental consequence of the decline in property standards and values in Toronto following the Second World War.

To suggest that Yorkville emulated, and was inspired by, Greenwich Village, implies, once again, that the role adopted by Canada in the folk revival was secondary and imitative. Indeed, Greenwich Village was a tremendous inspiration to those who flocked to Yorkville; as journalist and author Nicholas Jennings has remarked, it is important at least to take this factor into account and to acknowledge the reasons for its existence:

> There is this kind of love-hate situation between Toronto and New York, culturally and historically. Even to this day, you hear people talking about how Toronto is just like New York – a little smaller, cleaner and safer ... There is a long-standing tradition of Toronto wanting to see itself as a junior New York. So ... I do think that some of the coffee house owners, some of the artists, aspired for Yorkville to be 'our Greenwich Village'.[2]

There is certainly no doubt that, in terms of folk music, Greenwich Village was a great inspiration to Toronto musicians. However, the social and cultural conditions of post-war Toronto were also markedly different from those of New York, and the development of Yorkville as a bohemian 'village' was, accordingly, also in considerable contrast to that of Greenwich Village. 'Toronto the Good' was, during the post-war era, ostensibly, at least, in possession of a far more restrained character than New York, perhaps as a result of its strongly Protestant origins. It was, possibly, as a result of this that, in the mid-twentieth century, Toronto boasted a very rich underground culture, particularly where popular music was concerned; Yorkville emerged as a vital part of this subculture. In many ways, thus, the two neighbourhoods developed very distinct identities, with contrasting relationships to the cities in which they were established; in this way, folk music neighbourhoods were part of the long-standing popular music tradition of linking specific cities with specific sounds. Greenwich Village was to folk music as Liverpool was to the 'Mersey Beat', as Nashville was to country music, and as Haight-Ashbury would subsequently be to acid rock.

This association of place and musical culture was heightened during the 1960s; a sense of separate physical space seemed particularly crucial to the young rebels of the period. Perhaps as a result of their experiences of communal living at universities and colleges, young people with radical tendencies seemed to want to congregate and live among their peers in their own communities. Such communities abounded in this period, and perhaps the apex of this ideal was the Woodstock Festival of 1969; festival-goers considered the site of this festival to be their own city, in which values of love and peace prevailed. Music was always a crucial element of such ideal

---

2   Nicholas Jennings, in discussion with the author, Toronto, 2 December 2002.

communities; if young idealists were not gathering in places where music was to be found, then musical activity would soon arise wherever they congregated.

The purpose of this chapter is to explore the importance of Greenwich Village and Yorkville as attempts of the folk revivalists to create a community built upon the movement's ideals of unity in diversity and musical variety. As the previous chapter has shown, the coffee-house 'scenes' of neighbourhoods such as Yorkville and Greenwich Village served, importantly, both to further and shape the eclectic character of the revival in the early 1960s. Their promotion of all levels of talent and their proud exhibition of musical diversity were vital in developing further the all-embracing, pluralistic nature of the revival in the early 1960s.[3] In addition to this, however, the coffee-house scenes of these urban districts, so unique and individualistic in their origins, cultural conditions, and place within folk revival history, could be said to represent an attempt not merely to reflect the cultural interests of the revivalists, but also to make the revivalists' idealistic dream of unity in diversity, of true community, become a concrete reality. In many crucial respects, the development of Greenwich Village and Yorkville, both of which became known to their respective residents and regulars as 'the village', represented an attempt to manifest the myth of utopia in daily life. Both districts became residential centres for artists, musicians and refugees from conventional society, and developed distinct identities as alternative, 'beloved communities' of young people linked by their ideals and their love of the contemporary arts and music; and, at least for the first half of the 1960s, folk revival music was at the artistic and ideological centre of the utopian experiment.

The attempt to build unique societies founded upon the ideals of the youth movement would ultimately end in disillusionment and disappointment. Folk music, and the socio-political stance which it represented, a stance which appeared increasingly naïve as the decade progressed, began to pass through the neighbourhoods, hastened by the increased commercialisation of folk music, and its integration into the rock music scene. Folk musicians were, gradually, replaced by rock bands, biker gangs, under-aged runaways, and drug addicts and dealers. Those residents who tried to preserve the original vision and ideals of 'the village' found themselves at the mercy of an outraged public, a police force in search of scapegoats, and, eventually, property developers who perceived a dramatically different vision for the future of the neighbourhoods. The halcyon days of Greenwich Village and Yorkville were comparatively short, but an examination of their culture, their similarities and differences, and their development reveals much about the nature and ideals of the folk revival in the early 1960s – the myth of eclectic community, the failure of that myth, and, eventually, the consequences of this failure for the revival in Canada and in America.

---

3   See Chapter 2 discussion of coffee-houses.

Background: The Development of Greenwich Village and Yorkville as Bohemian Neighbourhoods

The existence of a neighbourhood such as Greenwich Village in post-war New York City is, perhaps, scarcely surprising. Less evident, however, is the development of Yorkville, the village which was annexed by the city of Toronto in 1883 and existed as a quiet residential district until the 1950s.

Greenwich Village had been an infamous 'bohemian' neighbourhood within New York since the 1890s. Artists, writers and social rebels of various kinds lived among the district's peculiar mixture of genteel urbanites and less prosperous Italian and Jewish immigrants; at one time these artists declared their community independent from the rest of the nation, a 'new territory of the mind and soul'.[4] According to historian George Chauncey, 'the Village' was, at the turn of the century, 'a prototypical furnished-room district, for it offered cheap rooms to unmarried men and women who wished to develop social lives unencumbered by family obligations and to engage in work likely to be more creative rather than numerative.'[5]

Greenwich Village also attracted homosexual men and women who sought to express their sexuality in a more liberated environment. Although he notes that not all 'bohemians' and free thinkers of the neighbourhood were welcoming or tolerant of homosexuals, generally the liberal, creative atmosphere of the Village enabled gay and lesbian people to find a comfortable home there.[6]

By the 1920s, Greenwich Village had become a popular destination for tourists who were attracted to the neighbourhood by the reports that 'free love' could be witnessed, and enjoyed, everywhere, and by the Italian restaurants and stores which, in defiance of Prohibition, sold cheap, home-made wine.[7] Therefore, from the turn of the century, Greenwich Village, like Harlem or Brooklyn, was an area of the city with its own well-documented, distinctive identity and mystique.

The distinctiveness of Greenwich Village continued into the post-1945 era, and, in the 1950s, the district became a haven for the bohemians of the beat movement. While Allen Ginsberg and Michael McClure recited poetry to enthralled audiences, jazz musicians such as Chet Baker and John Coltrane played in nightspots such as

---

4   Foreword by Robert R. MacDonald and L. Jay Oliva. In Rick Beard and Leslie Cohen Berlowitz (eds), *Greenwich Village: Counter and Counterculture* (New Brunswick, NJ, 1993), p. ix. For discussion of the early bohemian community of Greenwich Village, see Christine Stansell, *American Moderns: Bohemian New York and the Creation of a New Century* (New York, 2000). The original study of the Greenwich Village 'scene' was Caroline F. Ware, *Greenwich Village, 1920–1930: A Comment on American Civilization in the Post-War Years* (Boston, 1935).

5   George Chauncey, *Gay New York: Gender, Urban Culture and the Making of the Gay Male World, 1890–1940* (New York, 1994), p. 229.

6   Ibid., pp. 228–30.

7   Ibid., p. 233. For a general account of the rise of 'urban tourism' in America, see Catherine Cocks, *Doing the Town: The Rise of Urban Tourism in the United States, 1850–1915* (Berkeley, CA; Los Angeles, CA; London, 2001).

the High Spot and the Village Vanguard.[8] Establishments such as the White Horse Tavern, a former haunt of Dylan Thomas in which 'a tradition of chess, poets and beer remained', became popular among young people seeking alternative weekend entertainment.[9] Greenwich Village was also, according to musician and photographer John Cohen, a meeting-place for artists *per se* by the 1950s; small galleries run co-operatively by artists developed on Tenth Street, while abstract expressionist painters congregated in the Cedar Tavern, and aspiring photographers gathered in the Limelight Café.[10] Young people with artistic aspirations rented lofts around the neighbourhood, much to the chagrin of the older residents, particularly the owners of the original Italian coffee-houses, who, as folksinger Oscar Brand jokingly remarked, waged 'cold war' with their new neighbours in an attempt to curtail their activities.[11]

It was at this time, in the 1950s, that folk music, the presence of which in the city was already evidenced by the People's Artists activities of Pete Seeger et al., became central to the village. John Cohen recalls early folk music performances in some of the MacDougal Street coffee-houses such as the Café Bizarre – the Washington Square 'picking' sessions had also already been established by this stage – but Cohen maintains that one of the prime factors in the intersection of the village and the rising folk 'boom' was the establishment of Israel 'Izzy' Young's Folklore Center on MacDougal Street in early 1957.

Young, the son of Jewish immigrants and a former bookstore employee with a strong interest in folk music, developed particularly through involvement with Margot Mayo's Square Dance Society in the 1940s, intended his centre to be a folk music bookstore, but gradually the Folklore Center became a point of congregation, almost a place of pilgrimage, for folk music enthusiasts.[12] So integral did Israel Young become to Village life, in the eyes of young folk music fans, that he became known as the 'mayor' of Greenwich Village.[13]

Israel Young also began to organise concerts through the Folklore Center in the late 1950s, bringing lesser-known rural musicians such as Doc Watson and Joseph

8   Dan Wakefield, *New York in the Fifties* (Boston, MA; New York; London, 1992), pp. 298–318.

9   John Cohen (II) in Cohen (ed.), *Wasn't That a Time*, p. 178. The Limelight was the first photography gallery in the United States. See also the personal memoir of the owner of The Limelight Café, Helen Gee – *Limelight: A Greenwich Village Photography Gallery and Coffeehouse in the Fifties* (Albuquerque, NM, 1997).

10   Ibid.

11   Oscar Brand, *The Ballad Mongers: Rise of the Modern Folk Song* (Westport, CT, 1962), p. 157. Articles and items on artists' lofts in the Village are scattered throughout the *Village Voice* of the early 1960s. One example is 'Artists Fights to Save Lofts', *Village Voice*, 14 February 1963, cover story.

12   Young's involvement in Margot Mayo's dance group is discussed in Chapter 1.

13   Michele Wood, 'Music and the "Mayor" of the Village', *Cosmopolitan*, December 1963. Israel Young gave an extensive series of interviews with folklore student Richard Reuss from 1965 to 1969. Collectively, these interviews are an invaluable primary source for study of folk music in New York and beyond from the 1940s to the 1960s. They now form part of the collection of the American Folklife Center at the Library of Congress, Washington, DC.

Spence to an urban setting. Young also organised Bob Dylan's first New York concert, on 4 November 1961.[14] According to John Cohen, Young had the ability to address the interests of folk revival 'academics' and 'popularisers' alike; his centre was a crucial place of discourse in which demonstrations of square dancing, heated arguments and impromptu performances were commonplace.[15] The impact of the Center on the folk revival, and particularly the growing folk scene in New York, was crucial; gradually, creatively named coffee-houses featuring folk music performers were appearing all over the neighbourhood, among them The Gaslight, The Café Wha?, The Bitter End, Café Figaro, Gerde's Folk City and The Village Gate. In 1960, therefore, Greenwich Village was thriving as a vibrant centre, not merely for folk music, but also for modern art and drama, bohemian ideals and, increasingly, political idealism. It had, in many ways, passed into the hands of the baby boom generation, who viewed the Village lifestyle as an attempt to see whether one could live out one's ideals in reality.

The development of Yorkville as a folk music neighbourhood contrasted considerably to that of Greenwich Village. Not only did Yorkville lack such a storied past as a bohemian enclave, but, furthermore, Toronto had never been a city fabled for its rebellious character or artistic experimentation. Certainly, New York, rich in its artistic life, has always proclaimed its own importance in this respect, while Toronto has remained quite silent with regard to its cultural past. There have been few histories published on the subject of the expressive arts in Canada; those in existence, discussing 'high culture', have frequently, if inadvertently, highlighted the conformist character of the public cultural expressions of a country still tied to Anglicised society, hierarchy and values.[16]

By the mid-twentieth century, however, revolutionary changes in popular music in both America and Britain had spread to Canada. Leaving aside for the present issues of cultural ownership and derivation, cities such as Toronto, Montreal and

---

14   Israel Young in Cohen (ed.), *Wasn't That a Time*, p. 202. Young also discusses this concert, and his others, in his interview with Richard Reuss of 8 July 1965. Tape recording, from the collection of the American Folklife Center, Library of Congress, Washington, DC (Box 1, AFS 19 800). An original advertisement for the concert, along with a copy of 'Talking Folklore Center', a 1962 song which Dylan composed for Young about the Center, are included in the American Folklife Center's (Library of Congress, Washington, DC) sizeable Vertical File on Young.

15   John Cohen (II) in ibid.

16   See, for example, Maria Tippett's study *Making Culture: English Canadian Institutions and the Arts Before the Massey Commission* (Toronto; Buffalo, NY; London, 1990). However, this trend is beginning to change as new works are published with regard to working-class culture and other aspects of the city's cultural life. See, particularly, Carolyn Strange, *Toronto's Girl Problem: The Perils and Pleasures of the City, 1880–1930* (Toronto, 1995) and Keith Walden, *Becoming Modern in Toronto: The Industrial Exhibition and the Shaping of Late Victorian Culture* (Toronto, 1997). See also Steven Maynard's work on homosexual subculture in Toronto. '"Horrible Temptations": Sex, Men and Working Class Male Youth in Urban Ontario, 1890–1935', *Canadian Historical Review*, 78 (June 1997), 191–235, and David Churchill, 'Coming Out in a Cold Climate: A History of Gay Men in Toronto During the 1950s', (unpublished MA thesis, University of Toronto, 1993).

Vancouver became centres for aspiring popular musicians. Jazz taverns thrived in the St. Catherine Street area of Montreal and on Yorkville's Cumberland Street in Toronto, both of which would later become folk music districts. The live music scene in Toronto was particularly active during the post-war years, becoming famed for its white rhythm and blues bands playing along the 'strip' of wild nightclubs on Yonge Street which marked a contrast to the city's upright image. The Arkansas-born singer Ronnie Hawkins, searching out new audiences north of the border, assembled a backing band of promising Ontario musicians who became known as The Hawks. Much admired, The Hawks inspired many imitators and competitors, and soon a vibrant live music scene developed, transforming Toronto into 'a hip r&b town', presided over by Hawkins and by younger musicians such as Robbie Lane and the Disciples, David Clayton-Thomas, and The Mandala, all of whom became local heroes to aspiring performers.[17] Nevertheless, musical activity of this kind remained very much a subcultural, almost underground phenomenon, avidly followed by local teenagers but never publicised or advertised by the city except when members of the public expressed concern over decaying morals.

The neighbourhood of Yorkville became a bohemian neighbourhood almost coincidentally. The district remained a largely residential area until the 1950s, when small boutiques, edged out of the main shopping thoroughfares by major redevelopments and the creation of malls, relocated to Yorkville Avenue and Cumberland Street.[18] The properties on these streets, in a state of disrepair, were sold to shopkeepers at bargain prices. As the commercial character of Yorkville increased, a number of taverns, restaurants and coffee-houses began to appear in the neighbourhood. Initially, many of these establishments, such as the House of Hamburg on Cumberland Street, offered jazz music as entertainment, and, as a result, young 'beatniks', part of a small subcultural group which had hitherto congregated on Gerrard Street further downtown, began to frequent Yorkville.[19] A *laissez-faire*, bohemian atmosphere soon prevailed in the neighbourhood, making it 'an attractive place for subcultures to congregate'.[20]

As the popularity of Yorkville as a 'hip' place for young non-conformists grew, coffee-houses began, in the words of musician Ian Tyson, 'sprouting like mushrooms' throughout the neighbourhood.[21] These establishments, open to those below the age

---

17   Richard Flohil, discussion with the author, Toronto, 6 May 2003.

18   The first major mall to open in Toronto was Yorkdale, in the north of the city. James Lemon's work on Toronto's development as an urban centre, *Toronto Since 1918: An Illustrated History* (Toronto, 1985), pp. 113–87, portrays the mid-twentieth century as a period of tremendous expansion and transformation of the city.

19   An interesting glimpse of this early 'beatnik' subculture on Gerrard Street is provided by a short feature, broadcast on CBC Television on 17 February 1963, on The Bohemian Embassy coffee-house, which would later become important to folk musicians. The feature, entitled 'Toronto "Happening"', is now available online at <http://archives.cbc.ca/IDCC-1-69-1587-3080/life_society/60s/> (accessed 3 May 2004).

20   Charles Johnson, *Discussion paper No. 28: The Preservation of Yorkville Village* (Toronto, 1984), p. 7.

21   Quoted in Nicholas Jennings, *Before the Gold Rush: Flashbacks to the Dawn of the Canadian Sound* (Toronto; London; New York; Victoria, 1997), p. 21. Jennings' book,

of 21 who were barred from public houses, boasted a casual atmosphere and late opening hours which made them particularly attractive to young people. Among the earliest of the Yorkville coffee-houses were The Mousehole, The Gate of Cleve, The Fifth Peg, The Penny Farthing, The First Floor Club, The Cellar and The Village Gate, all named in emulation of their Greenwich Village counterparts. Later came The Mynah Bird, The Purple Onion, Bernie Fiedler's Riverboat, which would become the most celebrated and enduring of the Yorkville coffee-houses, and numerous others; by the mid-decade, there would be some 47 coffee-houses in the neighbourhood.[22] Richard Flohil, who witnessed this burgeoning development, noted the pragmatic motives behind the opening of many of these coffee-houses; their owners often encouraged folk musicians more for astute business reasons than as the result of artistic conviction. In discussing Bernie Fiedler, for example, Flohil remarked that he was simply 'a coffee salesman who said, "I can get a singer in here and I can make some more coffee!" ... It wasn't as if Bernie was a folk fan who said, "I should do this." He was a coffee salesman!'[23]

Some coffee-house owners were rather more interested in music than others. For example, the British-born John McHugh, who opened The Half Beat, a pioneering coffee house on Cumberland Street, was 'a little more ... into it for the music'.[24] However, he told Nicholas Jennings that his choice of entertainers was directed by his own personal tastes; hence, initially, he tended to book jazz and blues musicians rather than folk performers.[25] It is important to realise the mingling of economic and artistic motives in the development of neighbourhoods such as Yorkville; folk music, essentially, became integral to the neighbourhood as coffee-house owners began to respond to the demands of their young customers.

Folk music rapidly gained in popularity among the youth of Toronto, and the jazz music which the 1950s Yorkville patrons had favoured was rapidly displaced. As early as 1961, journalist Morris Duff noted this cultural shift. Only the previous year, Duff remarked, Toronto had still been 'a major jazz city', but by the end of 1961, 'only one bar, The Town Tavern, offered jazz as a regular policy', and many other jazz clubs had closed down. Folksingers now dominated; they were in demand as entertainers at exclusive parties and gatherings, and Yorkville had already begun to devote itself to folk music. 'Toronto has become North America's most important folk music city outside New York,' declared Duff. 'Americans imported here report the word is out, "Go to Toronto".'[26] As with Greenwich Village, however, folk music in Yorkville did continue to co-exist with other types of music and entertainment; jazz continued to be offered at venues such as The First Floor Club and blues at

---

intended principally for a popular market, is nonetheless very informative, and is based on a great deal of research undertaken by the author. I am indebted to him for sharing some of the findings of that research, and his own experiences of Yorkville, during my interview with him on 2 December 2002.

22   Johnson, *The Preservation of Yorkville Village*.
23   Flohil, discussion.
24   Ibid.
25   Jennings, discussion.
26   Morris Duff, 'Jazz Declines and Folk Music Soars', *Toronto Star*, 30 December 1961.

The Penny Farthing (run by John McHugh) and The House of Blues, where Lonnie Johnson frequently appeared. Former revivalists also recall poetry recitations at a number of clubs, such as the 'Poetry Hootenannies' held at The Bohemian Embassy in 1964.[27] During the early years of the 1960s, nonetheless, Yorkville, more than any other urban neighbourhood in Canada, attracted aspiring folksingers from all over the country, including a host of performers who would later move from the local clubs to find success and celebrity, from Neil Young and Joni Anderson (Mitchell) to Gordon Lightfoot, Ian and Sylvia Tyson, Bruce Cockburn and Murray McLauchlan.

Greenwich Village and Yorkville certainly differed in their origins, and they were, undoubtedly, different in many other respects. Greenwich Village was always considered the most desirable and successful of all the folk music districts of the continent; it was reputed to be more difficult to 'make it' in New York, and hence this should be the 'Mecca' to which the most talented would journey.[28] The headquarters for two of the major labels specialising in folk music, Vanguard and Elektra, were also to be found in New York; it was infinitely harder to make a successful record in Canada generally, let alone Toronto, considering the underdeveloped state of the music industry there.[29] It is also arguable that, while the folk music culture of Greenwich Village had grown from a rich, varied bohemian scene already in existence, the Yorkville folk scene had been created more as a consequence of the proliferation of coffee-houses in the district, and was therefore more commercial in origin and direction. Michael Van Dusen, who frequented Yorkville in the 1960s, suggested that Yorkville was 'a destination as opposed to a location'; it was not the fully developed community that Greenwich Village proclaimed itself to be, and Van Dusen felt that this was partly due to the lack of affordable accommodation in the vicinity, as well as the absence of a large gathering-place like Washington Square.[30] While this interpretation was contested by Nicholas Jennings, who did not agree that Yorkville lacked common space for musicians and participants, it is certainly worthwhile to consider such perceived contrasts between the two districts.[31]

Community Formation in Yorkville and Greenwich Village

Yorkville and Greenwich Village existed in very different cities, and had differing resources at their disposal; they developed differently as the result of internal and external factors. However, they also shared many similarities. Their cultural climate was shaped, during the 1960s, by the popularity of folk music, and by the success of artists, major and less well-known, black and white, who travelled to appear at clubs

---

27 Michael Van Dusen remembers being present at poetry recitations. The Bohemian Embassy's 'poetry hootenannies' are advertised in the *Toronto Telegram*'s 'After Four' section of 26 March 1964. (NB: The Bohemian Embassy was not located in Yorkville, but further downtown, on St. Nicholas Street near Wellesley Street, close to the original Gerrard Street beatnik 'scene'.)

28 Michael Van Dusen, discussion with the author, Toronto, 27 November 2002.

29 This will be discussed at length in Chapter 4.

30 Van Dusen, discussion.

31 Jennings, discussion.

in both neighbourhoods. The Riverboat, which became one of the most lucrative of the Yorkville coffee houses, featured every major performer from Bob Dylan, Simon and Garfunkel and Tom Paxton to The Staples Singers, Muddy Waters and Richie Havens, all of whom regularly graced the coffee-houses of Greenwich Village. The crowds of amateur and aspiring musicians, participants and onlookers were as crucial to the atmosphere of the neighbourhoods as any major performer.

More significantly, however, both Yorkville and Greenwich Village developed distinct communities, attracting music enthusiasts of conscience who were eager to share songs and ideas. Despite their differences, both, ultimately, represented attempts of young people to live out their ideals, ideals which both shaped and were influenced by the music of the revival. The music transmitted idealistic visions of rural utopias existing in the various regions of the continent; in Yorkville and Greenwich Village, the young residents tried to manifest such idealistic visions in urban reality.

Frequenters of the villages overtly displayed their sense of separateness and unconventionality through their style of dress, their language and behaviour, and through their overt flouting of moral strictures. It was this aspect of the districts that most intrigued and, apparently, amused journalists and members of the public who were attempting to understand youth culture at this time. Girls wore dark dresses and long, straight hair, looking, as Joan Baez herself once remarked, 'a little too grim for words'.[32] Young men sported berets, goatee beards, glasses, and frequently, wore sandals. Such young villagers, whose image was partially inherited from the beatniks who preceded them, also enhanced their look by consuming red wine and coffee and smoking marijuana – at this stage, there were comparatively few hard drugs circulating in either district.

As time passed, and as the number of young people frequenting the villages increased, their visual distinctiveness became something of a spectacle for outsiders. As has been demonstrated, this was not the first time in which tourists had 'gazed' upon Greenwich Village, but by the mid-1960s, the phenomenon of 'touring' the village became particularly popular. John Cohen recalled that 'people from the suburbs and uptown came to Greenwich Village with certain expectations of observing bohemian behaviour and people taking sexual liberties.'[33] Before long, tourist buses were driving regularly through the streets of Greenwich Village and Yorkville, enabling 'straight' but prurient North Americans to witness first-hand the permissive, flamboyant behaviour of their youth. As the singer Richie Havens remarked of Greenwich Village, 'it got to the point where even the Beatniks themselves, or so-called Beatniks, would stand on the side of the street and when the buses would go by they'd point at the tourists. It became a game.'[34]

The young villagers also claimed ownership of the physical landscapes of Yorkville and Greenwich Village – the names of cafés and coffee houses resonated

---

32 From an interview featured in the BBC documentary *Dancing in the Street: A History of Rock 'n' Roll*, Episode III: 'The Folk Revival' (BBC Television, 1997).

33 John Cohen II in Cohen (ed.), *Wasn't That a Time*, p. 178.

34 Quoted in Robbie Wolliver, *Bringing it All Back Home: Twenty-Five Years of American Music at Folk City* (New York, 1986), p. 12.

with their vocabulary, and they loitered at will on the street corners, front steps and alleyways of the districts. As Michael Van Dusen pointed out previously, the existence of large common space was a tremendous boon for Greenwich Village, promoting cohesiveness, community-building and music making. Danny Kalb, one early revival participant, remembered Washington Square as being 'like a Middle Eastern fair. You could choose which music you wanted to get involved with. There were easily ten or fifteen groups around there. Blues and Bluegrass predominated, even though people were interested in all kinds of music.'[35]

The melting-pot style of Washington Square's music sessions clearly served to promote actively the eclectic nature of the revival, as discussed in the previous chapter. Neil Rosenberg, in his history of Bluegrass, notes the manner in which the Washington Square 'sessions', initially involving banjo players, evolved naturally to become multi-faceted and thoroughly eclectic as more musicians were attracted there and began to join in the music. He quotes one participant, Arthur Jordan Field, as recalling that by the mid to late 1950s,

> ... the Washington Square Sunday singing had degenerated into a free-for-all competition ... [Tom] Paley and [Harry] West had become the leaders of an important segment of the younger group which they carried en masse into country music and away from such English ballads ... and political songs as were around before them ... By 1954 or so ... there were so many performers of all kinds and qualities that it would be impossible to catalogue the various cliques.[36]

Although Michael Van Dusen suggested that Yorkville possessed no comparable common ground, Nicholas Jennings suggested that the steps of local churches – particularly the now-demolished St. Paul's Church on Avenue Road – and shops served as substitute gathering-places.[37] Van Dusen himself also recalled the sharing of melodies and the furthering of musical friendships in the alleyways of Yorkville:

> People would be prepared to speak to you if they saw you with a guitar. If you saw somebody with a guitar there was no hesitancy going and chatting with them. If they weren't doing anything there was no problem in going down an alleyway and finding a spot where you could sit and play and swap music. I guess I was down there weekly for a number of years.[38]

Greenwich Village was, in the truest sense, a residential community for artists with a rich heritage, but Yorkville was not devoid of a comparable residential scene. It was, after all, a district of three-storey houses which were divided into apartments. Nicholas Jennings discovered, while researching for his own book on Yorkville, that, while coffee-houses were established on the ground floors of these buildings, countless artists and musicians rented rooms and apartments on the upper floors. One of these, the German-born John Kay, whose group, The Sparrow, was a mainstay of Yorkville,

---

35   Quoted in ibid, p. 15.
36   Quoted in Neil Rosenberg, *Bluegrass: A History* (Urbana, IL and Chicago, IL, 1985), p. 144.
37   Jennings, discussion.
38   Van Dusen, discussion.

described the district to Jennings in quite passionate terms as 'a youth community – where the people who lived and worked and played in Yorkville were all young people. It was our neighbourhood.' The neighbourhood, as Jennings explained, was truly a self-contained village for these young residents – within minutes' walk, they could access restaurants such as The Mont Blanc or The Upper Crust, corner stores such as The Grab Bag, clothing stores, and 'head shops' selling accessories for marijuana smokers.[39] This residential aspect of Yorkville would, however, develop more fully towards the end of the 1960s, when, after the heyday of folk music in the district, more hippies, bikers and 'greasers' moved into the neighbourhood, much to the consternation of the city at large. Nevertheless, those who lived in Greenwich Village and Yorkville, as well as those who visited on a nightly basis or hung around permanently, further enhanced the feeling of cohesiveness and community which pervaded both districts.

The coffee-houses of Greenwich Village, as well as Israel Young's centre, were alive with the most prescient contemporary debates of the revival. Michael Van Dusen also recalls the central importance of debate and discussion to the Yorkville scene. For him, The Riverboat, in particular, was as memorable for this aspect as it was for its musical events. He states that, 'the Riverboat wasn't just a place where you went and were entertained. My sense of the place is that it was a place of dialogue, and you encountered things, whether it was drugs, or the war in Vietnam, and you could actually talk about things.'[40] He recalls, in particular, exchanges with a volatile, stoned Tim Hardin, Joni Mitchell on the eve of her rise to stardom, and, in particular, Tom Paxton, with whom he had a memorable discussion about the situation in Vietnam. The intimacy of the coffee-house environment, it could be argued, served to lower the barriers between performer and audience in a unique manner which would later be lost as musicians performed at increasingly large venues. Nicholas Jennings would concur with such a notion; as a journalism student with a part time job washing dishes in the Riverboat kitchen, he was able to obtain interviews with many of the performers after their sets.[41] The association of Yorkville with the discussion of ideas and the dissemination of radical philosophies was heightened by the steady influx into the neighbourhood of Vietnam draft evaders from America. Brian Walsh maintains that draft resisters 'made an incredible contribution to Canadian culture':

> There's a certain intellectual class of people who are draft dodgers; these weren't just cowards. These were people who were saying, 'Hell, no, we won't go', we're not gonna fight in this war, we don't believe in America. So if we don't believe in America, we have to go some place where we can be safe, and develop an alternative. Well, Yorkville, in Toronto, was that place.[42]

The members of the 'beloved communities' of Yorkville and Greenwich Village took their utopian ideals very seriously indeed, and prided themselves on their commitment to equality of all descriptions. Ostensibly at least, black and white

39   Jennings, discussion.
40   Van Dusen, discussion.
41   Jennings, discussion.
42   Brian Walsh, discussion with the author, Toronto, 8 October 2002.

musicians co-existed and interacted with complete freedom, attempting to live in the spirit of their beliefs in the civil rights movement and their optimistic faith that society was undergoing tremendous changes for the better. In Yorkville, Estelle Klein, as president of the Canadian Folk Guild, went to great lengths to maintain as inclusive and as diverse a programme of artists at the 'hoot nights' as possible.[43] The goal of equal opportunities for all people ranked highly on the agendas of the folk music communities of both Greenwich Village and Yorkville. The previous chapter has discussed the central role played by black artists in the folk revival; in both Greenwich Village and Yorkville, blues artists such as BB King, John Lee Hooker, Lonnie Johnson, Big Bill Broonzy and Sonny Terry and Brownie McGhee were regular performers. Richard Flohil, who was responsible for bringing many of these artists to Yorkville and promoting their performances, acknowledged the misplaced romanticism with which many young white folk fans viewed such performers, but suggested that, overall, the showcasing of black artists in the folk clubs brought about a 'stunning kind of mutual self discovery' between white audience and black performer, in which a wide cultural gulf was somehow bridged, effecting a heightened mutual understanding in the process.[44] Black singer-songwriters who performed revival-style music were also central to both communities, among them Richie Havens, Jackie Washington, Al Cromwell, Len Chandler and Charles Roach.

Perhaps one of the most remarkable aspects of both communities, and, indeed, of the folk revival in general, was the large number of female performers who not only participated in the revival, but who proceeded to become highly prominent and celebrated professional performers. While rock 'n' roll music remained almost exclusively a male domain, especially where white musicians were concerned, the folk revival welcomed and actively promoted female singers and musicians. Joan Baez, Judy Collins, Odetta, Buffy Sainte-Marie and Mary Travers (of Peter, Paul and Mary), were mainstays of the Greenwich Village circuit, while Joni Mitchell and Sylvia Fricker (later Tyson) began their careers in earnest in the Yorkville coffee-houses. Numerous other women would become celebrities at least within the folk world, if not in international terms – Carolyn Hester, Barbara Dane and Maria Muldaur emerged from Greenwich Village to become very successful artists, while folksingers such as Donna Warner, Vicky Taylor, Susan Jains, Carol Robinson and Elyse Weinberg were all well known in Toronto circles. The folk revival movement provided these, and many other, female artists with a chance to be taken seriously as songwriters and performers. Joan Baez became one of the most active protest singers of the movement, taking such a prominent position in rallies, marches and gatherings that she virtually became the archetypical folk-protest artist, a role to which she remains fully committed. Buffy Sainte-Marie, a Canadian who began her career in New York but who played frequently in Toronto, became a crucial spokeswoman for the Native community, highlighting their plight through such songs as 'Now that the Buffalo's Gone', and encouraging the work of other Native folksingers such as Patrick Sky and Peter LaFarge.[45]

---

43 Ibid.
44 Richard Flohil, discussion with the author, Toronto, 6 May 2003.
45 See Wolliver, *Bringing it all Back Home*, p. 106.

In Yorkville, while Joni Mitchell and Sylvia Tyson grew in proficiency and popularity, eventually leaving to pursue careers in America, women such as Carol Robinson and Vicky Taylor inspired younger performers with their confidence, wit and talent. Nicholas Jennings describes Vicky Taylor as 'a social convenor' around Yorkville, allowing her apartment above The Night Owl coffee-house to become a 'crash pad' for other performers; she herself was a proficient and confident musician, possessing a very distinctive singing voice and performance style.[46] Her strength as a performer, according to Nicholas Jennings, served as an incentive to other aspiring female folksingers in the coffee-houses.

The high proportion of successful and prominent female artists who were initially nurtured by the communities of Yorkville and Greenwich Village would, indeed, suggest that the ideals of inclusiveness of the folk revival were truly being manifested in reality by the cultures of these neighbourhoods. As the folk revival began, by the mid-1960s, to integrate into the mainstream 'rock' scene, many of these women – Baez, Mitchell and Collins in particular – remained at the forefront of the industry, and their work encouraged the activities of female rock musicians such as Janis Joplin, Grace Slick (of Jefferson Airplane) and, later, Patti Smith (who began her own career in Greenwich Village during the late 1960s). Nevertheless, the recognition and fame received by female artists in the revival was not unquestioningly positive. Acceptance and appreciation of the talents of a female singer was not necessarily an indication that male performers considered such women with a true respect founded in egalitarianism. Greenwich Village performers talk at length about the demeaning male discourse concerning the activities of female artists in the neighbourhood. If the male musicians were not referring to the women in terms of their sexuality or sexual activities, then they were discussing the alleged rivalry among the various prominent 'chick' performers, in particular the 'Four Queens' – Joan Baez, Carolyn Hester, Buffy Sainte-Marie and Judy Collins. One man remarked that, '… they were all friendly. But if you put them on stage, sparks would fly. It was competitive. They were all friends until they got on stage.'[47] Such an allegation was denied by both Baez and Collins, but, notwithstanding its veracity or lack thereof, it is interesting and revealing that the idea of rivalry should be discussed at such length only with reference to female performers. Male performers could present themselves to a far greater extent in their own terms, while the female artists were frequently judged in terms of looks, behaviour and sexuality.[48]

---

46   Interview with Nicholas Jennings, 2 December 2002. Photographs of Vicky Taylor in performance are reproduced in Jennings' book *Before the Gold Rush*, p. 80.

47   Quoted in Robbie Wolliver, *Bringing it all Back Home*, p. 98. See also 'The Folk Girls', an article which featured in *Time*, 1 June 1962, which discussed Joan Baez, Bonnie Dobson, Judy Collins and Carolyn Hester.

48   There is a great deal of discussion in Israel Young's interviews with Richard Reuss about sexual liaisons among Village performers. A number of prominent male members of the folk revival 'community', including Alan Lomax and Irwin Silber, are identified as womanisers. Lomax, whom Young charges with having 'stolen' his own girlfriend, is accused of 'getting [his mistresses] to do his dirty work for him' (he is distracted before he can elaborate on this) and Silber's affair with folksinger Barbara Dane is discussed extensively throughout the interviews. Young himself makes suggestive jokes about young women of the Village

The situation in Yorkville was, similarly, less ideal for women than it appeared at the outset. Many of the most prominent Yorkville women, such as Susan Jains, Carol Robinson and Sylvia Tyson, performed in tandem with male artists; Tyson attained fame in partnership with her husband, Ian, while Jains and Robinson were vocalists with, respectively, The Stormy Clovers and The Dirty Shames, both of which consisted otherwise of men. However, for soloists such as Joni Mitchell, the path to success was difficult. Mitchell, too, was compared to Joan Baez and Judy Collins, and was aggressively heckled by male coffee-house goers when she first began to perform her own material.[49]

Particularly difficult was the situation for young female residents of Yorkville attempting to sustain a personal relationship with a man and a career in music or the arts. Nineteen-year-old aspiring model Eva Fallus told reporter Maggie Siggins about the situation for many of her peers: 'A girl can easily get work – as a waitress, go-go dancer or selling flowers – and a lot of the boys live off the girls. Of course nine out of ten girls in the Village live with their boyfriends. The worst word is marriage – it is forbidden to be spoken here.'[50]

Such an account would suggest that Yorkville's much-vaunted cultural freedom was very much defined by male villagers. Young women who came to Yorkville often found that they could not escape the lingering female stereotypes of society at large. The Penny Farthing coffee-house featured bikini-clad waitresses as an attraction, while the 'After Four' section of the *Toronto Telegram* featured an article on 'the belles of Yorkville' discussing various foreign waitresses and villagers in terms of their beauty and exotic desirability.[51] Female villagers were often at the centre of the ever-intensifying gaze of the tourists who flocked to Yorkville and to Greenwich Village; Maria Muldaur remarked that one of the main attractions of Greenwich Village was the reputation for promiscuity of the local women.[52] An extensive article on Greenwich Village in *Cosmopolitan* which appeared in 1963 also expounded, with a degree of prurience, on the promiscuity of 'chicks' who frequented coffee-houses.[53]

By the mid-1960s, Yorkville, in particular, became a destination for under-aged school pupils, much to the irritation of territorial villagers and the consternation of parents and city officials. Campaigns to curtail the activities of coffee houses and 'clean up' Yorkville were put into operation, bringing about the start of the community's metamorphosis into a prosperous commercial district. One of the main fears of the public was that the neighbourhood was not safe for women. On the front page of one of the Toronto newspapers in 1965, an article appeared in which

---

who are his 'protégées' (Young states that he won't 'incriminate himself' by elaborating). Interview of 24 August 1965. See also Jim Rooney's description of the 'dark beauty' of Joan Baez in Jim Rooney and Eric Von Schmidt, *Baby Let Me Follow You Down: The Illustrated History of the Cambridge Folk Years* (Garden City, NY, 1979), p. 42.

49   Jennings, *Before the Gold Rush*, p. 84.

50   Maggie Siggins, 'Yorkville: The Inside Story' from the *Toronto Telegram*'s 'After Four' section, 28 July 1966, p. 3.

51   Ibid., 16 July 1964.

52   Quoted in Robbie Wolliver, *Bringing it All Back Home*, 12.

53   Seymour Krim, 'Life in a Coffeehouse', *Cosmopolitan*, December 1963.

villagers declared that young women were at risk in the village at night, even when accompanied by a male escort.[54] Bikers were beginning to appear in Yorkville, and there were accounts of rape and intimidation. Shortly after this newspaper report, a by-law was passed prohibiting motorbikes in the main village at night; this would be the first of a string of legislation passed as a result of public concern about the district.

The extent to which such consternation was justified is difficult to gauge. However, it is important not to accept automatically the notion that sudden threats posed by 'outsiders' brought about the decline of Yorkville. The elitism inherent in the idea that there were 'genuine' villagers and 'outsiders' in many ways mirrors the 'exclusive' ideals of the folk revival, and should not go unnoticed in this context.

Whether the feeling of decline and threat was felt more keenly by original villagers, or by police and government officials, many would refute the notion that women were unsafe in Yorkville. Neither Michael Van Dusen nor Ken Whiteley, acknowledging that they, as men, would undoubtedly have differing perspectives from female participants, had personal memories of a threatening atmosphere in Yorkville, while Brian Walsh, remembering contemporary newspaper articles about the dangers of Yorkville, stated that

> I certainly did have the impression that most of the things that were written in the newspapers were written for middle-aged, middle-class people who just didn't understand, so … the fact that somebody had long hair meant that it was a dangerous place, right? … Did young girls get sexually taken advantage of? Undoubtedly; that happened. But, for example, I don't remember a teen sex trade in Yorkville. That was down on Yonge Street.[55]

The issue of female safety in Yorkville remains debatable; certainly, women were not, apparently, discouraged from visiting or residing in the neighbourhood by threats from bikers or predatory male tourists. As Brian Walsh, who worked at the Yonge Street Mission during this period, suggests, the culture of that district was more overtly rough and exploitative of women. The fact that physical and sexual dangers to women, historically and in the present time, may exist in their own homes also affects any argument about the security of a neighbourhood for females.

However, there is no doubt that the ideals of inclusiveness and equality were not manifested in reality for the female musicians and residents of Yorkville and Greenwich Village. The alternative societies promoted by these neighbourhoods proved itself to be little different from mainstream society in matters of gender equality, and, at times, it could be argued that a culture of promiscuity may have made matters somewhat worse, rather than better, for female villagers. Nevertheless, in spite of this, a greater degree of inclusiveness for women was present in Greenwich Village and Yorkville than in the rock 'n' roll culture of the time, and the neighbourhoods promoted the talents and careers of female artists to a very successful degree.

Whatever the reality of the internal dynamics of Yorkville and Greenwich Village with regard to gender equality, there is no doubt that villagers, male and female, identified with their communities as both physical and cultural entities. It

---

54   *Toronto Telegram*, 2 June 1965, front page.
55   Brian Walsh, discussion.

is interesting to note that, despite the great differences between the histories and cultures of Toronto and New York, the governments of both cities, at different times, saw fit to attempt a suppression of the youth activities of Greenwich Village and Yorkville.

In his primary account of the folk revival Oscar Brand recounts the heightening of tensions between local residents (who were outraged by the spectacles of nonconformist fashions, interracial couples and homosexuals on the streets of their neighbourhood) and members of the artistic community in Greenwich Village during the early 1960s.[56] This clash of interests culminated in police harassment of coffee-house owners and patrons.[57] The police claimed, among other things that the musicians in the coffee-houses were working illegally, and that they must possess licenses to perform; they insisted that cafés featuring folk singing be turned into legal 'cabarets' or be closed down.

As ill feelings increased, a riot broke out in Washington Square on the afternoon of Sunday, 9 April 1961. Under the orders of park commissioner Newbold Morris, police tried to break up the crowds of musicians who customarily gathered to participate in the sessions there, because they did not have licenses. Israel Young believed that local residents resented the crowds which gathered in the Square because, in spite of their regular presence, they did not live locally or eat in restaurants, and, thus, they '[didn't] support the economy of the Village.' Young also, interestingly, asserted that the objection to the Washington Square singers had, in his words, 'colour tones'; by the early 1960s, young black men and women were joining in with the music, and residents, resenting their presence, complained that the bongo drums which they used customarily were too loud.[58]

As the police attempted to remove the singers from the Square, scuffles ensued; several protesters were injured, and ten were arrested.[59] The police began to bar

---

56   Greenwich Village had been a vital centre for homosexual culture since the early century. Allen Ginsberg, beat poet and Village resident, was most public about his homosexuality, and members of the Mattachine Society, formed for gay rights in the 1950s, were based in the Village. For primary accounts of the gay culture of Greenwich Village, see Stephanie Gervis, 'Politics: A Third Party for the Third Sex?' *Village Voice*, 27 September 1962 and 'The Homosexual's Labyrinth of Law and Social Custom', *Village Voice* 11 October 1962, by the same author. A 1969 account of the Village's gay bar culture, Charles Wright, 'Two Queens, Unfurling', appeared in *Village Voice*, 22 May 1969. Yorkville does not appear to have had such a prominent homosexual culture. It seems that Toronto's gay culture was centred around the Church-Yonge Street area, and did not make a significant impact on Yorkville.

57   John Mitchell, owner of The Gaslight coffee-house, was one of the most prominent targets of such harassment, prompting him to seek an enquiry into the conduct of the Police, Fire, and other City Departments. See Dan List, 'Gaslight's Night-of-Travail Sparked by False Alarm,' *Village Voice*, 12 January 1961.

58   Israel Young, interview with Richard Reuss, 15 July 1965 (AFS 19,800).

59   The Washington Square 'riots' received extensive coverage from the Greenwich Village newspaper, *Village Voice*. Various articles appeared in the editions of 13, 20, and 27 April, in particular, Jan Kindler, 'Cops, "Beatniks", and Facts' (13 April), on the subject of the *New York Mirror*'s distortion of the story; 'Sunday Serenade in Square Causes Morris to Yield' (13 April, no author), which discussed the actions of Washington Square's commissioner,

musicians from entering the Square, and the future of the sessions was in jeopardy. However, the musicians prepared to defend their rights, and some 500 protesters participated in a 'Right to Sing' rally at Judson Memorial Church near the Square. Ultimately, when the Washington Square riots were televised, the sympathy of the general public was shown to be for the folk singers, and the musicians were permitted to continue with their activities in specially allocated sections of Washington Square.[60]

It was some years later, but again as the result of an issue of ownership of space, that the villagers of Yorkville would stage a similar protest. As has been demonstrated, by the mid-1960s, the officials of City Hall were becoming increasingly nervous about the activities of the neighbourhood, and newspapers, whether justifiably or not, began to raise the general alarm; in 1967 one newspaper described the neighbourhood as 'a cancer that is spreading through [the city]', enticing young people to 'live for pure lust'.[61]

It is certainly true that, by 1967, the heyday of the folk movement in the village was coming to an end. Clubs such as The Mynah Bird and The Purple Onion had become rock venues, attracting ever larger numbers of the Yonge Street crowd. As the crowds which flocked to Yorkville grew more diverse, and were perceived as being more threatening, the alarm was raised among the general public. Particular concern was expressed over the number of teenagers who defied their parents to visit Yorkville; in an attempt to counter this trend, efforts were made in the mid-1960s to pass by-laws preventing the opening of any new coffee-houses for two years, and prohibiting the presence in the neighbourhood of those under 16 after ten o'clock at night.[62] As public concern and outrage increased, so too did the presence of the police in Yorkville, and brutal clashes became regular occurrences.[63]

One of the most significant of these occurred in August 1967, when young 'villagers' staged a public demonstration on Yorkville Avenue in an attempt to force the authorities to close the street to traffic, particularly the tourist buses which drove

---

Newbold Morris; J.R. Goddard, '"Right to Sing" Rally Scores Ban by Morris; Ready to Fight' (20 April); J.R. Goddard, 'Big Turnout for Folksingers, Trouble Feared Next Sunday', which focused on the temporary relocation of the Sunday afternoon session to Thompson Street, and Mary Peart Nichols, 'Morris Ban on Singers in Square Divides Village' (27 April). A slightly more cynical appraisal of the disturbances was presented in *Time* magazine – see 'The Foggy, Foggy Don't', *Time*, 21 April 1961.

60 Brand, *The Ballad Mongers*. See also J.R. Goddard, 'Mayor Relents, Opens Square to Folksingers', *Village Voice*, 10 May 1961.

61 *Toronto Telegram*, 17 April 1967. The collection of newspaper clippings on Yorkville held in the Urban Affairs Department of the Toronto Public Library demonstrates the extent to which the press sensationalised the Yorkville situation and contributed to building public hysteria. Other articles from the 1966–67 period include the *Telegram*'s report on 'A World of LSD, Drugs, and … Sex' (*c.* April 1967) and the *Toronto Star*'s manipulative and sensational story on 'The Mirage that Drew Gloria, 16, to Yorkville … and the Streets', 4 June 1967.

62 Charles Johnson, *The Preservation of Yorkville Village*.

63 For an insider's perspective on the problems of Yorkville in 1967, see Ron Thody, 'Yorkville Needs its Heads Examined', from *Satyrday*, Vol. 2, No. 4, 1967. (*Satyrday* was an underground newspaper.)

regularly around the neighbourhood to stare at the inhabitants. The demonstration resulted in multiple arrests, violence and a heightened sense of public anxiety over the activities of Yorkville youth. The young people of Yorkville would not give up, however, and, led by the charismatic David DePoe, they gathered to discuss their plight and rally their peers in Queen's Park, and met with the Mayor in City Hall in an attempt to plead their cause.[64] By this stage, the city had become resolved to drive the subcultural elements out of the decaying Yorkville and clean up the blighted neighbourhood; as Nicholas Jennings has said, the 'death knell' had already been sounded for the district. Nevertheless, it is significant to note that, albeit at different times and in different circumstances, the young people who identified with Yorkville and Greenwich Village were prepared to fight for their physical claims to the districts. Many of these youth were already steeped in the culture of protest of the decade; it is interesting that this climate of rebellion affected so directly both of these distinctive experimental communities.

The utopian experiments of Greenwich Village and Yorkville, as envisaged by those who flocked to live, perform and attend concerts there, were, ultimately, not wholly successful. It is certainly true that much damage was done to both communities by local government smearing and interference, as well as by the drug dealers, bikers and tourists who began to frequent the area by mid-decade. However, as the trends and the political climate of the 1960s changed, so too did the folk revival; thus, neither Greenwich Village nor Yorkville could remain static. Indeed, folk music was never the sole defining music style of either neighbourhood. Although it was prominent in Greenwich Village, roughly, from 1957 until the mid-1960s, and in Yorkville from *circa* 1960 to 1965, the folk clubs and coffee-houses co-existed with jazz venues, poetry clubs and, eventually, rock venues and night clubs. Furthermore, as the folk revival began to enter the mainstream, many of the folk artists who had begun their careers in the clubs, basket-houses and coffee-houses of Yorkville and Greenwich Village attained recording contracts and moved beyond the local scene. The 1960s utopian experiments of both neighbourhoods would meet with failure; they were at the mercy of a rapidly changing political and cultural climate which, it could be said, valued individuality over community; by the late 1960s, the individual artist was now the star, far removed from his or her public in daily life and in a concert setting. The counterculture, through the LSD 'trip' and through its philosophy, placed a similar, central importance on the individual. In such a culture, neighbourhoods like Yorkville and Greenwich Village were no longer truly 'beloved communities' but fading entertainment districts.

---

64   The Yorkville riots are captured in the NFB film *Christopher's Movie Matinee* (1968), parts of which were later used to create a second film specifically about Yorkville, *Flowers on a One-Way Street*. Ken Whiteley, who features in the former film, talked about its significance in some detail, and lent me his personal copy. See also the short CBC Television report on the sit-in and unrest featured on the programme *Metro Extra* on 21 August 1967. Available online at <http://archives.cbc.ca/IDCC-1-69-580-3224/life_society/hippies/> (accessed 4 May 2004).

The Decline of Yorkville and Greenwich Village as Folk Music Communities

Nicholas Jennings says that many of the Yorkville musicians and participants whom he interviewed could identify 1965 as the year in which folk music lost its domination over the neighbourhood, and the music showcased in the area was more eclectic than ever before. This, of course, added to the appeal of the neighbourhood, and to its excitement. Many former Yorkville-goers comment on the aptness of Joni Mitchell's lyrics for the song 'Night in the City', apparently inspired by her Yorkville years, which describes music 'spilling out into the streets'.[65] The Yorkville crowds performed 'the Yorkville stroll' if on foot, and 'the Yorkville crawl' if travelling by car; so numerous were the clubs, and so diverse was the music on offer, that people were packed together on the pavements and cars were 'bumper to bumper'.[66] Such a phenomenon made the neighbourhood utterly unrivalled, at least among the urban musical districts of Canada. However, as has been stated, the change of music, and the changing of the times, brought different crowds to Yorkville, and the menacing aspects of the neighbourhood became more pronounced. Arguably, it was the increasing presence of hard drugs, more than any other factor, that changed the character of Yorkville. After the summer of love, Yorkville became a prime destination for hippies, many of whom were heavily involved in acid culture; numerous were the violent incidents between hippies and drug dealers to whom money was owed. It was also apparent that among the Yorkville hippy community, intermingled with bona fide, idealistic counterculture members, were increasing numbers of under-aged, highly disturbed runaways seeking refuge from their own chaotic lives.[67]

The presence of the newly created Rochdale College on Bloor Street, near the University of Toronto campus, did little to ameliorate conditions in Yorkville. Rochdale had been established as a utopian experiment, offering free and alternative education to anyone who wished it.[68] It became a centre for the counterculture, and there was much natural overlap with the Yorkville scene. However, as Brian Walsh, who eventually worked at Rochdale as a young Christian chaplain, remembered, the college soon became 'a place of death' for disorientated, directionless young people whose experimentation with drugs was leading them towards suicide, mental collapse and violence.[69] Biker gangs such as The Vagabonds became the security guards, and so many drug dealers operated within Rochdale that historian Doug

---

65   Joni Mitchell, 'Night in the City' from *Joni Mitchell* (Reprise RS 6293, 1968).

66   Jennings, discussion.

67   This is the conclusion of an interesting report on Yorkville by Reginald Smart, Gopala Ampur and David Jackson, *The Yorkville Subculture: A Study of Lifestyles and Interactions of Hippies and Non-Hippies* (Toronto, 1969). Gopala Ampur, an Indian anthropologist, posed as a hippy and lived in Yorkville for several months while accumulating 'findings' on the youth of the neighbourhood. See also the pieces on Yorkville contained within the interesting anthology *The Underside of Toronto*, ed. W.E. Mann (Montreal, 1970).

68   A useful outline of the early ideals of Rochdale is given in the first-hand account of Dennis Lee, 'Getting to Rochdale', printed in Gerald F. McGuigan with George Payerle and Patricia Horobin, *Student Protest* (Toronto; London; Sydney; Wellington, 1968), pp. 64–87.

69   Brian Walsh, discussion with the author, 8 October 2002.

Owram described the college as 'a drug dispensary of major proportions'.[70] The increasing chaos and nihilism of the Rochdale scene had a tangible impact on Yorkville, and public fears continued to increase. The neighbourhood had grown increasingly dilapidated, and there were concerns for the safety and hygiene of its residents, particularly the hippies who slept rough on the streets or who 'crashed' in run-down apartments with dangerous wiring and no sanitation. Medical facilities were brought in to combat apparent outbreaks of a strain of hepatitis which became known as 'hippy hepatitis', due to the fact that it was contracted through dirty dishes and general lack of hygiene.[71] Some have claimed that this was a government fabrication to drive the counterculture from Yorkville, although Michael Van Dusen, who eventually volunteered with the medical services, believed the threat to be considerable.[72]

Ultimately, however, the city acted to hasten the demise of Yorkville as the domain of young non-conformists. Developer Richard Wookey began to purchase and refurbish the properties of Yorkville Avenue and the surrounding streets, and within ten years the neighbourhood had become the upscale shopping district that it remains to this day.[73] Residents drifted away, some deciding to seek employment amid the 'establishment', and others continuing to pursue their ideals at Rochdale. One by one, the coffee-houses disappeared; often their owners could not refuse the lucrative offers made by Wookey and his associates, and, although folk music in Yorkville had maintained an eager audience, managers were forced to acknowledge that times were changing, and coffee-house culture was struggling in a new era of sophisticated, licensed nightclubs which could attract performers with promises of lucrative fees. As Ron Chapman, owner of The Groaning Board, a folk venue which transformed into a jazz-orientated nightclub, remarked in the late 1970s: 'It's a matter of staying abreast of the times. This is 1978, not 1968. What people want has changed.'[74] The Riverboat, one of the most celebrated and prominent of the coffee-houses, survived until late 1978, when it closed with a sell-out show featuring Murray McLauchlan,

---

70   Doug Owram, *Born at the Right Time: A History of the Baby Boom Generation in Canada* (Toronto; Buffalo, NY; London, 1996), p. 211. See also the short CBC News feature on the final collapse of the college, broadcast on 8 August 1977. Available online at http://archives.cbc.ca/IDCC-1-69-580-3224/life_society/hippies/ (accessed 4 May 2004).

71   See 'Hepatitis Spread Indicated as "Weekend Hippies" Affected', *Toronto Star*, 7 August 1968.

72   Van Dusen, discussion. Nicholas Jennings found, in his research, that 'hippy hepatitis' was more an invention than a reality.

73   See Charles Johnson, *The Preservation of Yorkville Village* and the documentary programme *Yorkville* (1986), part of a series on Toronto neighbourhoods produced by Paul De Silva and released via Criterion Videos. The programme on Yorkville was memorably presented by Carol Robinson.

74   Quoted in Kirk Makin, 'The Death Knell Sounds for Folk', *Globe*, c. November 1978 (Vertical File in Metropolitan Library of Toronto – no date provided.) See also Peter Goddard, 'David Rae Serenades Riverboat's Ghosts', *Toronto Star*, 13 November 1978.

David Rae and other local musicians who had remained committed to Yorkville.[75] With its closure, journalists decided that the Yorkville 'scene' was decisively over.[76]

Likewise, Greenwich Village, which had been, since the late 1950s, the stronghold of the folk revival, became a truly eclectic music neighbourhood and a haven for hippies.[77] The Village suffered particularly badly because of the rise in popularity of many of its artists; once the erstwhile mainstays of the coffee houses – Havens, Simon and Garfunkel, Baez, Dylan et al. – had obtained recording deals, the heart of the folk movement left Greenwich Village. As far as Israel Young was concerned, the Washington Square Riot had been a turning-point in the folk music community of Greenwich Village. In Young's view, the 'riot' was significant because it was

> the last time that America spoke up against folk music. Then, after that, it was perfectly legal, then it was okay to make money out of it. [The riot] was the last gasp of respectable America against folk music being left-wing or Communist or something like that.[78]

As with Yorkville, according to John Cohen, a more 'dangerous element' became attracted to the neighbourhood:

> Originally it was mostly Uptown and out-of-town couples on dates for a night out, but as MacDougal Street became sleazy, it also became an attraction for motorcycle gangs from New Jersey and for black groups from Harlem looking for excitement or trouble.[79]

Once again, it is worth noting that, in John Cohen's account of the 'decline' of the coffee-house scene, a narrative of 'outsiders' invading the 'insiders' appears to take shape. However, despite the bias inherent in the sense of 'decline' of the neighbourhood, it is clear that life in the Village was altering rapidly.

The *Village Voice* was forced to admit in 1967 that the coffee-house scene was in a state of terminal decline. As reporter Clark Whelton declared, the once 'incandescent enclave of sandal makers, coffeehouses, bars and bead shops that blossomed like a brassy Brigadoon along MacDougal and Bleecker Streets' had faded from prominence.[80] Whelton's article was prompted by the closure, in January

---

75   The block of buildings which once housed The Riverboat, The Grab Bag and the Yorkville-Hazelton commune was demolished in late 2004 to make way for a luxury hotel and apartment complex.

76   The Fiddlers' Green remained the main venue for folk music making in Toronto after the disappearance of the Yorkville scene.

77   Greenwich Village also began to reflect growing tastes for 'electric' music. The Electric Circus, which opened in 1966 under the supervision of Andy Warhol, presented psychedelic strobe-light shows and the 'art school' rock of the Velvet Underground and the Exploding Plastic Inevitables. See Terry Miller, *Greenwich Village and How It Got That Way* (New York, 1990), pp. 261–2. Israel Young also discusses the music of these groups in his interview with Richard Reuss of 17 June 1966.

78   Israel Young, interview with Richard Reuss, 15 July 1965.

79   John Cohen, quoted in Cohen (ed.), *Wasn't That a Time*, p. 185.

80   Clark Whelton, 'MacDougal and Bleecker: The Scene that Ended', *Village Voice*, 9 January 1969. 'Sandal makers' is a reference to Allan Block's Sandal Shop, a vibrant gathering place for musicians.

1969, of the Café Figaro, a long-established and highly successful coffee-house; the writer feared that the remaining coffee-houses would soon meet the same fate, now that the neighbourhood's traditional 'chess-playing, coffee-sipping crowd' had been replaced by 'swarms of tourists, teenage runaways, drug pushers and derelicts'.[81] He blamed the increasing commercialisation of the counterculture for the decline in the district's attractive distinctiveness. Whereas, before, Greenwich Village had been a celebrated enclave for bohemians and anti-establishmentarians, now its mores had become fashionable and commonplace. As one observer wryly remarked, 'every Kresge's and Woolworth's has a psychedelic counter and sells freak-out buttons. Casual clothes can be worn just about any place in town and if you want to get laid without too much hassle there are the singles bars on the upper East Side.'[82] Some of the folk clubs, such as Gerde's Folk City, struggled on, but the folk revival had passed through the community to enter the music industry.

However, unlike Yorkville, Greenwich Village was not automatically or immediately transformed into a 'respectable' district. In July 1969, the neighbourhood was, once again, at the centre of press attention when police raids of The Stonewall Inn, a popular gay nightspot in the Village, and harassment and arrest of patrons ('the Stonewall Riot'), led to the formation of the Gay Liberation Front, another vital manifestation of the spirit of social protest of the era.[83] Homosexual culture, always a vital component of the Village, remained strong in the district throughout the following decades, with the establishment of clubs and bars such as The Zoo and The Mineshaft.[84]

Remnants of the bohemian culture of the early portion of the twentieth century remained in the Village, co-existing with redeveloped, upmarket housing and shopping. Theatre groups such as the Women's One World (WOW) and avant-garde artists continued to be housed in the Village. The Judson Street Memorial Church, which had supported the protesters during the Washington Square Riot of 1963, maintained a radical activist profile and also nurtured the careers of musicians and artists.[85] A loft in the Waverly Place building in Greenwich Village (named after Sir Walter Scott's novel by nineteenth-century literary residents) became The

---

81   Ibid.

82   Ibid. Interestingly, an advertisement for Fifth Avenue tailor's shop I. Miller, which depicted two stereotypical '60s youths in casual clothing, and which was regularly featured in *Village Voice* throughout 1969, asserted that 'Uptown isn't Uptight Anymore'. (See, for example, the issue of 20 February 1969.)

83   A contemporary account of the riot is given in Lucian Truscott, 'Gay Power Comes to Sheridan Square', *Village Voice*, 3 July 1969. According to this article, folk revival performer and Village resident Dave Van Ronk joined the protest and was arrested for assaulting a police officer. Jonathan Black, 'Gay Power Hits Back', *Village Voice*, 31 July 1969, describes a gay rights march involving such groups as the Mattachine Society and the Daughters of Bilitis. See also Martin B. Duberman, *Stonewall* (New York, 1994); John D'Emilio, *Sexual Politics, Sexual Communities: The Making of a Homosexual Minority in the United States, 1940–1970* (Chicago, IL, 1998, 2nd edn); and Ian Young, *The Stonewall Experiment: A Gay Psychohistory* (London, 1995).

84   Miller, *Greenwich Village*, p. 162.

85   Ibid., p. 64.

Writer's Room, a space for New York writers to work, in 1985.[86] Alongside such vibrant remnants of the artistic past of the Village, redeveloped areas remain much in demand, exclusive residential districts. Therefore, although the Village did not maintain fully its identity as a bohemian enclave, certain crucial aspects of its past remained, and remain, in evidence.

Conclusion

The phenomenon of the folk music neighbourhood is an interesting one, and no equivalent to Greenwich Village or Yorkville has ever truly thrived since. While Haight-Ashbury was an important magnet for musicians in the late 1960s, following the decline of the counterculture in the subsequent decade, the concept of the alternative community based around music had somehow lost its appeal and its cultural pertinence.

In discussing issues of nationality and sense of place in the revival, however, it is crucial to look at these neighbourhoods to see the extent to which the early folk revival's ideals of community, eclecticism and acceptance of diversity were attemptedly manifested in reality. Dreams of community would prove unrealistic as the decade ended with the hippy culture's individualistic style of communalism centred around the drug experience and following one's own path. However, for a few short years, the folk revival attached itself firmly to these two distinctive North American neighbourhoods, transforming them in the process and leaving a rich musical and cultural legacy.

---

86   Ibid., p. 44.

Chapter 4

The Post-Revival Folk: Canadian Dreams and American Nightmares in the Late 1960s and 1970s

Introduction

The state of affairs in Yorkville and Greenwich Village by the end of the 1960s was symptomatic of wider cultural trends within society and the music industry. The North America in which the folk revival had grown to become so popular had altered dramatically by 1970. The flexible eclecticism which the revival had nurtured began to seem out of place as American society, observed closely by Canada and the rest of the world, was plagued by internal strife and crises in foreign affairs. The optimism in which the folk revival had flourished seemed to have abated considerably, and, in protest situations, angry emotions were replacing rational arguments and ideals; as the Vietnam conflict escalated, protest rallies and marches swelled in size and were often followed by brutal backlashes from police and authorities. Prior to this time, the folk revival had been pluralistic and North American in its focus, embracing the unusual and the specific. By the late 1960s, however, the *meaning* of nation was changing for both Canada and America, to become both vaguer and more generalised. Canadians sought to explain their 'Canadianness' in an overriding sense, without recourse to regional differences, while dissenting young Americans no longer wished to define their country as a place of hope and justice, but sought, almost, to escape from the burden of being American. The shifts in thinking about nation would affect the nature and significance of folk music. As a general climate of optimistic nationalism emerged in Canada while chaos and disintegration appeared to exist in the United States, Canadians began to consider their own folk musicians in a different light, while Americans looked to their performers, no longer for political answers, but for artistic ideals of escape and beauty.

Changing Music, Changing Culture: The Demise of the Folk Revival and the Culture of the Late 1960s

Many historians and commentators assert that the folk revival came to an end, or at least lost its status and influence as a tangible movement, at some point in the mid-1960s.[1] Others have argued, however, that, given the eclectic, and factional, nature of the movement, it did not so much end as simply fragment further until it lost its semblance of a unified phenomenon. Specialists in particular named-system revivals, such as bluegrass or blues, continued to pursue their special interests, while many of the most successful of the folk performers obtained recording contracts and entered the mainstream music business. Their admirers followed them, leaving behind them the more faddish and trite aspects of the movement.

Of all those who appeared to outgrow the revival, it was Bob Dylan who did so most publicly. It is often suggested that Dylan single-handedly destroyed the movement with his 'folk rock' performance at the 1965 Newport Folk Festival; such a contention has attained quasi-mythical status in the narrative of popular music history.[2] By ascending the stage at Newport with the backing of the raucous Paul Butterfield Blues Band, Dylan had boldly and publicly indicated that he was tired of the perceived constrictions of the folk movement and desired a dramatic change of direction. Reactions among the folk music fans were mixed, but many of the old guard were outraged.[3] In reality, however, Dylan was merely responding to changing times and trends; just over a month before he assailed the Newport audience with his uncompromising performance, The Byrds, a group which included former folk musicians Roger McGuinn and David Crosby, released 'Mr. Tambourine Man', a reputedly Beatles-inspired rock version of Dylan's poetic acoustic masterpiece.[4] This song, with its distinctive sound, particularly the memorable, inimitable opening guitar line which evidently owed much to the melodic riffs of the Beatles, was tremendously influential, inspiring other groups, including, among others, The Turtles and Manfred Mann, to record 'electric' versions of Dylan songs. Dylan had

---

1   Daniel Gonczy, 'The Folk Music Movement of the 1960s: Its Rise and Fall', *Popular Music and Society*, 10/1 (1985), p. 28; Stephen N. Gottesman, 'Tom Dooley's Children: An Overview of the Folk Music Revival, 1958–1965', *Popular Music and Society*, 5/5 1977, pp. 61–78; Jerome L. Rodnitzky, 'Popular Music as a Radical Influence, 1945–1970', in Leon Borden Blair (ed.), *Essays on Radicalism in Contemporary America* (Walter Prescott Webb Memorial Lectures) (Austin, TX and London, 1972), pp. 13–16.

2   See, for example, Gonczy, 'The Folk Music Movement of the 1960s', p. 28; Paul Wolfe, 'Dylan's Sell-Out of the Left', in R. Serge Denisoff and Richard A. Peterson (eds), *The Sounds of Social Change* (Chicago, IL, 1972), p. 147; and Charlie Gillett, *The Sound of the City* (London, 1996, 3rd edn), p. 299. Ronald Cohen discusses the 1965 Newport Folk Festival on pp. 233–42 of *Rainbow Quest: The Folk Music Revival and American Society, 1940–1970* (Amherst, MA and Boston, MA, 2002). First-person accounts of musician Eric Von Schmidt and others of Dylan's performance at Newport '65 are reproduced in Eric Von Schmidt and Jim Rooney, *Baby Let Me Follow You Down: The Illustrated Story of the Cambridge Folk Years* (Garden City, NY, 1979), pp. 258–65.

3   For instance, in the third episode of the BBC documentary *Dancing in the Street* (BBC, 1997) on the folk revival, producer Paul Rothchild recounts an often-repeated Newport '65 anecdote about Pete Seeger attempting to cut the wires of Dylan's amplifiers with an axe which he had been using in a log-cutting demonstration. Bob Dylan has recently given his own account of the events at Newport in Martin Scorsese's influential documentary *No Direction Home* (2005).

4   David Crosby discusses the influence of The Beatles on The Byrds in Episode 3 of the 1997 BBC documentary *Dancing in the Street*.

less brought about a revolution than he had helped to hasten a gradual evolution of the sound of popular music.

Folk revival performers had been drifting towards the 'mainstream' since the early 1960s, but once the major folk revival performers became part of the general popular music scene, they helped to pave the way for the intellectualisation of rock 'n' roll. As a result of the influence of such folk musicians and songwriters, a new emphasis was placed upon the intelligence and artistic value of the music and lyrics, on the discussion-provoking, rather than 'danceable', qualities of a song, and on the production of albums rather than hit-singles. The late decade was a golden era for the singer-songwriter, the period in which musicians such as Dylan, Buffy Sainte-Marie, Joni Mitchell, Paul Simon, James Taylor, Neil Young and countless other former folk revival participants attained great distinction for their poetic and 'meaningful' compositions. The folk revival, as Neil Rosenberg remarked, also elevated those musicians who possessed technical expertise and prodigious ability, and the wider music scene of the late 1960s would do much the same; guitar virtuosi such as Jimi Hendrix, Eric Clapton, Jimmy Page and Alvin Lee became heroes and role models for a generation of aspiring musicians.[5] The propensity of folk fans to discuss and debate their music also became a central factor in the wider popular music scene of the late 1960s. Rock journalism would effectively become a new literary form during this time, as magazines such as *Crawdaddy*, *Rolling Stone* and *Creem*, and individuals such as Ralph J. Gleason, Lester Bangs, Jon Landau and Richard Goldstein published sophisticated and insightful critical discussions of contemporary bands and their music.[6]

Thus, there was no point at which the folk revival suddenly vanished; rather, as revival-style folk music mingled with the sounds of other popular music, the two began to merge and enrich one another. Terminology for specific music styles at this point in the 1960s became rather vague, but one could use the generic term 'rock' to describe the conglomeration of folk-based and rock 'n' roll-based music which won the appreciation of intellectuals. The folk revival had much to offer the wider music scene, and, as it converged with rock 'n' roll, it would help to transform the scene irrevocably.

Nevertheless, it is important to recognise that certain of the social and cultural conditions upon which the folk revival of the late 1950s and early 1960s had been founded had, by the mid-1960s, altered and lost their compatibility with the original philosophies and goals of the movement, as the political climate changed. For instance, the folk revival had been fundamentally inspired by the civil rights struggle and encouraged by the belief that black and white people could work together to

---

5   Note that all of the aforementioned are male. There were no prominent guitar 'heroines' during this period, although both Joni Mitchell and Judy Collins were lauded for their ability to play the instrument 'properly'.

6   For examples of rock journalism of this, and subsequent, eras, see Clinton Heylin (ed.), *The Penguin Book of Rock and Roll Writing* (London, 1992) and Barney Hoskyns (ed.), *The Sound and the Fury: A Rock's Backpages Reader: 40 Years of Classic Rock Journalism* (London, 2003), as well as the magazines for which they wrote (for example, Peter Knobler, 'On the Nature of Rock Journalism', *Crawdaddy*, February 1973, which provides an eloquent account of changes in the world of the rock critic.)

create an equal society. By the mid-1960s, however, not only had many of the goals of the initial movement been realised with the passage of the Civil Rights and Voting Rights Acts by 1965, but it was also becoming evident that the fulfilment of legal equality was no longer sufficient, particularly for the black communities of the urban North. The Student Non-Violent Co-ordinating Committee, frustrated in the light of this knowledge, and under the influence of Stokeley Carmichael, author of the 'Black Power' slogan, began to expel its white workers. Malcolm X, another central figure in the growing Black Power movement, had directly questioned the utility of folk songs in his detraction of the integrationist civil rights movement: 'Whoever heard of angry revolutionists all harmonizing "We Shall Overcome" while tripping and swaying with the very people they were supposed to be angrily revolting against?'[7]

Then, in August 1965, the brutal riots in the Watts district of Los Angeles revealed the extent of rage among Northern blacks. The dreams of Martin Luther King and the civil rights movement of the early decade seemed, now, hopelessly naïve and inadequate. As Daniel Gonczy remarks, the voices of the SNCC Freedom Singers, once symbolic of hope and profound social change, and beloved of the folk revival, seemed, by 1965, to be 'drowned in the din of ghetto warfare'.[8]

The student movement was, simultaneously, altering its perspective on its other key concerns. Issues of nuclear testing, again vital to the movement and to the folk revival in the early 1960s, had faded from prominence once John F. Kennedy passed the Nuclear Test Ban Treaty in 1963. The question of war in Vietnam, on the other hand, had, after the major escalation of American involvement in 1965, shifted from its status as a secondary concern to become a major source of debate for almost all sectors of American society. As the 1960s progressed, opposition to the Vietnam War increased, and the anti-war movement encompassed 'an enormous breadth and diversity of people and perspectives', from religious groups to war veterans.[9]

It was, however, young people, and particularly students, who would remain at the forefront of the anti-war movement. Growing outrage at the actions of the United States in Vietnam increased the scope and nature of student activism considerably. The prospect of the draft for male students served to enhance anger and protest.[10] If the student left of the early 1960s had been a body founded on ideas

---

7   Quoted in Douglas T. Miller, *On Our Own: Americans in the Sixties* (Lexington, MA, 1996), p. 140. For more information on Malcolm X and on the Black Power movement on which his philosophies had a profound influence, see Malcolm X and Alex Haley, *The Autobiography of Malcolm X* (New York, 1965); Kolfi Natambu, *The Life and Work of Malcolm X* (Indianapolis, IN, 2002); Michael Eric Dyson, *Making Malcolm: The Myth and Meaning of Malcolm X* (New York, 1995); and Eddie S. Glaude, *Is it Nation Time? Contemporary Essays on Black Power and Black Nationalism* (Chicago, IL, 2002).

8   Gonczy, 'The Folk Music Movement of the 1960s', p. 28. For more on the Watts Riot, see Gerald Horne, *Fire This Time: The Watts Uprising and the 1960s* (Charlottesville, VA, 1995).

9   Edward P. Morgan, *The Sixties Experience: Hard Lessons About Modern America* (Philadelphia, PA, 1991), pp. 130–31. See also Charles De Benedetti and Charles Chatfield, *An American Ordeal: The AntiWar Movement of the Vietnam Era* (Syracuse, NY, 1990).

10   See John C. McWilliams, *The 1960s Cultural Revolution* (Westport, CT, 2000), pp. 52–3, for a discussion of the draft and its impact on students.

and philosophical debate, then it could be argued that the movement of the mid- to late decade became focused around emotions, principally those of frustration, anger and outrage.[11] The larger the student-based anti-war movement became, the less organised it grew, and the more sprawling the demonstrations became, the more violent was the suppression by the authorities and the more indignant the reaction of the protesters. Hatred of authority and of parents, and disgust with America and all it represented, clashed with the folk revival's calmly critical, yet ultimately positive, attitude towards its country, and with its respect for elders and their traditions.[12] As Students for a Democratic Society (SDS) president Paul Potter declared, in the watershed year of 1965, '[t]he incredible war in Vietnam has provided the razor, the terrifying sharp cutting edge that has finally severed the last vestige of illusion that morality and democracy are the guiding principles of American foreign policy.'[13] According to historian Edward P. Morgan, 'disassociation from American culture' accelerated rapidly as the Vietnam War escalated.[14] Thus, optimistic celebrations of the musical diversity of the country were no longer the most apt as the nation seemed to be undergoing a fundamental and violent generational rift.

The growth of the counterculture in the midst of all the angst of the 1960s also contributed to the fading of the politically focused folk revival. The counterculture, a movement which stressed non-conformity and rejection of societal strictures, placed its prime emphasis on the experiential rather than on the political. Timothy Miller, in *The Hippies and American Values*, states that the hippies (counterculture members) were essentially apolitical; although he acknowledges that there was some overlap between the political New Left and the counterculture, he argues that, fundamentally, 'the counterculture proposed not so much a confrontation with mainstream culture as a simple withdrawal from it'.[15] Others, however, would disagree with such a view, asserting instead that the hippies made a contribution to the politics of the era 'just by their existence'.[16] Certainly, their emphasis on 'peace and love' made them staunchly anti-war, and it could be argued that their very lives represented a political statement. However, they were apolitical in the sense that, compared to the New Left of the early decade, they had no political manifesto or coherently developed philosophy. Perhaps it is more accurate to say that the youth of the late decade expressed their

---

11   See Chapter 2 for a more detailed discussion of the New Left and student activism in the early 1960s.

12   Robert Cantwell has stated that the revivalists 'sought, or tacitly believed in, until deep political and social polarizations betrayed that belief, the blessing of the parent generation' (from Neil Rosenberg (ed.), *Transforming Tradition: Folk Music Revivals Examined* (Urbana, IL and Chicago, IL, 1993), p. 49). This possibly overstates the case, but it is certainly true that harsh and hateful criticism was not part of the folk revival, or early 1960s, mentality.

13   Paul Potter, 'The Incredible War', in Alexander Bloom and Wini Breines (eds), *Takin' It To the Streets: A Sixties Reader* (New York; Oxford: Oxford University Press, 2003, 2nd edn), p. 174

14   Morgan, *The Sixties Experience*, p. 127.

15   Timothy Miller, *The Hippies and American Values* (Knoxville, TN, 1991), p. 8. On pp. 10–15, Miller discusses the nature of the differences between the New Left and the counter culture.

16   Ibid., pp. 14–15.

political ideas through lifestyle and bold, rebellious actions rather than through the expression of ideas.[17] A Canadian article on the Woodstock festival illustrated this changing climate of youthful rebellion in its recounting of an anecdote concerning a young SDS member who was attempting to sell copies of the political *New Left Notes* to the departing festival crowds. One young 'dope freak' was heard to shout at him, 'Hey man, stop selling papers and join the revolution.'[18] Even Abbie Hoffman, leader of the influential 'Yippie' movement, which comprised a unique blend of radical politics and counterculture antics, and which had played a significant role in the development of the chaos surrounding the Democratic Convention in Chicago in 1968, found that it was difficult to talk to young hippies in terms of ideas. 'It's hard to reach them,' he stated. 'More and more, you've got to talk about magic.'[19]

The acid culture of the movement was a key factor in this 'magic', and it also served to emphasise further the apolitical, experiential nature of the movement. A whole subculture developed around LSD, with special nightclubs, such as those pioneered by Ken Kesey, which served 'electric koolaid' (LSD-spiked lemonade) and featured strobe lights and acid rock music performed by groups such as The Grateful Dead.[20] One of the key aspects of the drug culture of the late 1960s was indulgence and escape; the singer 'Country' Joe McDonald, when asked to comment on the response of young people to Vietnam, suggested that most would be unable to cope with the full reality of the situation. Instead, he remarked, 'you take drugs, you turn up the music very loud, you dance around, you build yourself a fantasy world where everything's beautiful.'[21] In this sense, the counterculture philosophy could not have been further from the responsibility-driven ethos of the folk revival in its heyday.

---

17   For more information on debates concerning the political implications of the counterculture, see Michael William Doyle, 'Debating the Counterculture: Ecstasy and Anxiety Over the Hip Alternative' from David Farber and Beth Bailey (eds), *The Columbia Guide to America in the 1960s* (New York, 2001), pp. 143–56. Doyle provides a succinct account of the debates concerning the impact of the counterculture upon the New Left, debates which began in the 1960s and which continue to this day.

18   Jack Batten, 'Stoned on Rock, Stoned on Drugs', *Saturday Night*, December 1969.

19   Ibid.

20   Neil Rosenberg notes the role played by the drug culture to the decline of the folk revival in his contribution to Cohen (ed.), *Wasn't That a Time*, p. 76.

21   Quoted in Jerome L. Rodnitzky, 'Popular Music as a Radical Influence, 1945–1970' from Leon Borden Blair (ed.), *Essays on Radicalism in Contemporary America* (Walter Prescott Webb Memorial Lectures) (Austin, TX and London, 1972), p. 16. It should be noted that 'Country' Joe McDonald was commenting on the 'scene' rather than advocating such an escapist response. He remained overtly political throughout the late 1960s; his 'I Feel Like I'm Fixin' to Die Rag', performed at Woodstock and featured in Michael Wadleigh's film of the event, dealt with the futility and human losses of Vietnam, while McDonald's group, Country Joe and the Fish, were outspoken in their opposition to the war. More detail on the anti-war stance of the group may be found in the reminiscences of Barry Melton, guitarist of the Fish who would later become an attorney in California: 'Everything Seemed Beautiful: A Life in the Counterculture', in Alexander Bloom (ed.), *Long Time Gone: Sixties America Then and Now* (Oxford and New York, 2001), pp. 146–57.

Meanwhile, many of those who did remain more politically orientated in the late 1960s exhibited a radicalism which at times bordered on nihilism and anarchy.[22] Such sentiments were equally at odds with the folk revival's stance of peaceful political awareness. A review of a 1969 Joan Baez concert which appeared in the *Village Voice* commented on the anachronistic nature of a singer who 'preaches non-violence to an up-against-the-wall generation. Believes in love, when love and the hippies are both obsolete.' In the wake of the violent Chicago Democratic Convention of 1968, and with the threat of the tragic Altamont Festival and the Weathermen looming, the music of Baez seemed, to the reviewer, 'out of style' and 'almost quaint'.[23] The enduring popularity of Baez was accredited to her status as a 'constant', an unchanging force in a world of change and a reminder of old ideals.[24] However, it is evident that, whether young people of the late decade had 'dropped out' altogether, or were anticipating 'the revolution', the ideals of the folk revival were no longer compatible with their culture or society.[25]

Similarly, while it is clear to see the legacy of the folk revival in the rock music of the late 1960s, in other respects the music scene veered away from many of the basic tenets of the movement. Musicians such as Bob Dylan had forsaken the folk revival, to a great extent, because they found that the ethos of community and adherence to left-wing political values interfered with their goals and aspirations as individual creative artists, just as the student movement of the late 1960s rejected many of the

---

22   This strand of radical politics was epitomised by the Weathermen, an anarchist splinter group of the SDS, whose 'days of rage' in Chicago, October 1969, were characterised by terrorism and brutal clashes with police. Ironically, the Weathermen allegedly took their name from a line in Bob Dylan's song 'Subterranean Homesick Blues' ('You don't need a weatherman to know which way the wind blows'). See Ron Jacobs, *The Way the Wind Blew: A History of the Weather Underground* (London and New York, 1997) and the 2003 Free History Project documentary *The Weather Underground*, produced by Sam Green and Bill Siegel.

23   During the 1968 Convention, the streets of Chicago became a battleground as police assailed young people who were protesting the country's involvement in Vietnam. See Mark Kurlansky, *1968: The Year that Rocked the World* (New York, 2004) and Charles Kaiser, *1968 in America: Music, Politics, Chaos, Counterculture, and the Shaping of a Generation* (New York, 1988). The Altamont Festival, held in December 1969, marked, in the minds of many, a decisive death-blow to the hippie ethos of Woodstock. Biker gang The Hell's Angels, who were hired by the Rolling Stones as security for the festival, performed their task with a brutality which culminated in the death, by stabbing, of a young black man. This disturbing incident was captured on film and became the central part of the Rolling Stones' documentary *Gimme Shelter* (1970). For more information, see the commentary of former *Rolling Stone* journalist Michael Lydon in his book *Flashbacks: Eyewitness Accounts of the Rock Revolution* (New York and London, 2003), pp. 173–84. See also the *Rolling Stone* editorial on Altamont, 'Let It Bleed', 7 February 1970.

24   Marlene Nadle, 'Joan Baez: The Pop Idol Who Wouldn't', *Village Voice*, 21 August 1969.

25   In 1968, Ralph J. Gleason heralded the end of the hippie era, noting that the movement had self-destructed when co-opted by the wider society, at least in terms of superficialities such as dress code. See 'Perspectives: Deathwish of the Hippie Ethos', *Rolling Stone*, 24 August 1968.

narrower political concerns of the early New Left in favour of a more personalised creed. The folk revival believed that music had a political and societal purpose, but many of the great rock musicians of the late 1960s were concerned first and foremost with the individuality of their sound, and political issues played a secondary role. The multi-faceted programmes and intermingling of amateurs and professionals in the coffee-house and the folk festival gave way to the concert tour in which single acts dominated (having been promoted vigorously by impresarios such as Bill Graham), and played to ever-larger crowds in huge venues such as the Hollywood Bowl, the Los Angeles Forum, and Madison Square Garden. The new rock music magazines and their journalists analysed these individuals and interviewed them extensively to uncover their artistic visions. The album became the dominant medium for groups and solo artists, rather than the 'single'. Thus, the concept of music as artistic expression had superseded the belief that music had, above all, a political responsibility. Most of the enduring, legendary performers of the late decade were those who pursued a unique artistic path – Dylan is perhaps one of the best examples of this. Other artists such as Jimi Hendrix, Janis Joplin, The Band, and Crosby, Stills and Nash, to name but a representative few, were acclaimed by the critics primarily because they 'did not sound like anyone else'. Hence, while the legacy of the folk revival was evident in music of the late 1960s, it is equally important to note the ways in which rock music diverged from the ethos of the movement.

Those who had embodied the spirit of the original folk revival found themselves confused and increasingly helpless in the midst of this period of transition. *Sing Out!* magazine, which had managed to survive by attempting to represent all sides of the revival and embrace its many facets, while leaving room for its readers to argue and opine amongst themselves, was forced to widen its horizons still further and include articles on the once-detested 'electric music' as folk-rock became too prevalent to ignore. For members of the 'old guard' such as editor Irwin Silber, eclecticism to this 'increasingly tenuous' extent became 'increasingly difficult to sustain'.[26] Silber, who had been involved with the magazine since the 1950s, and who subscribed to a traditional left-wing political position, ceased to be the editor of *Sing Out!* in 1967; since the mid-1960s, he had been criticising many of his fellow revivalists for failing to fulfil their political obligations through their music.[27] However, by 1967, Silber was prepared to admit that the folk revival, as it had once been defined, no longer existed, as his extensive review of the Newport Folk Festival of that year illustrated. He acknowledged the fact that the festival was no longer the crowd-drawing phenomenon that it had been even two years previously; people, it appeared, would not come unless they were promised a 'headline' act, and it was only when Joan Baez was booked to perform that ticket sales began to improve.[28] Once the

---

26   Quoted in Cohen (ed.), *Wasn't That a Time*, p. 103.

27   Silber had been one of the most severe and vocal critics of Bob Dylan from 1964 onwards, publishing a famous 'open letter' to the singer, printed in *Sing Out!*, Vol. 14 No. 5, November 1964, in which he accused him of wasting the time of his audience with his increasingly obtuse lyrics and receding sense of (overt) social and political responsibility.

28   Newport Folk Festival programmes for 1966–69 demonstrate that, in the wake of Dylan's electric performance of '65 and with large numbers of young people becoming

festival was underway, Silber noted that the old ideals of the revival were simply incongruous with the current political and social climate – a 'topical song' workshop seemed 'noteworthy for its lack of topicality', while other acts seemed lacklustre and superficial, and devoid of the constructive, eager, enthusiastic fighting spirit of the revival in its heyday. English singer Bob Davenport attempted to 'infuse some depth and perception into the superficialities, but America in the Vietnam summer was more prepared to snigger at a few raw words than to look into the mirror offered to it.'[29]

The old, celebratory cultural pluralism which the revival of the early decade had fostered also seemed irrelevant and almost quaint by 1967. Silber sadly remarked that the portion of the festival entitled 'New York City Folk Night', which featured samplings of the cultures of the many ethnic groups of the city, seemed, now, little more than an empty token gesture. Such celebratory performances had been a mainstay of the revival since the 1940s, but Silber no longer considered them to be appropriate. 'A few ethnic nationality performers do not a city's culture make,' he concluded. The despondent editor, noting that the car radios of departing festival-goers were tuned to upcoming singer-songwriter Janis Ian's biting and uncompromising commentary on interracial relationships, 'Society's Child', was forced to acknowledge that 'like it or not', the song was 'more relevant to America '67 than almost everything presented in the name of folk music up at Festival Field'.[30]

In the absence of Silber, and in the changing climate of the times, *Sing Out!*, though thriving (and still in print to this day), effectively became another contemporary music magazine, juxtaposing features on folk musicians with articles on rock stars.[31] In the view of scholar Serge Denisoff, this new approach was much to the disadvantage of the magazine; he found the articles 'awkward and unsophisticated'

---

attracted to rock music, the festival began to include more amplified musicians and groups. For example, in 1966, blues-rock band Blues Project and folk-rock group The Lovin' Spoonful were featured; in 1967 Buffalo Springfield performed at the festival, and in 1968, Big Brother and the Holding Company, most famous for becoming Janis Joplin's backing band, were featured (programmes from the collection of the American Folklife Center, Library of Congress, Washington DC).

29 Irwin Silber, Review of Newport Folk Festival, *Sing Out!*, Vol. 17 No. 5, October/ November 1967.

30 Ibid. Incidentally, a 16-year-old Janis Ian, interviewed for *Sing Out!* by John Cohen in 1968, reiterated Silber's view of the obsolescence of the Newport Festival: 'There are these old people who want to get in, the ethnic people [meaning traditional musicians]. Not only aren't they hip to what's happening, they don't know what's happening now. They do mostly the old songs', John Cohen, 'A Conversation with Janis Ian', *Sing Out!*, Vol. 18 No. 1, March/ April 1968.

31 According to Israel Young, who served on the editorial board of *Sing Out!* throughout the early 1960s, Silber's decision to resign was also the result of considerable in-fighting among magazine staff. In Young's view, the editorial board was comprised of two 'camps' in 1967 – one (Silber, Barbara Dane, and John Cohen) which wished to resist changing with the times, and one (Young, Julius Lester, Paul Nelson and Ethel Raim) which accepted and welcomed change (Israel Young. 1967. Interview by Richard Reuss. Tape recording. 20 December 1967. American Folklife Center, Library of Congress, Washington, DC, Tape AFS 19,807 Part 1, Box 2).

in comparison to the columns of *Rolling Stone* or *Crawdaddy* writers who specialised in the rock genre.[32] Ronald Cohen has elaborated on this sentiment, stating that, in the late 1960s, '*Sing Out!* dished out a mix of political articles, contemporary songs … historical pieces, record reviews, and current news. But the attempt to fatten newsstand sales produced rather dismal results.'[33]

➤ The original folk revival movement was, thus, the victim of changing trends, some, such as the Vietnam situation and Black Power, of a fairly traumatic, revolutionary character, others – such as the development of the music scene and the merging of rock 'n' roll and folk – more evolutionary, but nonetheless of a transforming nature for the movement. ➤

The 'great boom' of the folk revival may have declined by the mid-1960s, but by no means did the concept of folk music fade from importance in the music scene. The folk revival would provide the catalyst for a plethora of specific named-system revivals which would proceed to pursue their own course and attract their own particular audiences; revivals in Bluegrass music, Irish and Celtic music, Klezmer music and many other genres would flourish by the mid-1970s. This vital consequence of the folk revival will be discussed in the next chapter. For the present, however, the discussion will focus on those musicians whose roots lay in the folk revival but who proceeded to pursue careers as 'new aesthetic' performers, whether as soloists or in bands. Following the example of earlier songwriters such as Dylan, Tom Paxton, Gordon Lightfoot and Phil Ochs, it was these musicians – among them James Taylor, Joni Mitchell, Janis Ian, Paul Simon and Tim Hardin – who became the 'new folk' of the late decade. Most of them performed their own songs rather than traditional numbers, but the acoustic accompaniment, gentler sounds and linear, 'story-telling' nature of their songs were strongly rooted in revival-style folk music.[34]

Canadians and Americans were, by the late 1960s, perceiving the significance of the 'new folk' quite differently. The dream of an eclectic folk music of diversity and richness had lost its relevance as the original revival faded, and as the result of political and social events, the two nations of North America were, by 1967, standing at a crossroads in their respective and shared histories. Indeed, it does not seem excessively hyperbolic to suggest that, by the end of the 1960s, the *meaning* of 'Canada' and 'America', as nations and as concepts, had changed considerably. The situation in Vietnam and the increasing generation gap in the United States represented, or at any rate seemed to represent, serious threats to the fabric of American life and society. The summer of 1967 in the United States was Vietnam summer and the summer of love; conflict and the bold assertion of generational difference were the key elements of these months.

---

32   Serge Denisoff, *Great Day Coming: Folk Music and the American Left*, (Urbana, IL; Chicago, IL and London, 1971), p. 195.

33   Cohen, *Rainbow Quest*, p. 267.

34   Songs such as Joni Mitchell's 'The Fiddle and the Drum' and 'Circle Game' and Tim Hardin's 'If I Were a Carpenter' are good examples of the folk influence upon singer-songwriters of the late 1960s. Mitchell's 'Circle Game' contained a chorus designed for audience participation – a key element of folk revival performance style – and both Hardin's 'Carpenter' and 'The Fiddle and the Drum' were rich in archaic imagery and sung in a traditional style.

For many Canadians, however, that eventful summer represented a period of celebration and optimism, as they commemorated the hundredth anniversary of the existence of their nation. Canadians viewed events in America with a sense of distance and of relief; their pride in 'not being American' was considerably heightened during this troubled period. As Robert A. Wright has expressed it, 'just as Confederation had been consolidated in part out of disgust for the 'noisy' republic to the south, Canadians expressed their celebration of this anniversary in terms of the relief they felt at not being part of the United States.'[35] Thus, Canadians took advantage of the opportunity to celebrate themselves, to search and identify sources of national distinction and bring them to public attention. The press were instrumental in leading and enhancing this self-congratulation; throughout 1967 and beyond, magazines and newspapers were filled with pieces on the national psyche, with coverage of Centennial community projects and Expo 67 in Montreal, and with articles that consistently reminded their readers of their national origins and urged them to reflect on them with pride.[36]

The media (both the music press and news magazines such as *Time* and *Maclean's*) in Canada and America had, by the late 1960s, begun to take serious note of popular music, and, when the Canadian press began to acknowledge the considerable number of Canadian performers who were pursuing successful careers in the music industry – among others, Joni Mitchell, Neil Young, Leonard Cohen, Ian and Sylvia, Gordon Lightfoot, Buffy Sainte-Marie and The Band – they declared the unfolding of a veritable artistic revolution in Canada. Virtually all of these musicians had their roots in the folk revival, and now wrote their own songs to acoustic accompaniment. The Canadian press, filled with the jubilant spirit of the Centennial era, used the success of these musicians to persuade the public that there existed a 'Canadian sound', a music that was identifiably and tangibly Canadian. The folk elements of this music were key to its constructed 'Canadianness'. When the Canadian Radio-Television Commission, spurred on by the nationalist spirit of the late 1960s, passed the 'Canadian Content Regulation' in 1971 in an attempt to further the underdeveloped domestic music industry, journalists and nationalists became convinced that popular musicians, with the backing of a supportive industry, would take the 'Canadian sound' to new heights and help to create a rich musical culture in their homeland.[37] Musicians such as Bruce Cockburn, whose careers benefited from the regulations, were seen as exponents of this new sound – a sound that was described as gentle, introspective and folk-based. Although many of those musicians who were celebrated

---

35   Robert A. Wright, 'Dream, Comfort, Memory, Despair: Canadian Popular Musicians and the Dilemma of Nationalism, 1968–1972', in Beverley Diamond and Robert Witmer (eds), *Canadian Music: Issues of Hegemony and Identity* (Toronto, 1994), p. 285.

36   It is important to note that some journalists did consider those for whom the Centennial was less of a cause for celebration; *Saturday Night* contained articles on poverty-stricken and Native communities in Canada throughout 1967.

37   The Canadian Content Regulation legally required 30 per cent of all music played on AM and FM radio stations to be 'Canadian' – either the performer or songwriter was Canadian, or the song in question had been recorded in Canada. For more details see 'Special Section' on the CRTC Canadian Content Proposal in *Canadian Composer/Compositeur Canadien*, May 1970.

by the nationalists were equivocal about such praise, and although the intensity of the nationalist climate would wane as the 1970s progressed, there is no doubt that the new aesthetic folk genre became closely identified with the idea of 'Canadian' music. This association continued for many years, as new generations of songwriters working in folk-based music became successful. It is also significant that songwriters who came from 'the regions' of Canada (i.e. places other than Southern Ontario), such as Neil Young and Joni Mitchell, were now considered, by the press and by nationalists, Canadians first and foremost, and regional musicians secondarily. The creation of a national industry amidst a period of nationalism brought about a shift in focus and a new emphasis upon the creation of music that was 'Canadian'.

The press in the United States were equally fascinated by the developments in popular music, and in the proliferation of gifted singer-songwriters and groups who worked primarily in the folk music idiom. Just as the Canadian press placed upon its domestic musicians responsibility for leading a Canadian artistic revolution, so too did many American writers and chroniclers expect songwriters and performers to find answers to the problems of their country. Most musicians were, however, no longer interested in defending their country or even in discussing its flaws in detail, as they had been wont to do in the days of the revival; most of the former revivalists had given up on this venture. To sing of the cultural riches and natural splendour of their country seemed ludicrously incongruous now, and, by the early 1970s, in the wake of events such as the Kent State massacre, they appeared too jaded even to attack or criticise America.[38] The increasing complexity of popular music added to this reluctance to address political concerns; the genre was now considered an 'art form', and many of those who had formerly sung simple, linear political songs were now experimenting with more subtle, complex musical and lyrical approaches. Thus, to be an American folk musician now was to be an isolated and individualistic poet, one who focused far more on art rather than on contemporary concerns. Folk artists were more inclined, now, to lead their audiences in an escape from contemporary reality, in a quasi-subliminal artistic departure from their troubles, where once they would have rallied them, or at least been expected to rally them, to change their situations. Music that was now dubbed 'folk' in the mainstream industry tended to be performed by solo artists accompanied by acoustic instruments, and most of those who played music of this kind generally wrote their own songs, often eloquently poetic and dealing with personal experiences and self-expression, rather than perform the traditional material of the revival. Once bold and uncompromisingly proselytising, folk music was now the domain of 'new aesthetic' performers who were retiring, individualistic and sensitively self-revealing. In both Canada and America, this change led to a redefinition of the significance of folk musicians for national culture.

---

38   As will be demonstrated, this was true for many performers, but there were always exceptions. Neil Young's 'Ohio' will be discussed subsequently.

Canadian Nationalism and the Canadianising of Folk Music, 1967–80

The celebration of the centennial of the Canadian Confederation in 1967 gave rise to a wave of optimistic nationalism in Canada, a nationalism that was fuelled and encouraged by eager representatives of the media. While history and the recounting of narratives of the past played some part in the celebrations of the late 1960s, in many ways the official documenters and moulders of national sentiment during the Centennial maintained a stronger focus on the present, not as a product of a glorious past, but as the gateway to a great future which would witness the loosening of certain historical ties and the birth of a new Canadian nation with its own distinctive identity.[39] Such an attitude was fostered and enhanced by some of the most overt manifestations of celebration and commemoration during this time. For example, the country acquired, for the first time, its own flag and national anthem, thus removing some of the lingering vestiges of British influence; the Maple Leaf flag replaced the Union Jack, and 'O Canada' became the national anthem in place of 'God Save the Queen'. However, the largest and most evident of all the celebrations of the Centennial was, without doubt, Expo 67, which was hosted by Montreal in recognition of the anniversary. The focus of Expo was, again, not on the past of the country but on the present and the future; the purpose-built site boasted the latest technological and architectural wonders, the most recent industrial developments and the newest inventions. It was thoroughly international in its outlook, thus helping to locate Canada, the host of the exhibition, within a world-wide context, a context in which the country had previously played a more marginal role. The domestic effects of Expo on Canadian morale were considerable. Richard Flohil recalls the incredulous sense of pride felt by Canadians at the success of the exhibition: 'I can't tell you how surprised we were that we did [Expo] on time and that we did it so well! This was absolutely over the top, amazing, and the whole world came and [was] blown away.'[40]

Meanwhile, Robert Fulford, the *Toronto Star*'s Expo correspondent, in his triumphant account of the event, was proud to demonstrate that all doubts concerning Canada's ability to host the event (expressed mainly, according to Fulford, by Canadians themselves) had been dispelled:

> It seemed to me to mark the end of Little Canada, a country afraid of its own future, frightened of great plans. Despite the spectre of French-Canadian separatism that haunted Canada through the early and middle 1960s, Expo seemed to suggest that we were now entering a new and happier period in our history.[41]

---

39 Several histories of Canada were commissioned for the Centennial year. Donald Creighton's *Canada's First Century* (Toronto, 1970) is a good, representative example of the nationalistic tone of such works. See also *The Hundredth Year: The Centennial of Canadian Confederation, 1867–1967* (Ottawa, 1967); *Birthday of a Nation* (Time International of Canada, 1968); Vincent Massey, *Great Canadians: A Century of Achievement* (Canadian Centennial Publishing Company, 1965) and *Canada, One Hundred, 1867–1967* (Ottawa, 1967).
40 Richard Flohil, discussion with the author, 6 May 2003.
41 Robert Fulford, *This Was Expo* (Montreal, 1968).

The demands of the *Quebecois* separatists had indeed represented 'a spectre' for anglophone Canadians in the post-war period, and Expo 67, perhaps, attempted to resolve the situation by making grand, symbolic gestures of inclusiveness. However, in 1968, when Pierre Elliott Trudeau was elected Prime Minister of Canada, it seemed that more practical steps might be taken to keep the nation unified in its diversity. A francophone, Trudeau aimed to diminish separatist desires by emphasising and celebrating, on a national scale, bilingualism and biculturalism, building on the initial efforts of his predecessor, Lester B. Pearson.

Indeed, generally, Pierre Trudeau did a great deal to further the climate of national pride of the late 1960s. A popular, charismatic leader with a strong international profile, he strove hard to manifest the optimism of the period in political reality. He aimed to combat the extensive grip of America on the Canadian economy; in 1971, he established the Canadian Development Corporation to encourage the Canadian ownership and management of businesses, and in 1974, the Foreign Investment Review Agency was formed to examine all proposals for foreign take-overs of Canadian businesses.[42] Trudeau's pacifist outlook and sympathy for draft-dodgers won the hearts of many young radicals, and helped to convey the image that Canada was a peaceful land of tolerance, a peacekeeper representing an alternative to the aggressive, warlike American way.[43] As Robert A. Wright has pointed out, it was greatly to Trudeau's benefit that he began his career just at the time when that of Lyndon Johnson was in ruins.[44] By the late 1960s, therefore, Canada's profile and identity appeared to be undergoing great changes, and those who hoped that the country would gain control of its own destiny as a unique nation, autonomous in every respect and unified in spite of internal cultural differences, cast hopeful eyes upon a bright future indicated by Expo 67, and shaped by a popular and vibrant leader.

As it became apparent that a number of Canadians were at the forefront of the revolution in popular music that was unfolding coincidentally with the Centennial celebrations, journalists, immersed in and promoting the mood of Centennial national pride, began the process of identifying Canadian popular music with Canadian identity. Leading periodicals such as *Maclean's* and *Saturday Night* seized on the cultural and nationalist potential of popular music as interest in its creative developments grew and, more specifically, as journalists became aware that a number of Canadians – including folk revivalists Gordon Lightfoot, Leonard Cohen, Joni Mitchell, Ian and Sylvia, Neil Young and Buffy Sainte-Marie – were acquiring international reputations in the music world. The Band, a group comprised mostly of Canadians, had begun their careers in the rhythm and blues taverns of Yonge Street

---

42   Alvin Finkel, Margaret Conrad and Veronica Strong-Boag, *A History of the Canadian Peoples: Volume II, 1967–Present* (Toronto, 1993), pp. 494–5. See also Robert Bothwell, '"Small Problems": Trudeau and the Americans', in Andrew Cohen and J.L. Granatstein (eds), *Trudeau's Shadow: The Life and Legacy of Pierre Elliott Trudeau* (Toronto, 1998), pp. 207–21.

43   For a contemporary account of such attitudes, see Arnold Edinborough, 'Pierre Elliot Trudeau: The Leader Tomorrow', *Saturday Night*, March 1968.

44   Wright, 'Dream, Comfort, Memory, Despair', pp. 285–6.

as The Hawks, but after accompanying Bob Dylan on his controversial 1966 tour, they produced their own highly distinctive debut album in 1968.[45] Other popular musicians who were attaining international success included popular entertainer Anne Murray and The Guess Who, a group from Winnipeg who had reached the top of the US charts with their song 'These Eyes' in 1969. All of the aforementioned musicians had been forced either to move to America or to obtain US recording contracts in order to pursue their careers; the underdeveloped nature of the Canadian music industry made it impossible for musicians to gain international reputations while working domestically. There were no domestic music charts, no managers or official organisations for musicians, and no proper recording facilities; the major record companies in Canada – RCA, Capitol and Columbia – were American, and, like the major Canadian radio stations, they were interested primarily in the promotion and marketing of popular music which had been recorded and produced in America and Britain. Nevertheless, despite the fact that most of these famous musicians had been forced to leave their homelands to attain such distinction, many journalists of the period linked their success directly to their Canadian origins. They were anxious to use the names of Canadian musical celebrities to stimulate further a mood of national optimism. They used the common nationality of the musicians to create the concept of a 'Canadian sound', a concept which was extremely vaguely defined. Articles such as Courtney Tower's 'The Heartening Surge of a New Canadian Nationalism' and Jack Batten's 'Canadian Pop' were typical examples of such a tendency.[46] The latter claimed that the successful musicians were creating a sound which was 'as characteristically Canadian as the rolling western prairies or the gentle hills of the Ontario countryside'.[47]

The 'Canadian' element of this music was neither clearly defined nor supported by solid theoretical or musicological argument. However, the words used by the author to describe the music – the adjective 'gentle', and the references to specific place and rural location – could be said to represent an early example of the association between music in the folk vein and claims of Canadian musical distinctiveness. Robert A. Wright, one of the first, and the few, Canadian scholars to have documented and interpreted the consequences of the CRTC ruling for musicians, has drawn attention to this growing association of Canadian musicians with the folk music idiom in the Centennial era. He comments upon the perceived qualities of 'rurality [*sic*], directness and simplicity' which much of the music made by Canadians in this period possessed, and remarks that 'Canadian musicians have betrayed a deeply rooted reverence for rural life and for natural ecology, and very often these values

---

45   The Band, *Music from Big Pink* (Capitol CDP 7 46069 2).

46   Courtney Tower, 'The Heartening Surge of a New Canadian Nationalism', *Maclean's*, February 1970; Jack Batten, 'Canadian Pop', *Chatelaine*, September 1969. The scholar Barry K. Grant, in his article 'Across the Great Divide: Imitation and Inflection in Canadian Rock Music', *Journal of Canadian Studies* 21, (1986): 116–27, first drew attention to this trend in late 1960s journalism and discussed it in relation to the passing of the CRTC regulation.

47   Jack Batten, 'Canadian Pop'. The musicians in question were The Band, Leonard Cohen, Joni Mitchell, Gordon Lightfoot, and The Tysons. Two other expatriate successes, former Yorkville performer Zal Yanovsky (of The Lovin' Spoonful) and Steppenwolf (formerly The Sparrows, also of Yorkville) were also included.

were identified as "Canadian" and juxtaposed with urban America.'[48] Such values were also considered to appertain to the folk music genre as it was defined in the late 1960s, and so, gradually, an association was created between the 'folk' music of performers such as Joni Mitchell, Leonard Cohen and Neil Young and the concept of intrinsically 'Canadian' music.

While some journalists blissfully expounded upon the 'characteristically Canadian' qualities of music made by performers from Canada, others were more inclined to focus on the more negative fact that these musicians had been forced to leave Canada in order to pursue successful careers in the music industry. The Australian journalist Ritchie Yorke became something of a crusader on behalf of Canadian musicians. In 1969 he published a lengthy exploration of the shortcomings of the industry in Canada in *Billboard* magazine, conveying a picture of gifted aspiring Canadian musicians at the mercy of unsympathetic music corporations and heartless, unsupportive disc jockeys.[49] Certainly, it was true that few opportunities existed in Canada for musicians to attain major success domestically, but articles such as that of Yorke did not make any allusion to the vibrant local musical activities which existed in Canada, or to the extent to which young people loved and encouraged local musicians and groups regardless of their international status. A glance at the pages of 'After Four' in the *Toronto Telegram* displays the tremendous enthusiasm which local teenagers exhibited towards musicians such as Robbie Lane and the Disciples and Ronnie Hawkins; groups such as The Beatles certainly received a great deal of coverage from 'After Four', but coverage of activities and musicians in the city was considerable, conveying the impression that local teenagers were not inclined to think local musicians any less valid than those who had distinguished careers. Brian Walsh, who was a teenager in Toronto during this period, would concur with this suggestion:

> I think that our attitude was ... these guys are as good as anybody else that we're listening to. They're every bit as good. So I think we had a certain pride. The Ugly Ducklings ... Yeah, they've got a Stones kind of feel to them, but they're not the Stones. And the musicianship that was going on there was as good as anybody's. I mean, Domenic Troiano played with Mandala, and he could play the guitar beside Eric Clapton any day. So there was a sense of pride that we had. I didn't have the feeling of 'they're second best to anybody', but it was clear that they felt that to truly make it, they had to make it on the international stage.[50]

While, in general, radio stations may have been less than sympathetic to aspiring Canadian musicians, there were disc jockeys across the nation who were willing and keen to support local talent. Again, in 'After Four', a segment known as "The Canadian Sound Survey" was added in January 1967. This segment represented a survey of 'Canadian music coast to coast', and provided information on the programmes of local radio stations, from Calgary's CFAC to Vancouver's C-FUN,

---

48   Wright, 'Dream, Comfort, Memory, Despair', pp. 291–2.
49   Ritchie Yorke, 'Canada's Role in World Music Industry – Silent No Longer' from 'A Billboard Spotlight: Canada', *Billboard*, 24 May 1969.
50   Brian Walsh, in discussion with the author, Toronto, 8 October 2002.

which were 'concerned with promoting Canadian talent'.[51] Prior to the instigation of this feature in 'After Four', however, Bob McAdorey of CHUM had a regular column in the paper which provided commentary on the Toronto scene and its key performers. Therefore, while it is true that the Canadian music industry was primitive and underdeveloped prior to 1971, it is important to acknowledge that it may be excessively simplistic merely to assume that Canadian musicians were always 'victims', entirely devoid of supporters, as Ritchie Yorke would suggest.

Both those who condemned the lack of domestic support for Canadian music and those who enthused over the success of Canadian musicians internationally were excited and optimistic as it became clear that the Trudeau government was beginning to take an interest in the development of the popular music industry. This interest was part of the broader movement, during the Trudeau era, to generate a greater internal control over the Canadian economy, but, in the sphere of musical activity, the Composers, Authors and Publishers Association of Canada (CAPAC) had been pushing for greater Canadian content on the radio for some years, and had managed to assist in convincing the government that new, protective laws were necessary.[52] Articles anticipating the effects, cultural as well as practical, of the CRTC Canadian Content Regulations were in abundance; the regulations seemed, to many, the ideal way to ensure that Canadian popular music would become fully a 'Canadian' form of expression.[53] The regulations took effect on 18 January 1971, after extensive public and governmental debate in Ottawa.[54] With the passing of the regulation, the anticipated economic revolution in the hitherto disadvantageous conditions for musicians in Canada took place, and, effectively, the regulations provided the foundation of the first profitable, organised Canadian music industry which was largely liberated from American control. Musicians could work domestically, hear their music promoted on the radio, record in newly built recording studios in Canada, and aspire to win a 'Juno' Award (the Canadian equivalent of the 'Grammy', named

51   See, for example, the 'Canadian Sound Survey' of the *Toronto Telegram*'s 'After Four' section, Thursday 16 February 1967.

52   See 'CAPAC Proposals incorporated in CRTC's new Radio Regulations', *Canadian Composer/Compositeur Canadien*, September 1970. (*Canadian Composer* was the official journal of CAPAC.)

53   See Courtney Tower, 'The Heartening Surge of a New Canadian Nationalism', *Maclean's*, February 1970; Peter Goddard, 'A Maple Leaf on Every Turntable Means Made-in-Canada Pop Stars', *Maclean's*, November 1970; and Lyman Potts, 'Horizons Expanded for Our Musicians', *RPM*, 9 January 1971.

54   The CRTC regulation is outlined in full in Roger Bird (ed.), *Documents of Canadian Broadcasting* (Ottawa, 1988). Details of the adjustments which radio stations were forced to make to accommodate the regulation are outlined in "Learning to Live with Canadian Content", *Canadian Composer/Compositeur Canadien*, February 1971. Indeed, much can be learned of the impact of 'Can-con' within the music industry from the issues of *Canadian Composer* between 1970 and 1971. The magazine began, simultaneously, to feature more items on popular musicians; prior to this, it had focused almost exclusively on classical composers and musicians.

in honour of Pierre Juneau, the head of the CRTC).[55] Pierre Juneau himself shared the straightforward faith of the press that the regulation would lead to the creation of a nationally distinctive popular music:

> [The purpose of the CRTC] is to ensure that Canadian broadcasting develops as a system of us [*sic*] to communicate with one another about our problems and the problems of the world; about our ideas and our views of the world, about our past and our hopes for the future, about our environment, about the quality of our lives, about our role in this area of the universe.[56]

The Canadian music industry was, thus, boosted by the government largely as a consequence of the increase in nationalist sentiment during the late 1960s. The search for a 'Canadian' music became a prominent concern more than ever before.

For music industry representatives, disc jockeys and some performers, however, an alliance between popular music and government agencies seemed ridiculously incongruous during such an era of musical individualism and political agitation. Disc jockeys and radio stations resented the governmental interference, and were convinced that the CRTC was thoroughly misguided in its belief that Canadian people wanted more Canadian music. They continued to display their hostility to 'Cancon' either by fulfilling the 30 per cent quota very late at night, or by playing songs by successful American-based groups such as Crosby, Stills, Nash and Young or The Band, groups which were classed as Canadian, but whose work made a mockery of the notion that the music of Canadians must sound obviously 'Canadian'.[57] Artists themselves tended to consider the ruling as a crutch on which the less successful and less talented had to lean. Gordon Lightfoot, who remained resident in Canada, and who was a recipient of the Governor General Award in 1970, expressed this viewpoint when asked about the regulations. At least two of his compositions, 'Canadian Railroad Trilogy' and 'The Wreck of the Edmund Fitzgerald' reflected his Canadian roots and his apparent interest in the history of his country, but he was seemingly reluctant to be cast in the role of nationalist icon:

> Canadian content is fine if you're not doin' well. But I'm in the music business and I have a huge American audience. I'm going to do Carnegie Hall for the second time. I like to

---

55 'Juno Awards: Pop Music Up Front', *Canadian Composer/Compositeur Canadien*, April 1971.

56 Quoted in John Lehr, 'As Canadian as Possible ... Under the Circumstances: Regional Myths, Images of Place and National Identity in Canadian Country Music', in Diamond and Witmer (eds), *Canadian Music*, p. 271. Juneau was interviewed several times on CBC radio about the consequences of the CRTC ruling. Some of these may be heard online at the CBC Archive website, including a News Special of 22 May 1970 <http://archives.cbc.ca/IDCC-1-68-1150-6312/arts_entertainment/canadian_content/> and a 'Sunday Supplement' edition of 26 April 1970 <http://archives.cbc.ca/IDCC-1-68-1150-6311/arts_entertainment/canadian_content/> (accessed 4 May 2004).

57 See Grant, 'Across the Great Divide', p. 122. NB: CSNY would be considered 'Canadian' if a song by Neil Young was played, and The Band were four-fifths Canadian.

record down there, but I like to live up here. I really dig this country, but I'm not going to bring out any flags.[58]

Many industry representatives, artists and audience members would continue to sneer at Canadian Content for the next three decades, whether as a result of objections to the ruling itself or, possibly, as a symptom of the national 'inferiority complex' which many Canadians believe exists in their own country. Some, according to Richard Flohil, believed that the Cancon regulation was giving money to people without considerable talent simply by virtue of their nationality, and thus were creating a mediocre industry. As Flohil remarks, 'there is still a school of thought, in radio and in the music business, that the only reason Canadians score at all is [the CRTC regulation].'[59] However, despite the objections, the Canadian music industry was boosted tremendously – indeed, effectively created – by nationalist sentiment. While, as the 1970s progressed, the nationalism of the centennial years would abate somewhat, and the Canadian content regulations would cease to be a source of vociferous debate, the search for 'a Canadian music' would never completely end. In particular, during the post-Centennial period, ideas concerning the endowment of the music of folk-based performers with intrinsically 'Canadian' qualities would continue to be expressed. Artists who, in the late 1960s, might have found such ideas limiting and damaging to their careers would often warm to such notions, albeit fitfully, thus helping to 'Canadianise' the folk genre. The belief that folk music was the most compatible musical genre for the expression of Canadian culture was also enhanced by the music of three singer-songwriters whose careers were blossoming in the early 1970s (although not necessarily as a consequence of the ruling) – namely, Bruce Cockburn, Murray McLauchlan and Stan Rogers. Vague though it is, the notion that folk music provides the best mouthpiece for the Canadian experience, born during the period of Centennial nationalism, has persisted even to this day.

Although the CRTC regulation served to boost the careers of several notable Canadian rock bands – such as Lighthouse, Crowbar and Edward Bear – those musicians who attained the greatest success in the post-Centennial period, and who attracted the most attention, tended to be soloists who performed their own material.[60] Unlike those who had become successful in the 1960s, however, these musicians did not have to leave Canada to pursue their careers, and they expressed great pride in their homeland. Bruce Cockburn, from Ottawa, had begun his career in Yorkville, proceeding from there to attain considerable success as a songwriter and performer. Murray McLauchlan, born in Scotland but brought up in Toronto, also frequented Yorkville until he was able to produce his own albums featuring songs about his

---

58 Robert Markle, 'Early Morning Afterthoughts: Gordon Lightfoot and the Canadian Dream', *Maclean's*, December 1971. This excerpt is also cited by Robert A. Wright in 'Dream, Comfort, Memory, Despair'.

59 Flohil, discussion.

60 The majority of the rock bands which were boosted by the CRTC ruling were only comparatively successful, and tended to be derivative in their sound. Groups such as The Poppy Family, Edward Bear and Crowbar were among the first rock bands to benefit from the ruling; articles on them and on other post-CRTC newcomers are abundant in *Canadian Composer/Compositeur Canadien* throughout the early 1970s.

home city and its culture. Stan Rogers, the Ontario-born son of Nova Scotians, devoted himself to a musical portrayal of the land of his parents, immersing himself in Maritime culture while simultaneously displaying interest in the other distinctive regions of Canada. His untimely death solidified his reputation as a hero, not only to the people of the Maritimes, but also to Canadians in general, because of his sensitive and enthusiastic interpretations of their real or hypothetical/romanticised experiences. These folk artists became the focus of nationalist sentiment after the Centennial climate had waned; their 'new aesthetic' music helped to enhance and continue the belief that music in the 'folk' vein represented the true musical expression of Canadian identity.

Bruce Cockburn was one of the first musicians to benefit from the CRTC regulations. His very acoustic, gentle, reflective music was met with great appreciation from Canadian audiences, in particular, and for a period of time he became the darling of the nationalists, proof of the fact that tremendous talent existed in the country and was just waiting to be discovered. Soft-spoken, thoughtful and articulate, Cockburn was portrayed by writer Myrna Kostash, in her 1972 *Saturday Night* interview, as the quintessential Canadian – a man who appeared in every respect the antithesis of the aggressive, macho American man. Kostash questioned him on the differences between Canadians and Americans – a fashionable topic at the time – and, while Cockburn was not willing to draw simplistic comparisons, he expressed the common belief that Canadians were more in tune with country living, and talked about the concept of 'space' and its significance for Canada:

> Space may be a misleading word because it is so vague in relation to music, but maybe it has to do with Canadians being more involved with the space around them than trying to fill it up as Americans do … The more Canadians fill up their space the more they will be like Americans.[61]

The romantic idea that Canadians were an ecologically aware and rural-minded people was particularly appealing at this time, perhaps because of the growing fears in the early 1970s concerning environmental abuse, fears which focused especially upon the activities of the United States government. Bruce Cockburn, although never overtly or stridently patriotic, embodied, in his gentle early albums, this rural spirit which many considered a 'Canadian' quality. Generally, the Canadian press, and perhaps elements of the public, seemed to like to hear their musicians express love for the land at this time.

Canadians, of course, did not possess the monopoly on rural-sounding music or on pastoral desires at this time. Since the late 1960s, American musicians, too, had been singing about the benefits of country life – Don Maclean's 'Castles in the Air', and Canned Heat's 'Goin' Up the Country', which was used as background music in the film *Woodstock*, were popular manifestations of the desire to return to nature. Meanwhile, throughout the 1970s, country music performers such as Emmylou Harris and Bonnie Raitt expressed rural sensibilities through the imagery and roots

---

61   Myrna Kostash, 'The Pure, Uncluttered Spaces of Bruce Cockburn', *Saturday Night*, June 1972. This interview is also cited by Wright in 'Dream, Comfort, Memory, Despair', pp. 291–2.

of their music.[62] Joni Mitchell and Neil Young, in songs such as 'Woodstock', which proclaimed that 'we've got to get ourselves back to the garden', and 'Helpless', which was full of natural imagery, were as much a part of an American, or even international, 'return to nature' as they were part of any Canadian expressions of this impulse.[63] However, neither of these performers was purely 'rural' in his or her imagery – for instance, one of the most celebrated songs on Mitchell's first album was 'Night in the City', allegedly about Yorkville, and she would subsequently paint pictures of urban scenes in her mid-1970s, jazz-inspired albums. Furthermore, by the late 1960s, the notion of Canada as the preserve of a rural lifestyle was only partially accurate, for it was during the 1960s and '70s that many Canadian cities, particularly Toronto, Vancouver and Montreal, experienced considerable growth and expansion, their landscapes changing as suburbs expanded and high-rise buildings dominated the skyline.[64]

Nevertheless, the image of Canada as a natural and pure land was persistent in the views of the nationalists and the press in the late 1960s and early 1970s, when the desire to 'Canadianise' native-born musicians was strongest. For example, in an article about his brother Neil, Bob Young conveyed an image of the songwriter not unlike that of Bruce Cockburn; he stated that, as far as he was concerned, the immensely popular Neil would always remain the boy who loved 'simple things such as trees, getting up early [and] mornings in the country'.[65] Similarly, in an interview with fellow folksinger Malka Himel, Joni Mitchell expressed her pride in being Canadian and implied that there was 'a lot of prairie in [her] music and in Neil Young's music as well ... both of us have a striding quality to our music which is like long steps across flat land.' Describing herself as 'definitely a Canadian', Mitchell also discussed her decision to settle in rural British Columbia, and expressed her love for the 'beautiful loneliness' which she had encountered there.[66] Cockburn, too, frequently articulated his empathy for the land. In his interview with Kostash he made it clear that he preferred 'the country to the city' and his first album featured the song 'Going to the Country', a simple, joyful ode to country living. Other early pieces by Cockburn evoked feelings of alienation experienced in Toronto and, in general, utilised imagery which evoked rural life.[67] In many respects, Cockburn, Mitchell and Young, in expressing their love for nature, were essentially in tune with general developments in the music industry at large in this period; countless artists, American, British and Canadian, were turning to rural life for escape and for

---

62 For more information on country music in the 1970s, see Chapter 11 of Bill C. Malone's seminal study *Country Music, USA* (Austin, TX, 2002), pp. 369–415.

63 'Woodstock' from *Ladies of the Canyon* (Reprise CD 6376, 1970) and a live version of 'Helpless' is on a recording of The Band's farewell concert in which Neil Young was a guest artist. See *The Last Waltz* (Warner Bros 7599-27346-2, 1978).

64 For a detailed history of the urban development of Toronto from the 1950s to the 1970s, see James Lemon, *Toronto Since 1918: An Illustrated History* (Toronto, 1985), pp. 113–87.

65 Bob Young with Jon Ruddy, 'Neil Young: My Brother The Folk Singer', *Maclean's*, May 1971.

66 'Face to Face: Joni Mitchell in Conversation with Malka', *Maclean's*, June 1974.

67 Bruce Cockburn, *Bruce Cockburn* (True North TNBD 0001, 1970).

enrichment.[68] However, in the immediate post-CRTC period, Cockburn's thoughtful music was perceived as a veritable Canadian alternative to mainstream rock music. He would subsequently experiment with many different styles of music, but throughout his career he has continued to be perceived as an icon for Canadian songwriters.

Both Murray McLauchlan and Stan Rogers, whose careers would not blossom until the mid- to late 1970s, were more pointed and specific in their expressions of Canadian pride. In many ways, their songs reflected something of the spirit of the folk revival of the early 1960s, to the extent that they chose to write and sing about specific places within their country, and were proud to speak of their love for those places. Rogers's music, in particular, found a place within the Maritime music revival which was occurring simultaneously in the 1970s, although his music was an interpretative 'new aesthetic' response to the music of that region, rather than being traditional in the strict sense of the word.[69] By this stage, long after the spirit and ethos of the original folk revival had waned, the place-specific folk music of McLauchlan and Rogers was interpreted, by nationalists of the CRTC and the press who supported Canadian music, as distinctively 'Canadian' in the broad sense, rather than in the regional sense.

Murray McLauchlan, brought up in the suburbs of Toronto, had been a performer and a songwriter for many years before he attained any tangible success. CRTC was helpful to him, but, like Cockburn, he was initially reluctant to describe himself as a nationalist, declaring that he reacted to the concept 'very, very badly'.[70] However, as McLauchlan matured as a songwriter, he appeared to gain inspiration from his home city and its culture, and endeared himself to Canadian audiences by writing and performing songs, such as 'On the Boulevard', 'Immigrant', 'Shoe-Shine Working Song' and 'Down by the Henry Moore', which dealt with life in Toronto and contained specific references to landmarks and locations.[71] McLauchlan explained in a 1979 interview that Toronto was 'the source of all [his] cues and all [his] signals, everything that [made him] tick', and, apparently, people in Toronto responded to his sense of local pride. As the journalist J.C. Alspector stated, 'suddenly, here [were] song[s] about their hometown instead of yet another ode to San Francisco.'[72] McLauchlan himself challenged the traditional fascination of urban young people with the rural myths of North America when he commented, in the early 1970s, '[t]here are lots of songs about hoboes and bums. But these people I'm talking about

---

68   For example, Ian McKay notes that, in the late 1960s and early 1970s, young counterculture members from Canada and America (including a number of draft-resisters) experimented with life in rural Canada, particularly Nova Scotia, as part of the 'back to the land' movement. (Ian McKay, *Quest of the Folk: Anti-modernism and Cultural Selection in Nova Scotia* (Montreal; Kingston; London; Buffalo, NY, 1994), pp. 283–9.

69   There were also, reportedly, some people from the Maritimes who rejected his music because he was Ontario-born.

70   Richard Flohil, 'Murray McLauchlan: Coming to Terms with a New Art Form', *Canadian Composer/ Compositeur Canadien*, May 1974, p. 18.

71   See Murray McLauchlan, *Greatest Hits* (True North TNK 35, 1990).

72   J.C. Alspector, 'The City Minstrel: Murray McLauchlan's Toronto is something to rock 'n' roll about', *Toronto Star*, 4 March 1979.

in my songs are the middle class – not the middle class of our parents' generation but of our own age.'

A skilled songwriter who performed music in the folk vein, McLauchlan experimented with 'harder' sounding rock music in the early 1980s, but his popularity had been built on his ability to reflect local culture through acoustic songs, and he returned to this idiom subsequently. Even if Murray McLauchlan had disliked to call himself a nationalist, his music displayed a pride in his home city and in its culture that was more heartfelt and unique, and hence more successful and more highly acclaimed. Once again, the public, guided as always by journalists looking to note and enhance 'trends' in music, looked to a 'new aesthetic' songwriter to become a representative of Canadian culture and qualities, and, in the case of Murray McLauchlan, the songwriter seemed pleased and proud to oblige his audience.

Arguably, the songwriter whose work crystallised the notion that Canadian culture was best expressed through folk music was Stan Rogers. One of the most prolific Canadian writers and performers of the 1970s, Rogers, too, had begun his career in coffee-houses; gradually, he developed an interest in writing songs which, in his own words, reflected 'the Canadian spirit'.[73] In particular, he desired to depict historical incidents and specific Canadian locations from the point of view of one person. Such was the perspective of some of his best known songs, such as 'Field Behind the Plow', the story of a prairie farmer, 'Barrett's Privateers', on the subject of privateering in Maritime waters during the eighteenth century, and 'The Mary Ellen Carter', a song about a shipwrecked sailor which became something of an anthem after Rogers's death.[74] Rogers was particularly associated with the culture of the Maritimes, for a large number of his songs dealt with that region, and particularly with the lives and activities of sailors and fishermen there; he was often credited as a central figure in the 'commercial flowering of traditional East Coast music' which developed from the 1970s onwards.[75] However, most journalists and admirers perceived Rogers as a Canadian musician above all, and he seemed very proud of this fact. As he told Ken Waxman,

> folk musicians like me are spreading Canadian culture throughout the world and giving people outside the country an idea of what this country is. The funny thing is that we're doing it almost completely on our own, but we're doing it better than any number of government-sponsored projects.[76]

Rogers's words display, once again, the ambivalence of Canadian artists towards 'government sponsored' music. Nevertheless, Rogers did not appear to mind being called a nationalist. To a far greater extent than McLauchlan or Cockburn, Rogers promoted himself as a 'Canadian' folk musician who was proud to sing about his native land.

---

73   Mark Miller, 'Singer's Loss Stuns Folk Scene', *Toronto Star*, 4 June 1983.

74   Some of these songs are featured on Stan Rogers, *Between the Breaks ... Live!* (Fogarty's Cove Music, FCM-002D, 1979).

75   Alexandra Gill, 'Canso Reels in Fans of Stan Rogers', *Globe & Mail*, 4 July 1997.

76   Ken Waxman, 'Stan Rogers's Music Goes Abroad – Thanks to Himself' (pre-1983 – from the collection of the TPL Vertical Files. No date or source provided.)

In 1983 Stan Rogers was tragically killed, aged only 33, in an aircraft fire while en route from Detroit to a concert in Toronto. His unexpected demise seemed to transform him into a Canadian hero; newspaper tributes and obituaries abounded, all of which emphasised the tremendous contribution which Rogers had made to Canadian music and culture, and the extent to which he had been reputed to understand and express 'the Canadian experience'. One of the most emotive of such tributes, written by Silver Donald Cameron for *Quest* magazine on the first anniversary of Rogers's death, stated that the artist's 'chronicles of Canada' were 'songs that seem[ed] to come from inside the [Canadian] people. ... He spoke for all Canadians [–] he belong[ed] to everyone. ... We all needed him.' A key factor in the success of Stan Rogers was his status as a folksinger, a status of which he seemed very proud. In one interview, he noted the ways in which perceptions of folksingers had changed since the days of the 1960s revival; he jokingly described the stereotypical folksinger as being 'someone who wears faded jeans and a torn t-shirt, can't tune a guitar, sings off-key and lectures the audience on politics'. He proceeded to state, 'I'm none of these things. But I don't deny the charge. I'm a folksinger and proud of it.'[77]

By the time the careers of Murray McLauchlan, Bruce Cockburn and Stan Rogers had begun, the definition of folk music, and of what constituted a 'folksinger', had indeed altered considerably. However, Rogers and McLauchlan, at least, seemed proud to belong to the folk genre as it was now broadly defined, and all three artists, working in a solo capacity on very distinctive types of songs, helped to emphasise the notion that the folk idiom was best suited to reflecting and defining the Canadian experience.

Cockburn, Rogers and McLauchlan were three of the most notable and critically acclaimed of those folk songwriters who were said to embody Canadian culture and values. However, in any discussion of folk artists who devoted themselves to the expression of Canadian identity, it is imperative to include the career and music of 'Stompin'' Tom Connors. Connors, born and brought up on Prince Edward Island, exhibited a nationalism which was more vocal and uncompromising than that of virtually any other artist. He, however, was equally proud of his status as a worker and as a representative of the 'ordinary' working people; as Richard Flohil stated in an article on Connors from the early 1970s, his music represented 'a kind of blatant working-class Canadian nationalism'.[78] His music was deliberately and triumphantly simplistic, the very antithesis of the artful compositions of Joni Mitchell or Bruce Cockburn – songs such as 'Sudbury Saturday Night', containing only two chord changes, and 'Tillsonburg' were designed for audiences to sing along as raucously as possible, while Connors maintained the beat via his 'stomping board' on the floor. Their lyrics dealt with workaday situations; 'Tillsonburg' described the conditions for workers in the tobacco fields of Southern Ontario, while 'Sudbury Saturday Night' joyfully celebrated the weekend revels of a northern working community. Although

---

77 'Maverick Stan Rogers was "a folksinger and proud of it"', 5 June 1983 (from the TPL Vertical File collection – no author or source provided).

78 Richard Flohil, 'Stompin' Tom: Canada's Unlikely National Symbol', *Canadian Composer/Compositeur Canadien*, (85) November 1973, p. 36.

his music clearly, and perhaps purposely, lacked the sophistication and depth displayed in the work of the aforementioned Canadian songwriters, and although he is frequently, and justifiably, viewed as being part of the Maritime country music tradition, Connors might still be described as a folk artist in the 'new aesthetic' vein. His songs were linear and 'storytelling' in structure, and his performances echoed folk revival concerts in their emphasis on community singing and audience participation (although they were usually devoid of the sort of earnestness often found at folk revival gatherings!). Certainly, his pride in his Canadian identity was fierce, and he lost no opportunity to vocalise his opinions on Canadian musicians who pursued their careers in the United States, only to be lauded as national heroes upon their return home. He spoke out against the awarding of 'Junos' to these artists with such vehemence that he was eventually barred from the award ceremony. An utterly inimitable performer who has now become something of a legend in his homeland, Tom Connors was another artist whose music helped to enhance the association between folk music and Canadian identity, albeit in a manner which contrasted dramatically with the approaches of other songwriters.

The idea that folk music is an ideal medium for the expression of Canadian culture and values has persisted beyond the 1970s. At least one work has been published which ostensibly articulates the link between Canadian identity and folk music. The poet and journalist Douglas Fetherling observed the number of Canadian solo performers who were both distinguished and successful, and wrote an article on their music which eventually became a full-length book in the early 1990s. Fetherling characterised the music of Neil Young, Joni Mitchell, Robbie Robertson and others as distinctively Canadian; he claimed that their work exhibited recognisable qualities of 'sincere gentleness', 'polite, distracted anguish', and 'abstraction and introspection'.[79] He considered it highly significant that most of these performers had been most successful as soloists – even Robbie Robertson, the guitarist and principal songwriter for The Band, had, according to Fetherling, always been torn between group and individual musical activity. Fetherling linked this soloistic tendency to the 'loneliness of the [Canadian] landscape'. His book, though eloquent and thoughtful, was highly subjective and interpretative, yet it clearly reflected and reinforced the persistent belief that the work of Canadian songwriters was both distinctive and recognisable. It is unlikely that the work was widely read, but it remains one of the few published studies of Canadian songwriters and their music, and thus, at present, it appears in the public realm as a source of some authority. Many people would be inclined to agree with Fetherling that Canadian 'new aesthetic' songwriters produced 'Canadian' music; the notion has now been prevalent for almost four decades, reinforced initially by the media and, subsequently, by musicians themselves. Thus, as the folk revival waned in popularity and as the meaning of folk music appeared to change, Canadians created a new significance for folk music as it was now broadly defined, giving it a unique place in their culture and national identity.

---

79   Doug Fetherling, *Some Day Soon: Essays on Canadian Songwriters* (Kingston, 1991), Introduction.

Artistic Individualism in a Time of Turmoil: Folk Performers in the United States from the late 1960s to 1980

In the United States, the careers of singer-songwriters, many of whom were former folk revivalists, also flourished towards the end of the 1960s. Where once they were willing to offer criticisms of their country and dream of its regeneration as a multi-faceted and tolerant nation, however, by the late 1960s, singer-songwriters were largely growing disillusioned with such a stance. While Canadian folk-style musicians were being linked by the press and by the CRTC to their native land, their American counterparts were retreating from any kind of optimistic stance on the United States. This is not to suggest that protest songs were no longer in existence by the end of the decade. Many anti-Vietnam songs were written and sung, among them Joe McDonald's 'Fixin' to Die Rag', memorably performed at the Woodstock festival, and Pete Seeger's 'Waist Deep in the Big Muddy'.[80] Joan Baez remained staunchly and overtly committed to political causes; her husband, David Harris, went to prison for resisting the draft, and she herself was arrested many times for her part in anti-war demonstrations. John Fogerty of the group Creedence Clearwater Revival reflected the legacy of the folk revival in his political songs, most notably 'Fortunate Son', on the subject of class discrimination in the draft.[81] Don McLean, whose career as a singer-songwriter began at the very end of the 1960s, campaigned with Pete Seeger for environmentalist causes, a crusade which was reflected in his 1968 debut album *Tapestry*.[82] Other important topical songs of the late decade included 'Ohio' by Neil Young on the subject of the Kent State shootings, and Joni Mitchell's 'The Fiddle and the Drum'.[83] Countless other musicians would compose and perform songs on political topics.

Nonetheless, it is clear that many of those who began their careers immersed in the protest music of the folk revival were moving away from political concerns as the years progressed. They seemed, in this sense, no longer interested in the optimistic view of America projected by the folk revival of the early 1960s; they no longer spoke of desires to improve the country, or to teach others about the true meaning of democracy and equality.

Bob Dylan was, of course, the most strident in his rejection of political music, and those interviews which he gave in the mid- to late 1960s demonstrate just how reluctant he was not only to discuss politics, but also to have his music classified in any way. In his *Rolling Stone* interview of December 1967, Dylan simply evaded answering questions regarding 'messages' in his music, and, when asked why he had begun to play folk-rock music, he merely replied, 'I don't play folk-rock.'[84] Dylan

---

80   For more information on songs written about the Vietnam conflict, see Barbara Dane and Irwin Silber (eds and compilers), *The Vietnam Songbook* (New York, 1969). A very interesting interview with Lt. Barry Sadler, the singer of the most famous pro-Vietnam song, 'Ballad of the Green Berets', appeared in *Crawdaddy*, August 1973.

81   See Ralph J. Gleason, 'John Fogerty: The *Rolling Stone* Interview', *Rolling Stone*, 21 February 1970.

82   Don McLean, *Tapestry* (Capitol BGO CD 232, 1994).

83   The fact that both of these songwriters are Canadian will be discussed subsequently.

84   'Bob Dylan: The Rolling Stone Interview', *Rolling Stone*, 14 December 1967.

was, certainly, always a notoriously difficult interview subject, but his extreme reluctance to answer such directly posed questions about his music and its 'purpose' was also indicative of changing times. Bob Dylan desired his music to be accepted and received in its increasing complexity, and he was tired of being forced, time and again, to explain it.

It could also be argued that Dylan, and other musicians who began to respond to political questions in a similar manner, were developing something of an ambivalent attitude towards the press. Rock journalism, as has been stated, had essentially become a new literary and journalistic form by the late 1960s, and it was certainly responsible to a considerable extent for the elevation and intellectualisation of rock music which occurred during this period. Simultaneously, however, musicians like Dylan appeared to feel pressurised into answering endless, and often excessively probing or misdirected, questions by the very journalists who had first supported them and bestowed on them accolades of artistic integrity. Music journalists now wielded a great deal of power; a negative review from a respected rock journalist was a blow even to the most blasé of musicians. Thus, many popular musicians developed a certain wariness of the music press, and evasiveness in interviews could be said, in part, to result from this, at least in Dylan's case. Nevertheless, evidently Bob Dylan was no longer willing to represent the role of the politically conscious folk musician, either through his music or in interviews. His 'country music' album *Nashville Skyline*, released in 1969, was considered by many to be his decisive statement to this effect. As one biographer of Dylan has stated,

> *Nashville Skyline* found pop's greatest poet apparently abandoning allusion, allegory and anything approaching deep meaning or mystery in favour of trite blandishments … The music, too, was … mostly perfunctory; a series of routine country arrangements that wouldn't have sounded out of place on a Merle Haggard or Charley Pride record.[85]

The album was not received well; however, it did not, as many feared, represent the end of Dylan's career as a 'pop poet'. Rather, it could be argued that, at this stage in his career, and influenced by the external social and political climate, Dylan felt more need to escape from his erstwhile persona and circumvent the intensely political, intellectualising discourse that had surrounded him since his folk revival days.

Other 'new aesthetic' singer-songwriters were certainly not as aloof as Dylan when they discussed their music with the press, but, when interviewed, it was clear that many of them no longer felt certain that they, as musicians, should be instructing or radicalising their audience when it came to American political affairs. *Rolling Stone* contained extensive editorials on current affairs throughout the late 1960s and 1970s; the magazine provided coverage of all the major socio-political events of the period, from Vietnam and the Altamont Festival to Watergate and beyond. Yet the musicians whose lengthy interviews were the prime attraction for the readership of the magazine were, by comparison, tentative and vague when it came to the subject of politics. David Crosby, an ex-revival musician, revealed to editor Ben Fong-Torres, in the wake of the Kent State shootings, 'I don't dig politics. I don't

---

85 Andy Gill, *My Back Pages: Classic Bob Dylan, 1962–1969* (London, 1998), p. 137.

think politics is a workable system any more. I think they gotta invent something better.'[86] Singer-songwriter Arlo Guthrie, the son of Woody Guthrie, voiced similar sentiments in an interview of 1969. As he stated, 'all political systems are on the way out. Peace is the way. I don't get involved in the world outside. I create my own. I stay with my friends. We're in the same boat and we don't believe we should get out of the boat.'[87]

Paul Simon, another former revivalist who subsequently became one of the most distinguished songwriters of his generation, displayed a dislike of proselytising when he attempted to explain his position with regard to 'messages' in his music and the question of whether he was obliged to 'teach' his audience:

> Everybody's woken up. We're right in the middle of a nightmare; everybody is wide awake ... I'm just writing the way I feel and the way I feel reflects the part of society that I'm in. It's not a teaching thing, or I'm not trying to hip somebody to something they don't know because everybody knows that.[88]

Simon's response to the question of politics and music seemed to reflect a mixture of unwillingness and confusion. He would remain more politically conscious than many of his peers, particularly towards the end of the 1970s, when he began to work with South African musicians and to compose songs which depicted their culture and plight. Towards the United States, however, Simon seemed to maintain a more uncertain stance. His song 'American Tune', written in 1973, illustrated this confusion. The song was composed to the tune of a Bach chorale which was often used as a hymn, and its lyrics, while evoking images of the Pilgrim Fathers and describing the hopes of immigrants and their forebears, depicted a world in which souls are 'battered' and dreams 'shattered and driven to [their] knees'. In his analysis of the song, which comprised part of a study of images of the United States in popular song, Timothy Scheurer perceived a message of ultimate disillusionment, which he linked to the events in American politics which coincided with the composition of the song – namely, Nixon's re-election, Vietnam, Altamont and Kent State:

> ... [Simon] closes [the song] with a reference to those who come 'in the age's more uncertain hours' singing an 'American Tune'. He is seemingly trying to make a universal assumption about Americans and how this song of our American spirit seems to come forth during times of trial, but Simon does not see regeneration of the trial as the Pilgrims did.[89]

While 'American Tune' may be interpreted rather less pessimistically, for Simon too, the innocence and optimism of the folk revival days were apparently no more, and,

---

86 Ben Fong-Torres, 'David Crosby: The *Rolling Stone* Interview', *Rolling Stone*, 23 June 1970.

87 Quoted in Jack Batten, 'Stoned on Rock, Stoned on Drugs', *Saturday Night*, December 1969, 20. See also Pat Morris, 'Guthrie the Goatherd', *Crawdaddy*, June 1973.

88 Lorraine Alterman, 'Paul Simon: The *Rolling Stone* Interview', 28 May 1970.

89 Timothy E. Scheurer, *Born in the USA: The Myth of America in Popular Music from Colonial Times to the Present* (Jackson, MI and London, 1991), p. 188.

as his songs grew increasingly complex, so too did his view of his homeland become more ambiguous and uncertain.

Even two of the most politically active revivalists, Joan Baez and Phil Ochs, softened their straightforwardly political stance. Baez (although accused by *Village Voice* journalists of anachronistic political naivety) was, by 1968, prepared to admit that a changing musical climate required a new creative approach which was not simply comprised of political beliefs set to music: '[T]here are two approaches to music. One is, "Man, I'm a musician and I got nothin' to do with politics. Just let me do my own thing." And the other is that music's going to save the world ... I think that music's somewhere in between.'[90]

Phil Ochs had been one of the darlings of the 'great boom'; his song 'I Ain't Marching Anymore' became an anthem for the 1960s generation.[91] However, Ochs found that, by the early 1970s, his very straightforward style of protest songwriting was no longer appropriate or acceptable. In order to adapt to changing times, he became a nostalgia artist, performing songs of the 1950s; he recognised that the style of songwriting which had brought him to prominence in the early 1960s was simply outdated: '[The old protest songs are] too obvious, too easy. Just say what Nixon's doing and putting it into a rhyme scheme. And it's embarrassing to sing.'[92] As the 1970s progressed, however, Ochs found that the new musical order of 1970s had fatally damaged his creativity. Steeped increasingly in alcoholism and despair, Ochs committed suicide in 1976. Brian Walsh, who saw Phil Ochs perform at the Toronto Riverboat, considered the singer's story to be symbolic of the fate of 1960s idealism:

> Phil Ochs kind of personified the pathos, for me, of the 'sixties. Here's the guy who ... was writing protest music that was better than Bob Dylan's ... His protest music was incredible, powerful stuff. And then the Chicago Convention happens, in 1968. And it breaks him. It breaks him how ... how so many of the hippies were all talk and no action. Dylan breaks him by ... by releasing *Nashville Skyline* ... For Ochs it was ... not the electric guitar, that wasn't the problem. It was ... that he was making music of no consequence. That was the sell-out.[93]

In general, therefore, as a result of changing political, social and cultural trends, American songwriters who had begun their careers during the folk revival were no longer willing to associate themselves with political crusades or commentary on American society. Though they felt angered and outraged at the tumultuous events which were unfolding in their country, they no longer seemed eager to campaign or fight. The optimism which had characterised the folk revival of the early decade, and the vision of a united, diverse nation which it had engendered, were no longer

---

90   John Grissim, Jr, 'Joan Baez: The *Rolling Stone* Interview', *Rolling Stone*, 7 December 1968.

91   The songs of Phil Ochs were frequently featured in the magazine *Broadside*, the most overtly political of early 1960s revival magazines. See, for example, the edition of October 1962.

92   Billy Altmarr, 'Phil Ochs Marches it All Back Home', *Crawdaddy*, January 1974.

93   Brian Walsh, in discussion with the author, Toronto, 8 October 2002.

compatible with the more introverted stance of these musicians. Now, like David Crosby and Arlo Guthrie, musicians sought to escape from 'the system' altogether.

Escape was, indeed, a key factor in much of the music of American performers and songwriters during this time. Psychedelia and its drug culture associations, with which some former revivalists, such as The Grateful Dead and Scottish-born folk performer Donovan, experimented, represented one avenue of escape for musicians. Other folk-based songwriters, in evading political topics, chose to focus on themselves and escape into their own inner worlds of emotional turmoil and introspection. James Taylor serves as a representative example of such a songwriter. In March 1973, Taylor was the subject of *Time* magazine's cover story; he was considered by the writers to be the epitome of the 'bittersweet and low' sounds of a 'softening' rock music world.[94] A recovering drug addict who had spent some time in a mental hospital, Taylor wrote many acoustic, new-aesthetic folk-style songs about his personal experiences and difficulties. 'Fire and Rain', from the album *Sweet Baby James*, described his anguished reaction to the suicide of his girlfriend; 'Hey Mister That's Me Upon the Jukebox' recounted feelings of alienation and pain experienced while hearing one of his own songs played on a San Francisco jukebox. Janis Ian, Don McLean and, indeed, Joni Mitchell, were also confessional and introspective songwriters whose work largely consisted of complex illustrations of inner states of mind and personal experiences and troubles. Many of those musicians who were, by the turn of the decade, being described as 'folk', were writing music in this personalised style, a style that contrasted greatly with the socially focused music of the earlier revival folk performers. As far as *Time* magazine was concerned, this new sound represented 'a progress toward harmony and thoughtfulness or a tragic slide into a mood of enlightened apathy'.[95]

As has been stated, escape into the tranquillity of rural life was another important trend for musicians in the late 1960s and 1970s. In the Canadian context, this concern with the countryside was frequently perceived as quintessentially 'Canadian', but, in reality, this was a trend which was reflected in the music and lifestyles of popular musicians throughout America, Canada and, indeed, the United Kingdom during this time. Few were the songwriters who chose to base themselves entirely in an urban setting; countless popular musicians retreated to the country to write songs and escape from the pressures of celebrity. Rural imagery and celebration of tranquillity were common in the work of many songwriters of this period, from Bob Dylan to Tom Paxton. However, one of the most unique examples of this rural music was that of The Band.

The Band, all the members of which were Canadian (with the exception of Arkansas-born Levon Helm, the drummer and singer) had not been part of the folk revival *per se*. Although, during their years in Toronto as The Hawks, they had been acquainted with Yorkville and its music, they had played rhythm and blues, and, when they provided the backing music for Bob Dylan on his 'electric' tour in 1966, they were perceived by many purists as the very enemies of the folk revival. However, after the group settled with Dylan in Woodstock, New York, in the late

---

94   'James Taylor: One Man's Family of Rock', *Time*, 1 March 1973.
95   Ibid.

1960s, they began to experiment with acoustic music, performing together with unamplified guitars, fiddles, mandolins and accordion. Their principal songwriter, Robbie Robertson, developed an interest in American history, an interest which was reflected in his compositions. The Band performed songs such as 'The Night They Drove Old Dixie Down' and 'King Harvest Has Surely Come', which evoked images of nineteenth-century rural America, utilising acoustic instruments. Photographs of the group which appeared in the late 1960s depicted them almost as characters from the songs they sang; the black-and-white pictures showed moustached men in hats and suits, grouped together in rural settings. The debut album of the group, *Music from Big Pink*, was heralded as an artistic triumph, a remarkably unique departure from other contemporary albums. The reverence for traditional American folk styles, from both black and white cultures, was certainly in keeping with the spirit of the folk revival of the early decade, but The Band were a reclusive group whose music could be said to represent a deliberate evasion and retreat from all that was going on in the contemporary world. As Canadians who played music that seemed recognisably American in its origins, it appeared to be the intention of The Band to transcend all nationalist concerns and avoid being perceived so narrowly as neither American nor Canadian. The Band certainly retreated from politics and society, but they also retreated from their musical peers, leading their listeners to escape from the present society and all its conflicts into a peaceful, hazy rural setting.[96]

Until the advent of punk rock, with its harrowingly direct social messages, much of popular music of the 1970s would provide escape for the audience into quasi-mythical worlds. British groups which were very popular and influential at this time in North America – including the phenomenally successful rock band Led Zeppelin, and 'progressive rock' groups such as Pink Floyd, The Moody Blues, Yes, and Jethro Tull – also borrowed from folk traditions, but, in doing so, were inclined, like The Band (although in some cases with a far lesser degree of sophistication), to use those traditions to create countries of the imagination.[97] In the case of many of these groups, this process would enter the realms of mythology and become grossly overblown, to the extent that it became the subject of humorous parody in the 1984 film *This Is Spinal Tap*.[98] The folk idiom, in these instances, was associated with

---

96 For a contemporary account of the ethos of the Band, see Jay Cocks, 'Down to Old Dixie and Back', *Time*, 12 January 1970. The Band had the distinction of being the first rock group to be featured on the magazine's cover.

97 For example, Jethro Tull performed on stage in medieval-style costumes and evoked the medieval era through such songs as 'The Witch's Promise'. Led Zeppelin's most famous song, the evocative 'Stairway to Heaven', used recorders to create a folk sound and was allegedly inspired by the works of fantasy writer J.R.R. Tolkien. The Moody Blues produced a number of successful 'concept albums' with philosophical lyrics, Indian instrumentation and lush orchestrations.

98 *This is Spinal Tap*, dir. Rob Reiner (1984). Many punk rockers were intensely critical of the 1970s rock music which had preceded their movement. See 'Anthems of a Blank Generation', *Time*, 11 July 1977. Canadian popular music critic Jack Batten also expressed a sense of jadedness in his critique of the 1970s rock world, 'Confessions of a Retired Rock Critic', *Saturday Night*, March 1973.

history, myth and imagination, rather than with what was most pertinent, pressing and rooted in reality.⁹⁹

It is evident, therefore, that American 'new aesthetic' folk musicians had moved beyond concerns of politics by the end of the 1960s. The optimism which had surrounded the work and vision of the folk revivalists of the early decade was no longer present. Folk-style musicians no longer perceived their purpose to be that of instructing or informing their audiences in the direct manner which had been employed by folk revivalist musicians, and many chose to evade all societal, and national, concerns by creating new worlds in which to situate their music.

In discussing the differences between Canadian and American folk musicians at this time, at least in so far as they were perceived by journalists and their audiences, it is worthwhile to discuss briefly the position of performers such as Joni Mitchell and Neil Young, who were perceived as integral to the American scene, no matter how strongly Canadian journalists believed in their 'Canadian' qualities. Robert A. Wright has made their situation, and the situation of other prominent Canadians such as Gordon Lightfoot and Bruce Cockburn, the subject of his short study. In his opinion, their music, though perceived and celebrated as Canadian, during the 'euphoric nationalism of the Centennial era', 'owed less to the benevolence of the newly-created CRTC and the adulation of the nationalist music press in Canada than it did to the influence of American folk-protest music'. He considers songs such as Young's 'Ohio' and Mitchell's 'The Fiddle and the Drum' to be examples of the American protest tradition which had been 'co-opted' by Canadians, but proceeds to argue that

> [m]uch Canadian pop music in these years appeared stridently anti-American, but, in truth, thoughtful Canadian song-writers like Gordon Lightfoot, Joni Mitchell and Neil Young were suspicious of the new Canadian nationalism and profoundly ambivalent about the United States. Revulsion for 'official' America and sympathy for American youth combined in the songs of these musicians to produce some of the most poignant pop music of the Sixties generation.¹⁰⁰

Robert Wright is correct in his estimation of the music of these folk performers. It could be argued, furthermore, that these musicians, being eager neither to be considered 'typically Canadian' nor American, were, like many of their successful peers in both countries, eschewing national labels altogether. The label of 'Canadian', though at times perceived by musicians such as Gordon Lightfoot as limiting and frustrating, was perhaps more benign and positive, and so it was sporadically adopted by these musicians, particularly after the frenzied nationalism of the Centennial period had begun to wane. However, when Mitchell and Young rejected the label of 'American', they did not only do so as Canadians, but also in company with their American peers, who now wished, especially considering the current political climate, that their music move beyond all such considerations and associations.

99 For more information on the progressive rock 'movement', see Kevin Holme-Hudson (ed.), *Progressive Rock Reconsidered* (New York and London, 2002).
100 Wright, 'Dream, Comfort, Memory, Despair', p. 283.

It is clear, therefore, that, in the wake of the folk revival, those musicians whose work continued to display the influence of folk music had very different objectives from those who had embraced and adopted the ethos of the revival movement in the early 1960s. This is not to suggest that the folk revival in America had been profoundly nationalist, or that the revival in Canada had never considered nationalist values. Rather, the revival in both countries, as has been demonstrated, adhered to a very loose definition of nation which embraced and celebrated many diverse kinds of music and cultures. 'Nation' in the folk 'boom' was a secondary concern; when defined, it was defined, basically, as a collection of varied peoples whose collective music styles were embraced by the revival. By the late 1960s, views of nation had been forced to change in both countries, ironically as the result of political, social and cultural events which had partially contributed to the demise of the folk revival itself. 'Nation', in both cases, became increasingly abstract, increasingly all-encompassing, and less considerate of diversity and detail. America became a force against which the young should now fight, and Canada was to be perceived as a rising, youthful, unified land. Folk music performers were considered in Canada to be typically Canadian, but in America they were frequently alienated and disillusioned. As this shift took place, the spirit of eclecticism and the definition of nation as varied and all-embracing, which had been so integral to the folk revival, was no longer so prevalent.

Conclusion

The demise of the 'great boom' of the folk revival was the result of internal and external factors. Younger revivalists had grown discontented with the perceived narrow agenda of the movement, and began to experiment with new, often 'electric' styles of music, while, simultaneously, changes to the political climates of both America and Canada undid much of the optimism and pluralistic character of the 1960s movement. As a consequence, folk music changed in scope and outlook, and issues of national identity crept into popular music expression. Young American musicians frequently retreated from politics, increasingly frustrated by the social unrest and political chaos of their nation, while Canadian musicians found themselves forced to contend with an enthusiastic, nationalist press and fledgling music industry which were determined to promote them as inherently 'Canadian' artists. The pluralistic dream of the early 1960s revival had faded as it grew outdated, and in the subsequent decade, 'folk music' though expanded as a musical category, had become fragmented in its outlook and purpose.

Chapter 5

Folk Since the 1970s: Diversity and Insularity

Introduction

The emergence of singer-songwriters was the most visible and prominent consequence of the folk revival from the late 1960s onwards. However, the 1970s also witnessed a dynamic growth of the branch of revival folk music which folklore scholar Neil Rosenberg identified as 'named-system': that is, music which could be said to belong traditionally to a particular regional, social or ethnic group, but was often revived and performed by musicians who did not belong to the group in question.[1] The 'great boom' of the folk revival promoted the growth of interest in traditional music styles such as bluegrass, 'old time' music and the blues. Performers such as The New Lost City Ramblers, who replicated the sounds of old-time Appalachian string-bands, and John Hammond Jr, son of a distinguished Columbia Records Executive, who sang the blues and, according to Ellen Stekert, 'def[ied] the ear with the eye', were at the forefront of these facets of the revival.[2] In the 1970s, although the 'boom' period of the popularity of folk music had passed, innumerable other genres of traditional folk and ethnic music enjoyed fruitful revivals. Jewish klezmer music underwent a dramatic renaissance in popularity, as did Celtic music from the British Isles, Ireland and Maritime Canada, and other, more obscure types of music such as ragtime. While the origins of these revivals may be traced to the folk revival of the previous decade, their scope and nature differed in many respects from the 'boom'. While interest in musical diversity had frequently been motivated by political concerns during the 'great boom', the ethnic revivals of the 1970s possessed no such motivation. In some ways, they could be viewed as nostalgic, even retrogressive, in their outlook and ethos. Such an interpretation seems to fit conventional notions that the 1970s was a period of apolitical escapism and introspection.

While there may be some evidence to confirm such an interpretation of the era, it is also true to state that the increasing interest in different styles of ethnic music,

---

1   The term is employed by Neil Rosenberg in his introduction to Neil Rosenberg (ed.), *Transforming Tradition: Folk Music Revivals Examined* (Urbana, IL and Chicago, IL, 1993), p. 4. The label is apt here, but it should be noted that many of those who did take part in 'ethnic revivals' did, in fact, 'belong' to the ethnic group in question, although in some cases 'membership' was tenuous or distant.

2   Ellen Stekert, 'Cents and Nonsense in the Urban Folksong Movement, 1930–1966', from Rosenberg (ed.), *Transforming Tradition*, p. 97. Stekert referred to named-systems revivalists as 'imitators' or 'emulators' (see ibid., p. 90).

and experimentation with various genres, during the 1970s was a precursor of the highly pluralistic, multi-generic 'world' music sounds of the late twentieth and early twenty-first centuries.

The Growth of the Ethnic Revival

The ethnic revivals which flourished in the 1970s were certainly a significant consequence of the folk boom of the previous decade. Mark Slobin, one of the first (and few) scholars to examine ethnic music revivals, believed that the folk revival of the 1960s, and the socio-political climate in which it was nurtured, created an ethnic awareness that, in turn, allowed the named-system music revivals to flourish in the subsequent decades. In his view, 'the humane internationalism and political activism which marked the folk revival's ideology fed directly into the civil rights movement, which in turn spurred on the new ethnicity.'[3] The main purpose of Slobin's work was, however, to question the utility of the term 'revival' with regard to the resurgence of ethnic music genres; he preferred to see so-called revivals as the 'reshaping' of culture, rather than as revivals of customs and cultures that had somehow disappeared. Slobin consequently asserted that the flourishing of ethnic revivals had come about as the result of the activities of dedicated and charismatic individuals who promoted the music genres in question until communities were reminded of their heritage and experienced a renaissance of ethnic pride. He focused particularly upon the klezmer revival of the 1970s, noting that it was as the result of the activities of a small group of individuals – 'historian-researcher types' such as Martin Schwartz and Henry Sapoznik, traditional musicians or 'repositories of traditional repertoire' such as Dave Tarras, and 'performance acolytes and band-creators' such as Andy Statman, Lev Liberman and the Klezmorim – that the klezmer revival came into being. These significant and energetic individuals 'laid the groundwork' for what would become 'a nationwide craze in the Jewish community'. Slobin added that, 'for smaller groups, like the Latvians [whose music was also revived in this period] it may take only two [activists] to create a movement.'[4] Slobin even applied his theory of community activists to the 1960s folk boom itself:

> Even in the case of a monster movement like the good old American 'folk revival' of the forties to sixties, about the same number of hard-core influential enthusiasts provided the spark for a musical explosion: the Lomaxes as collectors, Guthrie and Leadbelly as the sainted repositories, and Seeger, Seeger and more Seegers as popularisers and definers. It sometimes seems to me that one only needed Mike and Pete Seeger, the one [Mike] combing the hills for talent, learning every conceivable instrument, while the other [Pete] brought his charismatic presence to the job of pulling in both acolytes and the masses.[5]

The Canadian folk revival musician I. Sheldon Posen concurs with Slobin's view of the origins of the ethnic boom. In his view, those who had, throughout the folk

---

3   Mark Slobin, 'Rethinking "Revival" of American Ethnic Music', *New York Folklore*, 9/3–4 (1983), p. 41.
4   Ibid., p. 39.
5   Ibid.

revival of the 1960s, satisfied their hunger for roots through the adoption of the music of 'other' cultural groups, now found that 'they didn't have to go to "outside" groups for what they sought':

> Using criteria they had learned to apply to others, they could recontext and essentially validate a folk group they already belonged to, one that usually turned out to be their ethnic group. (I am thinking, for example, of the urban, Jewish, blues or bluegrass revival musicians who foregrounded their identity as the children of immigrants, invoked a small-town, East European, Jewish past, and founded Yiddish-singing klezmer bands.)[6]

The revival of Irish instrumental music in the 1970s and 1980s also enabled many Americans of Irish extraction to rediscover and validate their sense of heritage. While the 'great boom' did acknowledge and promote Irish music in North America, it had tended to focus mostly on vocals and ballad singing. Although Irish instrumental groups such as The Chieftains were established and known in North America in the 1960s, they did not generate the same interest as song-focused artists such as the popular and influential Clancy Brothers and Tommy Makem. The catalyst for the revival of Irish instrumental music in America was the celebration of the national Bicentennial in 1976. As part of the wealth of celebrations and commemorations of all aspects of American life and culture, the Smithsonian Institution sponsored a Festival of American Folklife, in which some 52 Irish musicians, singers and dancers from across the country participated. Their performances in numerous concerts and sessions during the weeklong festival not only pleased those who had gathered to hear them, but also gave the musicians themselves a chance to meet and perform with their fellows from other parts of the country. A formal reception at the Irish Embassy was provided for the musicians, an honour which Irish-born flautist Jack Coen considered to be the first real acknowledgement and gesture of appreciation for instrumentalists of his generation.[7] Furthermore, between 1976 and 1977, the traditional music company Rounder Records issued, for the first time, field recordings of Irish-American instrumentalists, and the recently-formed Folk Arts Department of the National Endowment for the Arts (NEA) funded a series of nationwide tours for a troupe of various Irish musicians calling themselves 'The Green Fields of America'. These successful tours continued to run for the next decade, reawakening interest in Irish roots music, and a sense of ethnic pride, for Irish Americans throughout the United States.[8]

---

6 I. Sheldon Posen, 'On Folk Festivals and Kitchens: Questions of Authenticity in the Folksong Revival', from Rosenberg (ed.), *Transforming Tradition*, p. 128. Mark Slobin also noted the fact that, in the klezmer revival, the 'remarkably talented pool of young Jewish-American instrumentalists' who had previously been playing bluegrass or American folk styles, 'could switch their allegiance to klezmer music from the repositories they were playing' (Slobin, 'Rethinking "Revival"', p. 40).

7 See the entry entitled 'USA' in Fintan Vallely (ed.), *The Companion to Irish Traditional Music* (Cork, 1999), p. 415.

8 Ibid. See also Steve Winick, 'The Musical Life of Mick Moloney', *Dirty Linen*, 48 (October–November 1993) for more on 'The Green Fields of America' and on the career of banjoist Mick Moloney, one of the key figures in the Irish-American music revival.

Irish-American musicians were not the only ones to benefit from this sort of federal sponsorship and support. The NEA's Folk Arts Department, headed by folk revival participant Bess Lomax Hawes, would provide similar opportunities for many American musicians of particular ethnic backgrounds; to this day, it continues to sponsor and promote a vision of American culture the eclecticism of which would have delighted the most idealistic of 1960s folk revivalists. The American Folklife Center of the Library of Congress in Washington, DC, also founded in 1976, has done similar work to ensure that American folklife and folk music is represented and accessible to the public in all its diversity.

It was not, however, merely those who 'belonged', ethnically and culturally, to the group in question who participated in ethnic revivals in the 1970s, as Neil Rosenberg pointed out in his essay on bluegrass revival music. Drawing once again upon the example of klezmer music, Rosenberg states that '[a]mong those who have enthusiastically embraced revived klezmer music are people who are either not Jewish or consider themselves Jewish but are considered by some other Jews to be Jewish in name only, or to be lapsed or marginal Jews.'[9]

As Slobin, Posen and Rosenberg have pointed out, the klezmer revival represented, in part, a rediscovery of ethnic identity on the part of revival musicians who had hitherto been interested in other, indigenous American, musical genres. It is perhaps risky to use the klezmer revival as a 'typical' example of ethnic revival music, since, as has been demonstrated throughout the study, the considerable Jewish involvement in the revival did arise, to a great extent, from unique socio-cultural circumstances. The sense of being integrated and yet separate which prevailed among Jewish youth who participated in the revival and in radical politics also, undoubtedly, influenced the klezmer revival. As Mark Slobin noted, the formation of the first klezmer bands occurred in 1976, the same year in which Irving Howe published his phenomenally successful history of the Eastern European Jewish experience, *World of Our Fathers*, a work which would also serve to enhance the reawakening ethnic consciousness and pride among Jewish Americans.[10] This pride, was, however, of an especially nostalgic character; many began to glorify the world of the *shtetl* and romanticise its intense hardships. Slobin does suggest that the klezmer revival reflected a 'streak of leftism' rather than being conservative or apolitical. Nevertheless, as previous chapters have shown, the secular Jewish left of the early twentieth century was dynamic and focused on present and future, while the world depicted by the klezmer revival was, often, that of bygone days. The activism celebrated was part of history. Indeed, some of the early klezmer performers themselves dressed in clothing and performed melodies which evoked the Eastern European past of their ancestors. For example, The Klezmorim were featured in a cartoon on the cover of their first album clad in immigrant dress and standing on a ship in New York harbour.[11]

9   Neil V. Rosenberg, 'Starvation, Serendipity and the Ambivalence of Bluegrass Revivalism', in Rosenberg (ed.), *Transforming Tradition*, p. 195.

10   Slobin, 'Rethinking "Revival"', p. 40. See Irving Howe with Kenneth Libo, *World of Our Fathers* (New York, 1976).

11   This is pointed out by Mark Slobin. See *The Klezmorim: First Recordings, 1976–78* (Arhoolie CD 309, 1989).

However, in other respects, the klezmer revival shared with other ethnic revivals similarities of outlook and agenda. As Rosenberg pointed out, it was not only Jewish people who warmed to the klezmer revival. For many non-Jews, the rediscovery of klezmer was undoubtedly linked to the popularity of the 1973 film of the musical *Fiddler on the Roof*.[12] The nostalgia of the film's themes of exploitation in the Old World and the promise of the New struck chords with the American viewing public at large, regardless of their ethnicity. Such ideas were also mirrored in other ethnic music revivals of the period, most notably the Irish music revival in America. According to Mark Slobin, the summer school of the Irish Arts Centre, located in Ireland, would become flooded annually by both Irish Americans and those of different heritage, who were attracted to the romantic ideal of the Irish past.[13]

A certain amount of nostalgia could also be perceived in some of the Canadian named-system revivals of the 1970s, or at least in the activities of groups who worked to preserve certain regional or ethnic traditions and to teach them to the wider population. The traditional folk scene in Canada, as represented by the quarterly bulletin of the Canadian Folk Music Society, was small in scale, but vibrant and thriving. Proponents of certain traditional music styles found eager audiences at the many Canadian regional folk festivals, from Mariposa and the Owen Sound Festival to the New Brunswick Miramichi Festival and the Edmonton Folk Festival. Often the performers, such as The Friends of Fiddler's Green (affiliated to the Toronto coffee-house Fiddler's Green) and the group Maple Sugar, were proud to call themselves the preservers of tradition. The former specialised in traditional Canadian folksong styles and dances (particularly Ontario clog dancing), while the latter described its music as 'pure traditional Canadian folk music'.[14] The performers were anxious that their forms of music be passed on to the next generation as 'their own' traditions – thus, the format which worked best for the named-system performers was the workshop, rather than the large stage.[15]

There is ample evidence that many traditional Canadian performers, such as Newfoundland bands Figgy Duff and The Wonderful Grand Band, were willing to experiment and to intermingle traditional and popular styles of music. Stringband, a folk group led by Bob Bossin, performed a mixture of original arrangements of Native, Anglophone and Francophone Canadian songs, and witty, satirical political songs. However, many named-system performers often found themselves accused of excessive conservatism and retrogressive traditionalism. The Canadian Folk Music Society, which represented and publicised such musicians, was attacked on more than one occasion for its 'stale' and excessively academic attitude towards folk music.[16] One young critic, writing in 1975, felt that the Society and its activities continued

12 *Fiddler on the Roof*, directed by Norman Jewison (United Artists, 1973)

13 Slobin, 'Rethinking "Revival"', p. 42.

14 Dorothy Hogan, 'Maple Sugar', *Canadian Folk Music Society Newsletter/Bulletin*, Vol. 13 No. 3, Fall 1978.

15 Tim Rodgers reported on the aptness of the workshop format for such musicians in 'Focus on Festival' in *Canadian Folk Music Society Newsletter/Bulletin*, Vol. 16 No. 3, July 1982.

16 Interesting correspondence on this topic was featured in Vol. 14 No. 1 of the *Newsletter* (Spring 1979).

to purvey the 'stodgy' belief that true 'folk music' constituted the performances of 'untrained, non-professional musicians.'[17] Not only did such a contention demonstrate that the debates over the scope and purpose of folk music – rampant since before the 'great boom' – had failed to be resolved, but it also illustrated the continuing links, whether actual or perceived, between traditional, named-system folk music activities and a romanticised view of the past with its purist view of folk culture.

Therefore, while the klezmer movement possessed particular aspects which were peculiar to its origins within the Jewish community, many of the ethnic revivals of the decade were characterised by a similar nostalgia which reinvented the pasts of a particular community as simpler, happier times.

Ethnic Revivals and the Culture of the 1970s

It is clear that the growth of ethnic revivals in the 1970s owed a great deal to the folk revival of the 1960s. Mark Slobin, as has been demonstrated, believed that the 'monster movement' of the 1960s and the ethnic revivals had sprung from fundamentally similar socio-cultural impulses. Concerns over authenticity and the middle-class romanticisation of the lower classes were also characteristics which the ethnic revivals shared with the folk revival of the 1960s. To emphasise the similarities among the movements, however, risks minimising the immense social and cultural changes which had taken place between the early 1960s and the 1970s, the era in which ethnic revivals began to flourish. As has been demonstrated, many former revivalists who became singer-songwriters in the late 1960s divorced themselves from political idealism and sought to create a music which was intensely individualistic and which could afford its listeners some escape from the contemporary world. Likewise, the ethnic revivals of the 1970s could be said to be manifestations of the same climate of escape, a climate which was created by the sentiments of disillusionment among Americans during this period.

While political activism was not completely absent during the 1970s, particularly with regard to the women's movement and environmental issues, there is no doubt that much of the idealism of the previous decade had been replaced by disappointment and bitterness. Richard Nixon's presidency, which had begun amid the tumult of 1968, ended with his disgraceful impeachment over the Watergate conspiracy. The Vietnam War, despite ever-growing protests from pacifists and war veterans alike, was escalated during Nixon's presidency, and would finally grind to a halt in 1975, bringing to a close one of the most bloody and controversial conflicts in American history. Such events had not only destroyed Nixon's reputation, but had also led to an unprecedented distrust of politics in general among the American public. Voting statistics showed a dramatic drop in the number of ballots cast during post-Nixon elections; one poll revealed that, in 1975, some 69 per cent of Americans believed that, over the previous ten years, US leaders had 'consistently lied to the people'.[18]

17 Barbara Long, 'Argue the Case for a New Definition of Folk Music', *Canadian Folk Music Society Bulletin*, Vol. 10 Nos. 1 and 2, December 1975.

18 Quoted in Peter N. Carroll, *It Seemed Like Nothing Happened: The Tragedy and Promise of America in the 1970s* (New York, 1982), p. 235.

According to Peter Carroll, this sense of disillusionment was not confined to the world of politics; people were now inclined to look upon doctors, lawyers, scientists, corporate leaders and all representatives of 'the dominant institutions of society' with suspicion.[19] This disorientating sense of pessimism and doubt was exacerbated by the fluctuations of the economy during the 1970s; unemployment, particularly among the young, was rife, and led both to an increase in crime and a decrease in university enrolment. Many young people, the spearheads of social change during the 1960s, had, apparently, become disillusioned and bitter by the 1970s.

In Canada, too, the optimism of the late 1960s had begun to wane somewhat. The northern nation of the continent also suffered economically during this period, but more disheartening still was the threat posed to national integrity by the increasingly volatile and militant *Quebecois* separatists. The gloom and anxiety of the decade was also, therefore, pervasive in Canada.

It could be argued that, during the 1970s, escapism and retreat became the preferred reaction to societal difficulties and economic uncertainties. Commentators and historians have described the many ways in which this escapist tendency manifested itself. For example, involvement in religion increased dramatically during the 1970s. While attendance at churches and synagogues was boosted, more remarkable were the many 'alternative' faiths and modes of religious expression which gained in strength at this time. The 1970s witnessed the growth in membership of cults and sects, the increased exploration of Eastern faiths such as Zen Buddhism and Hare Krishna, and the growing popularity of alternative Christian modes of expression such as charismatic movements, Pentecostalism and televangelists.[20]

In a similar manner, people sought to escape from harsh reality through an increased focus on themselves, both in physical and internal, psychological terms. The 1970s saw the increase in popularity of dieting, health foods, workouts, aerobics, martial arts and yoga.[21] More curious, perhaps, was the strong tendency towards self-analysis, and the desire for self-awareness and personal fulfilment which were exhibited by increasing numbers of people during the 1970s. Therapy sessions, self-help books and group counselling became popular as people sought greater self-awareness. As this aspect of Seventies culture blossomed, many contemporary critics such as Daniel Yankelovich, Edwin M. Schur, Christopher Lasch and Jim Houghan were disgusted.[22] Lasch declared that the self-awareness movement promoted nothing but 'the pursuit of happiness to the dead end of a narcissistic preoccupation with the

---

19 Ibid., pp. 235–6.

20 Ibid., pp. 247–9. See also Richard Michael Levine, 'Who's Your Guru?', a 1973 *Rolling Stone* article about the craze for religious experimentation. Reprinted in Ashley Kahn, Holly George-Warren and Shawn Dahl (eds), *Rolling Stone: The Seventies* (Boston, MA; New York; Toronto; London, 1998), pp. 102–5.

21 Douglas T. Miller, *On Our Own: Americans in the Sixties* (Lexington, MA, 1996), pp. 340–1.

22 Daniel Yankelovich, *New Rules: Searching for Self-Fulfillment in a World Turned Upside-Down* (New York, 1981); Edwin M. Schur, *The Awareness Trip: Self-Absorption Instead of Social Change* (New York, 1976); Christopher Lasch, *The Culture of Narcissism: American Life in an Age of Diminishing Expectations* (New York, 1978); Jim Houghan, *Decadence: Radical Nostalgia, Narcissism, and Decline in the Seventies* (New York, 1975).

self'.[23] More hopeful, Daniel Yankelovich suggested that people should focus less on themselves in their search for awareness, and should, instead, use newfound insights towards the creation of 'an ethic of commitment'.[24] However, most critics could see only destructive selfishness in the awareness movement, and, in 1976, the radical writer Tom Wolfe summed up their sentiments in a *New Yorker* magazine article of August 1976 when he dubbed the era 'the Me-Decade'.[25] In comparison to the previous decade, it certainly seemed as though people were, in increasing numbers, turning inwards and avoiding political and societal responsibility.

Another important manifestation of the tendency towards escape was an increasing sense of nostalgia in popular culture. The past, like religion or the self-awareness quest, was supposed to provide people with 'a sense of direction' for the present.[26] However, ultimately, in the hands of the media, history became romanticised, and the glorification of the past served as a panacea for the ills of the contemporary world. As Jim Houghan remarked, nostalgia for the past may have begun as an 'unselfconscious perception of loss', but it quickly became 'an industry' in 1970s America, something to be 'served, rather than felt'.[27] Nowhere was this more evident than in the many celebrations held to commemorate the American Bicentennial in 1976; according to Peter Carroll, the national past was, during the celebrations, frequently trivialised, popularised and made into 'mass entertainment'.[28] Besides the Bicentennial festivities, Americans enjoyed a diet of nostalgic television programmes and films during the 1970s. *The Waltons*, the tale of a large family living in the Blue Ridge Mountains during the Great Depression, romanticised traditional values, poverty and rural simplicity. A wave of nostalgia for the 1950s led to the immense popularity of the comedy series *Happy Days* and the films *American Graffiti* and *Grease*.

Perhaps the most astonishing manifestation of the nostalgic climate of the period was the unprecedented success of the ABC television miniseries *Roots*, first broadcast in January 1977. The creation of African-American writer Alex Haley, *Roots* recounted the history of a black family, beginning with its pre-slavery origins in Africa. The series proved tremendously popular; it was estimated that over 130 million people (more than half of the US population) saw at least one episode, while Haley's book sold some 900,000 copies in just one month.[29] *Roots* inspired a craze for genealogy, as well as a growing industry of historical romance novels; it helped to ensure that preoccupation with and romanticisation of the past and of one's own ethnic and cultural background were powerful trends among Americans in the 1970s. However, the past which was being celebrated was, in many respects, a version of history which was less a dynamic precursor of the present than it was a comforting means of escape from a troubling contemporary world.

---

23   Lasch, *Culture of Narcissism*, p. xv.
24   Yankelovich, *New Rules*, p. xviii.
25   Quoted in Carroll, *It Seemed Like Nothing Happened*, p. 250.
26   Ibid., p. 298.
27   Houghan, *Decadence*, p. 195.
28   Carroll, *It Seemed Like Nothing Happened*, p. 297.
29   Statistics from ibid., p. 297.

It is possible, then, to link the growth of ethnic revivals in the 1970s to this escapist and nostalgic fascination with the past. As Slobin and Posen have demonstrated, the ethnic revivals came about, in part, as the result of former revivalists turning back to their own cultures rather than focusing on 'other' musical genres. As they rediscovered their roots, they did so often with a conservative and retrogressive agenda. For example, the klezmer revival brought back to life a genre of music which had almost disappeared with the *shtetl* culture of Eastern European Jews. Its revival, thus, though highly fruitful and timely, essentially represented the romanticisation by middle-class, urban Jews of their forebears' poverty-stricken past. Similarly, other ethnic revivals, such as the Celtic revival, harked back to a simpler, rural past as a reaction to the troubles of the contemporary world.

Burt Feintuch, an American musician who participated enthusiastically in the revival of Northumbrian pipe music in the north-east of England, has noted the continued romanticising tendencies of certain named-system revivals. He suggests that named-system revivalists remain far more conservative and preservation-orientated than are those musicians who are dubbed 'traditional' performers of the genre.[30] Believing that they are 'bolstering a declining musical tradition', the named-system advocates become preoccupied with that sense of tradition and of the past.[31] As a result, they effectively 'recast' the musical culture in question, setting at the centre of their redefined canon for the genre those 'model' musicians who fit their definition of an archetypical old master. As Feintuch states, revivalists 'tend to see models as representing grass-roots communities of musicians. Idiosyncrasy wouldn't work; models are representations of an idealized view of musical sound, technique, and social setting as they exist in a romanticized organic community.'[32] For example, in the context of Northumbrian piping, Feintuch notes the central role played by 1920s traditional piper Tom Clough in the historical canon of the revivalists; he is idealised as 'a man of the earth, a true Northumbrian' by virtue of the fact that his repertoire of music was passed down to him by the elder members of his family.[33] According to Feintuch, the fact that Clough learned his music from his elders actually makes him the exception rather than the rule in the context of Northumbrian piping. However, the romantic revivalists have reinvented the history of the genre to suggest that, in fact, the reverse is the case.

Such curious reinterpretations of the past seem to have been commonplace in the named-system revivals of the 1970s onwards – a sense of history and a romantic sense of place became paramount concerns amid a general climate of social dislocation and uncertainty. While it is true that the folk revival of the previous decade had exhibited similar romanticising tendencies with regard to the music of the inhabitants of the Southern and Western states, their reinventions, though often romantic in nature, were, to a considerable extent, informed by the social and political activism of the

30   Neil Rosenberg calls this sort of neo-conservatism in named-systems revivals 'romantic purism'. See 'Starvation, Serendipity and Ambivalence', p. 197.
31   Burt Feintuch, 'Musical Revival as Musical Transformation', in Rosenberg (ed.), *Transforming Tradition*, p. 184.
32   Ibid., p. 189.
33   Ibid.

present.[34] However, during the 1970s, named-system revivals seemed to represent more of a retreat from the present, the embracing of a romantic, semi-fictitious world and identity in order to escape from the demands of the age. North Americans in the 1970s were in search of strong anchors, and, for many, the rediscovery of one's ethnic roots represented one such anchor. The musical results of such a rediscovery were often interesting and rich, but simultaneously, to some extent at least, they conveyed the strong retrogressive and escapist characteristic which was prevalent during the 'me decade'.

Towards a 'World Music': The Other Side of the 1970s and Beyond

While there seems to be much validity in the view that revivals in traditional folk music reflected an escapist tendency in 1970s culture, such an interpretation does not do full justice to the folk music activities, and to the activities of the music industry in general, in that decade. While there were, undoubtedly, elements within the many named-systems revivals which desired to preserve their chosen genre and keep it rooted in a nostalgic conservatism, very few of the major 1970s ethnic revivals remained in a static or insulated condition, particularly as they continued to gain strength in the last two decades of the century. For example, Andy Statman and Dave Tarras, founder figures within the klezmer revival, far from being preservationists of 'pure' examples of the genre, produced an album of their own, innovative, klezmer-styled compositions in 1984.[35] Such experimentation paved the way for latter-day klezmer bands such as The New Orleans Klezmer All-Stars, a group which fuses the sounds of traditional klezmer with cajun, jazz and other styles of music.[36] In the Irish music revival, Dublin-based group The Chieftains, who had attained a large following in North America, and who epitomised, for many, traditional Irish music, became more experimental by the 1980s, moving from 'pure' Irish folk music to recording with major rock musicians such as Sting, Van Morrison and Mick Jagger.[37] Minnesota-born banjoist Leroy Larson, a key figure in the revival of Scandinavian music in the 1970s, mingled traditional and 'old time' Scandinavian music with original jazz-banjo and ragtime compositions.[38] Maritime Canadian music, particularly in the hands of the younger generation of musicians who came to prominence in the 1980s, also attained an experimental streak, and fiddlers such as Natalie MacMaster have now begun to fuse their traditional music with bluegrass, classical and electronic music styles.[39] The immense popularity of *Riverdance*, the stage show which mingles traditional Irish dancing and music with African-

---

34 See Chapter 2.

35 The Andy Statman Klezmer Orchestra, *Klezmer Suite* (Shanachie 21005, 1984)

36 The New Orleans Klezmer All-Stars, *Flesh Out the Past* (Shanachie 9015, 1999).

37 See The Chieftains, *The Wide World Over* (RCA/Victor 09026-63917-2, 2002), for an anthology of the group's collaborations with other musicians.

38 See 'European-American Music' in Stanley Sadie and H. Wiley Hitchcock (eds), *The New Grove Dictionary of American Music* Vol. 2 (New York, 1986), p. 74.

39 See, for example, Natalie McMaster, *In My Hands* (WEA, 1999) and Ashley MacIsaac, *Hi How are you Today?* (A&M Records, 1996).

American, Russian and Spanish song and dance, has helped to strength associations of Irish music with musical eclecticism and multi-culturalism.

Evidence of experimentation and growing multi-culturalism was also present in the 'mainstream' popular music scene of the 1970s. Despite the fact that the era was frequently characterised as a period of banality and overblown, escapist rock music, the 1970s also witnessed many important new musical innovations. For example, during the '70s, a new generation of black musicians, with unique and influential styles, came to prominence – in particular, The Wailers from Jamaica, who were largely responsible for the surge of interest in reggae in the mid-1970s, Sly and the Family Stone, who led the 'funk' movement of the early decade, and Stevie Wonder, whose sophisticated *Songs in the Key of Life* (1976) was the first American album to enter the US charts at number one.[40] White musicians were experimenting too – although progressive rock was often dismissed as pretentious, musicians in this genre, such as Jon Lord of Deep Purple and Rick Wakeman of Yes, were attempting to fuse classical and popular music.[41] Led Zeppelin's experimentation with 'world' music styles was, similarly, criticised and dismissed, but the group was heavily influenced by the music of North Africa and India, to the extent that, in 1994, guitarist Jimmy Page and vocalist Robert Plant travelled to Morocco to re-record some of the group's original songs with local musicians.[42] Paul Simon, likewise, became deeply interested in the music of South Africa, and his work with musicians there culminated in his award-winning *Graceland* album of 1986.[43] The 1970s were also notable for the advent of punk rock. Although critics debated its 'artistic' credentials, there is no doubt that the punk movement, with its minimalist musical style and provocatively violent lyrics, was markedly innovative, a dramatic contrast to the music which had preceded it.[44] Therefore, the notion that the 1970s was, above all, a reactionary and retrogressive period for music is disproved by an examination of some of the musical activities of this era. While there may have been elements of conservatism in the origins of some of the ethnic revivals of the 1970s, these revivals were destined to progress beyond their traditional boundaries in a general music scene which was becoming increasingly pluralistic.

The development of 'world music' in the late 1980s would enable many roots music styles to develop further and to encounter new and growing audiences. The concept of 'world music' as a distinctive genre was developed in the mid-1980s, essentially

40 Joe Stuessy, *Rock & Roll: Its History and Stylistic Development* (Englewood Cliffs, NJ, 1990), pp. 341–6.

41 Jon Lord composed a Concerto for Rock Group and Orchestra in the late 1960s, a piece which Deep Purple continues to perform with orchestras today. Rick Wakeman specialised in ambient keyboard compositions such as those which appeared on his 'concept album' *The Six Wives of Henry VIII*.

42 Jimmy Page and Robert Plant, *No Quarter* (Fontana 526 362-2, 1994).

43 Paul Simon, *Graceland* (Warner Bros CDW 46430, 1986).

44 Critic Noel Coppage, for example, was doubtful about the merits of punk: 'A mass music, the late Seventies demonstrate, cannot be Art and will not very long even try to be' ('Requiem for the Seventies', *Stereo Review*, July 1979). Lester Bangs was a little more optimistic about the future of punk in his article 'Pop Music in the Eighties', *Stereo Review*, January 1980.

as a marketing strategy through which to promote global (particularly non-Western) styles of music.[45] It is certainly true that the folk revivalists of the 1960s were aware of, and interested in, global music styles – *Sing Out!* contained features on little-known folk traditions from around the world during the early 1960s, and musicians such as Pete Seeger and The Weavers experimented with international songs and instruments from the immediate post-war era onwards. However, the primary purpose of world music distributors and record labels was to make available the work of hitherto unknown traditional musicians from around the globe; certain world music companies, such as Putomayo and the 'Rough Guide' series of recordings produced by the World Music Network, were established primarily as fund-raising sources for the frequently deprived and troubled communities from which world musicians came. Since the late 1980s, music from around the world has become increasingly familiar to Western audiences in all its diversity, although very few artists promoted through world music are well known individually in the West, perhaps because, as has been suggested, global music styles, though widely appreciated, tend not to generate a mass appeal. Indeed, it is possible to argue that world music as a genre encourages the sort of educated elitism and exclusivity promoted by the 1960s folk revival. Simon Frith demonstrates that, as world music developed as a genre in the late 1980s and early 1990s, it was presented to audiences as a serious alternative to 'predictable' popular music. Ethnomusicologists provided 'liner notes' for world music CDs, giving the genre intellectual gravitas and demonstrating to consumers that 'proper appreciation' of world music depended on knowledge of 'real' culture as opposed to what Frith terms 'tourist memories'.[46] Such claims, of course, resurrect the familiar 'authenticity debate' once again; the very academics used to endorse world music expressed concerns that artists were being promoted and valued only if they performed according to 'authentic' standards set by their Western listeners, and that listeners would only appreciate those who managed to appear sufficiently 'exotic' and 'other'.[47] On the other hand, despite such concerns, it has been argued that world music, with its unique blending of the small-scale and local with international marketing forces, represents 'a remarkable decentralization, democratization, and dispersal of the music industry at the expense of the multinational and national oligopolies'.[48] Frith also notes that world music recognises, to a greater degree than did folk revivalists of the 1960s, that change and innovation form part of traditional musical cultures.[49] Despite continued debates over 'authenticity', therefore, there is

---

45   The 'creation' of world music as a genre is apparently directly traceable to the summer of 1987, when eleven independent record company representatives met in London, UK, to discuss marketing strategies for their international pop music. See Simon Frith, 'The Discourse of World Music', in Georgina Born and David Hesmondhalgh (eds), *Western Music and its Others: Difference, Representation, and Appropriation in Music* (Berkeley, CA; Los Angeles, CA; London, 2000), pp. 305–6.

46   Ibid., p. 307.

47   See ibid. and 'World Music' in John Shepherd et al. (eds), *The Continuum Encyclopedia of Popular Musics of the World* Vol. 1 (London and New York, 2003), p. 197.

48   Peter Manuel, quoted in Frith, 'The Discourse of World Music', p. 315.

49   Ibid., p. 312.

more recognition and tolerance of musical experimentation and 'fusion' than there was among certain factions of '60s revivalists.

The relationship between Westerners and non-Western 'world musicians' is, similarly, not always based on a straightforward recognition of 'difference'. Musicians who began their careers within the Westernised popular music industry – such as Peter Gabriel, Paul Simon and Robert Plant – have created new artistic identities for themselves, not as 'imitators' or as 'advocates' of world music styles, but as Western musicians interested in merging their own musical pasts and backgrounds with those of other cultures, and in finding linkages among global musical styles while considering themselves to be part of 'global' culture.[50] They seek, perhaps, to undo some of the damage caused by the worst excesses of Western cultural and musical colonisation by seeking to be informed by, and find a mutual understanding with, musicians of non-Western cultures. World music, despite continued debates over cultural imperialism, appropriation and authenticity, has offered viable and genuine alternatives to the music industry and to the public. It is possible to argue that it represents, in many ways, something of a fulfilment of many of the pluralistic, multi-cultural aspirations of the 1960s folk revival; it has become a vibrant facet of twenty-first-century folk music. Modern-day resources, marketing, technology and the forces of globalisation have enabled some musical barriers to be broken down, and allowed Westerners to interact more directly, in more varied ways, and with more genuine mutuality, with musical cultures otherwise far removed from their own.

Conclusion

Revivals of particular musical styles, such as klezmer, Maritime Canadian and Celtic music, thrived from the 1970s onwards. Their prominence, in some ways, seemed more of an escape from contemporary society than the manifestation of an optimistic pluralist perspective, although many of the ethnic revivals of the 1970s did not remain static by any means, and fused with other styles of music while maintaining a vibrant distinctiveness. By the 1980s, world music had emerged as a new, pluralistic approach to the musical cultures of the globe, offering new influences to Western musicians and a new way of understanding musical cultures and processes. Alongside, and often overlapping with, the singer-songwriters and the ethnic music revivalists, world musicians offer, and continue to offer, new ways of understanding and defining folk music.

---

50   Robert Plant, initially a devotee of American blues music, has subsequently become preoccupied with finding linkages between this genre and African music styles. See web-based article 'Robert Plant Finds Blues Roots in the Sahara' on the 'Eye for Talent' website <http://www.eyefortalent.com/index.cfm/fuseaction/artist.articles_detail/artist_id/70/article_id/42.cfm> (accessed 13 October 2005). Peter Gabriel, former singer with British group Genesis, founded the World of Arts, Dance and Music (WOMAD) Festival in 1980 and the Real World record label in 1989. Paul Simon's *Graceland* has been discussed earlier in the chapter; his interest in world cultures, and in fusing world sounds in his music, remains strong.

Conclusion

From the first stirrings of folklore exploration in North America during the late nineteenth century, folk music has always maintained some relationship with the concept, and identity, of the nation. While, in other lands, folk music has been utilised by those in possession of a right-wing agenda – the case of Nazi Germany being the most dramatic – it is curious to note that those who have promoted the worth of folk music in twentieth-century North America have often been leftist in orientation. Because the agenda of the North American left has included the promotion of the dignity of the working classes, and, to an increasing degree, agitation for racial equality and an end to discrimination, their adoption of folk music has promoted a vision of nation which portrays the country as a patchwork of multifarious ethnic and regional cultures, and which celebrates this diversity as a source of strength. This vision was promoted most strongly during times in which the left wing was flourishing – as Chapters 1 and 2 have demonstrated, the pluralistic interpretation of folk culture gained in initial strength during the Great Depression, a period in which left-wing expression was prominent in America, and reached its apex during the early 1960s, which was the golden age of the civil rights movement and the New Left.

At various points in the work, it becomes difficult to compare the situation of folk music in Canada and America. This is particularly the case when charting the early development of the folk revival in the early twentieth century and inter-war period. It certainly seems that many of the crucial foundations for the revival were laid in the United States and resulted from the social and cultural conditions of that country. To attempt to force Canada into a comparison could prove reductive for both nations concerned. However, from the 1950s onwards, the folk revival grew in influence and popularity in both Canada and America, and proved significant and relevant for both countries in similar and contrasting ways. The study of Yorkville and Greenwich Village, presented in Chapter 3, illustrates the way in which the folk revival nurtured distinctive communities which formed unique relationships with the cities in which they had developed, and which represented attempts to manifest the ideals of diversity and fraternity in daily life.

Chapters 4 and 5 have illustrated how the folk revival's optimistic and pluralistic vision of North America was damaged by events of the late 1960s, and the ways in which folk music became more conservative and retrogressive during the 1970s, when it had lost many of its links with the left. It is equally important to note that, whatever its purpose had become during the 1970s, folk music, however it might be defined, had become an integral part of popular culture in North America. The folk revival had helped to give it a broad definition, a definition which encompassed everything from the modern music of singer-songwriters to the most purist and traditional of named-system revivals. Even if the agenda of its promoters had changed, the generic category of folk music in North America was now synonymous with pluralism and diversity. Indeed, it remains so to this day, and over the past three decades, it has become desirable for artists to continue to expand the pluralistic character of popular music, widening its boundaries ever further by fusing disparate genres and types of folk music. Experimentation and the defying of conventional boundaries have become desirable, challenging activities for contemporary popular musicians, and much of this spirit constitutes the legacy of the folk revival. If the folk revival intended to portray the North American continent as a rich patchwork of interweaving cultures, as a place where unity was achieved through diversity, then modern popular music is certainly striving to widen this vision to global proportions.

Since the folk revival, the presence of the solo singer-songwriter in the popular music scene has been constant. Not only have veteran Canadian and American solo performers such as Bob Dylan, Joan Baez, Neil Young, Joni Mitchell and Paul Simon remained phenomenally popular, in many cases continuing to attract huge concert audiences, but they have also inspired subsequent generations of soloists. To this day, singer-songwriters such as Sheryl Crowe, Alanis Morrissette, Tracy Chapman, Bryan Adams and Sting continue to be associated with introspective, socially conscious lyrics and acoustic instrumentation (or at least a sound which avoids the louder excesses of rock music). While some are denounced by critics for excessive seriousness and derivative music, many treat the modern folk-style performer with respect, considering him or her to be a worthwhile artist who, as Neil Rosenberg has said, 'trades broad commercial success for intellectual integrity, someone who deals with difficult social issues in the forum of popular culture'.[1] The folk revival was largely responsible for the association of solo performers with proficiency in songwriting and 'meaningful' messages. It is also worthwhile to note that many of the most successful solo performers are of Canadian origin – including Bryan Adams, K.D. Lang, Alanis Morrissette and Celine Dion (who, though not principally a songwriter, has attained immense popularity as a ballad singer). This helps to perpetuate the post-1967 myth that solo, folk-derived performance is a style particularly suited to Canadian musicians.

Suggestions for Further Research

While the study has attempted to explore many of the facets of the folk revival and its legacy in relation to the subject of national identity, there remains much that still needs to be uncovered and researched. Primarily, more focus is needed on the development of the folk revival in Canada. While the comparative perspective of this work has enabled a relatively developed historical outline of the revival in Canada, it remains necessary for scholars to delve into the rich history of the Canadian movement and to reveal the extent of its tremendous variety. This work has tended to focus above all on events in and surrounding Toronto, while vibrant folk music 'scenes' developed across the country, from Vancouver and Calgary to Halifax and St. John's. Histories of the revivals within individual regions and cities, and their

---

1   Neil Rosenberg, 'Introduction', in Neil Rosenberg (ed.), *Transforming Tradition: Folk Music Revivals Examined* (Urbana, IL and Chicago, IL, 1993), p. 10.

relationship to the folklore of that particular area, would prove invaluable. A study of the folk revival in Quebec, and its relationship to regional identity, and to the separatist movement, would be perhaps more significant still. This work has focused exclusively on English-speaking Canada, but no full understanding of the nationwide revival can be attained without knowledge of events and cultural movements within Quebec and among French-speaking minorities across the country. While in many ways the *Quebecois* revival movement embodied and represented issues and concerns that were peculiar to that province, it also formed an important part of the national movement, and must therefore be studied with its dual perspectives in mind.

More work is also needed on the various branches of the revival, in particular the revivals of specific musical genres. Both Robert Cantwell and Neil Rosenberg have published studies of bluegrass music which include detailed discussions of the revival of the 1960s and beyond. Histories of blues and country music have also examined the significance of the folk revival in the development of these genres. However, the many other ethnic and regional music revivals, such as klezmer, Celtic music, Eastern European music styles and others – which occurred in the late 1960s and early 1970s – require further study. In particular, scholars should focus on the correlation between these revivals and of the position, politics and outlook of the ethnic community in question at the time. They should also look at the motivation of those who became involved in particular ethnic revivals despite being unable to claim 'membership' of the ethnic community from which the music originated. Not only would such studies shed light on individual ethnic revivals in terms of basic history, membership and repertoire, but they would also raise important questions of identity and belonging which are raised, to a considerable extent, by this study in its discussion of the general folk revival of the 1960s.

Chapter 4 has also illustrated an interesting aspect of post-revival rock music history which could benefit from further exploration; namely, the 'imaginative landscapes' of rock groups of the late 1960s and early 1970s which were dubbed 'psychedelic' or 'progressive'. These groups, as has been demonstrated, developed a style of music which evoked rural and historical imagery and often made use of folk-style idioms. It would be worthwhile exploring some of the reasons behind such choices; although they are commonly attributed to the drug culture of the period, more might be said about the philosophies behind, and societal context for, such imagery, and the relationship between rock music of this kind and the folk revival, which, by this stage, was on the wane as a popular movement. The folk revivalists had, for reasons of their own, embraced rural music with a strong historical context; rock musicians would experiment with similar worlds, shaping them according to their own unique interpretations. Psychedelic and progressive rock music may, thus, represent another key to understanding the link between the folk revival of the early 1960s, and the broader music scene of the later decade.

Finally, it is important to consider the tremendous impact of the British music scene upon North America. Because much of this impact was felt most keenly in the realm of commercial, chart 'pop' music, it has played only an incidental role in the study. Nevertheless, folk music thrived in Britain, not merely through the music of revival performers such as Donovan, Bert Jansch or Martin Carthy, but also through revivals of specific music styles, as described in Chapter 4 – for example,

Northumbrian piping, Gaelic singing and traditional fiddling. Furthermore, the opinion of British audiences mattered a great deal to 'name' revival performers such as Bob Dylan, Pete Seeger and Joan Baez. Indeed, it was during Dylan's visit to the United Kingdom in 1965 that he first experimented with folk-rock, and, the following year, in Manchester, he would encounter the most powerful reaction against his electric sound while on tour with The Hawks. British musicians played a crucial role in the shaping of the music scene, not merely by influencing American and Canadian artists, but also by integrating themselves into the North American scene and helping to direct its future course. Therefore, a study which managed to incorporate the perspectives of British, American and Canadian musicians during the folk revival, and its aftermath, would be, if overly ambitious, a very worthwhile task.

It is hoped that this study of the folk revival and national identity in Canada and America has begun to shed light on important social, cultural and musical questions and considerations. There is no doubt that many of the questions addressed in the study continue to be pertinent to the music scene of today.

Bibliography

Adams, Henry, *Thomas Hart Benton: Drawing from Life* (New York: Abbeville Press, 1990).

Adria, Marco, *Music of Our Times: Eight Canadian Singer-Songwriters* (Toronto: James Lorimer & Co., 1990).

'After Four' Teen Section, *Toronto Telegram*, 1964–71.

Agee, James and Evans, Walker, *Let Us Now Praise Famous Men* (London: Peter Owen, 1965, 1st British Commonwealth edn).

Albright, Thomas, 'Visuals: The Album Art', *Rolling Stone*, 6 April 1968.

Allen, Barbara and Schlereth, Thomas J, *Sense of Place: American Regional Cultures* (Lexington: Kentucky University Press, 1990).

Alspector, J.C., 'The City Minstrel: Murray McLauchlan's Toronto is Something to Rock 'n' Roll About.' *Toronto Star*, 4 March 1979.

Alterman, Lorraine, 'Paul Simon: The *Rolling Stone* Interview', *Rolling Stone*, 28 May 1970.

Altmarr, Billy, 'Phil Ochs Marches it All Back Home', *Crawdaddy*, January 1974.

Anderson, Benedict R, *Imagined Communities: Reflections on the Origins and Spread of Nationalism* (London; New York: Verso, 1991, 2nd edn).

Anderson, Terry H, *The Movement and the Sixties* (New York: Oxford University Press, 1995).

——, 'The 1960s Benefited American Culture', in Mary E. Williams (ed.), *Culture Wars: Opposing Viewpoints* (San Diego, CA: Greenhaven Press, Inc), pp. 76–84.

'Anthems of a Blank Generation', *Time*, 11 July 1977.

'Artists Fights to Save Lofts', *Village Voice*, 14 February 1963.

Austin, Wade, 'The Real Beverley Hillbillies', *Southern Quarterly*, 19 (1981): 83–94.

Baker, Lindsay T., *The WPA Oklahoma Slave Narratives* (Norman: Oklahoma University Press, 1996).

Bangs, Lester, 'Pop Music in the Eighties', *Stereo Review*, January 1980.

Barbeau, Marius, Interview. Ottawa: Canadian Museum of Civilisation <http://www.civilization.ca/academ/barbeau/basteng.html> (accessed 14 March 2004).

Barker, Gerry, 'Folk Singing Buffs Get "the Fifth Peg"', *Toronto Star*, 20 October 1961.

Batten, Jack, 'Canada's Rock Scene: Going, Going...', *Maclean's*, February 1968.

——, 'Canadian Pop', *Chatelaine*, September 1969.

——,'Confessions of a Retired Rock Critic', *Saturday Night*, March 1973.

——, 'New Sandpiper Aims At Audience Contact', *Globe and Mail*, 21 April 1975.

——, 'Stoned on Rock, Stoned on Drugs', *Saturday Night*, December 1969.

Bauchman, Rosemary (ed.), *The Best of Helen Creighton* (Hantsport, Nova Scotia: Lancelot Press, 1988).

'Bob Dylan: The Rolling Stone Interview', *Rolling Stone*, 14 December 1967.

Beard, Rick and Berlowitz, Leslie Cohen, *Greenwich Village: Culture and Counterculture* (New Brunswick, NJ: Rutgers University Press for Museum of the City of the New York, 1993).

Becker, Jane, *Selling Tradition: Appalachia and the Construction of an American Folk, 1930–1940* (Chapel Hill; London: North Carolina University Press, 1998).

Bell, Leslie, 'Popular Music', in Ernest MacMillan (ed.), *Music in Canada* (Toronto: Toronto University Press, in co-operation with the Canadian Music Council/ Conseil Canadien de Musique, 1955), pp. 208–15.

Bennett, Michael J., *When Dreams Come True: The GI Bill and the Making of Modern America* (Washington, DC; London: Brassey's Inc., 1998).

Benton, Thomas Hart, *An Artist in America* (Columbia: University of Missouri Press, 1968, 3rd edn).

Berger, Carl, *The Sense of Power: Studies in the Ideas of Canadian Imperialism, 1867–1914* (Toronto; Buffalo, NY: University of Toronto Press, 1970).

Bernstein, Paul, 'Earl Scruggs: Foggy Mountain Father', *Crawdaddy*, May 1973.

Biderman, Morris, *A Life on the Jewish Left: An Immigrant's Experience* (Toronto: Onward Publishing, 2000).

Bindas, Kenneth J., *All Of This Music Belongs To The Nation: The WPA's Federal Music Project and American Society, 1935–1939* (Knoxville: University of Tennessee Press, 1995).

Bird, Roger (ed.), *Documents of Canadian Broadcasting* (Ottawa: Carleton University Press, 1988).

Bird, S. Elizabeth (ed.), *Dressing in Feathers: The Construction of the Indian in American Popular Culture* (Boulder, CO: Westview Press, 1996).

Birthday of a Nation (Time International of Canada, 1968).

Black, Jonathan, 'Gay Power Hits Back', *Village Voice*, 31 July 1969.

Blackman, Carolyn, 'Camp Naivelt Celebrates 75 Years', *Canadian Jewish News*, 20 July 2000.

Bloom, Alexander (ed.), *Long Time Gone: Sixties America Then and Now* (Oxford; New York: Oxford University Press, 2001).

—— and Wini Breines (eds), *Takin' It To the Streets: A Sixties Reader* (New York; Oxford: Oxford University Press, 2003, 2nd edn).

Bluestein, Gene, *The Voice of the Folk: Folklore and American Literary Theory* (Cambridge: Massachusetts University Press, 1972).

Bossin, Bob, 'The Ups and Downs of a Great Canadian Peace Festival', *Maclean's*, July 1970.

Bothwell, Robert, Drummond, Ian and English, John, *Canada Since 1945: Power, Politics and Provincialism* (Toronto; Buffalo, NY; London: University of Toronto Press, 1989).

——, '"Small Problems": Trudeau and the Americans', in *Trudeau's Shadow: The Life and Legacy of Pierre Elliott Trudeau* (Toronto: Random House of Canada, 1998).

Botkin, Benjamin A., *Sidewalks of America: Folklore, Legends, Sagas, Traditions, Customs, Songs, Stories and Sayings of City Folk* (Westport, CT: Greenwood Press, 1954).

——, *A Treasury of American Folklore: Stories, Ballads, and Traditions of the People* (New York: Crown Publishers, 1944).

——, *A Treasury of New England Folklore: Stories, Ballads, and Traditions of the Yankee People* (New York: Crown Publishers, 1947).

——, *A Treasury of Railroad Folklore: The Stories, Tall Tales, Traditions, Ballads, and Songs of the American Railroad Man* (New York: Bonanza Books, 1953).

——, *Western Folklore* (New York: Crown Publishers, 1964).

Bourke-White, Margaret, and Caldwell, Erskine, *You Have Seen Their Faces* (Athens: University of Georgia Press, 1995; originally published in New York, 1937).

Bradshaw, Michael, *Regions and Regionalism in the United States* (Basingstoke; London: Macmillan, 1988).

Brand, Oscar, *The Ballad Mongers: Rise of the Modern Folk Song* (Westport, CT: Greenwood Press, 1962).

Breines, Wini, 'The New Left and the Student Movement', in Alexander Bloom (ed.), *Long Time Gone: Sixties America Then and Now* (Oxford and New York, 2001).

Broadside, New York, selected editions, 1962–76.

Brocken, Michael, *The British Folk Revival, 1944–2002* (Aldershot, Hants.; Burlington, VT: Ashgate, 2003).

Bronner, Simon J., *American Folklore Studies: An Intellectual History* (Lawrence: Kansas University Press, 1986).

——, *Following Tradition: Folklore in the Discourse of American Culture* (Logan: Utah State University Press, 1998).

Brown, Alan and Taylor, David, *Gabr'l Blow Sof': Sumter County, Alabama Slave Narratives* (Livingston: Livingston Press, University of Alabama, 1997).

Brown, Dona, *Inventing New England: Regional Tourism in the Nineteenth Century* (Washington, DC; London: Smithsonian Institution Press, 1995).

Cameron, Silver Donald, 'When the Dory Failed to Make it: The Legacy of Stan Rogers', *Quest*, June 1984.

Campbell, Rod, *Playing the Field: The Story of the Edmonton Folk Music Festival* (Edmonton: B. Evan White Publications, 1994).

Canada, One Hundred, 1867–1967 (Ottawa: The Division, 1967).

Canadian Composer/Compositeur Canadien, 1963–80.

Canadian Content Regulations, CBC Radio News Special, 22 May 1970 <http://archives.cbc.ca/IDCC-1-68-1150-6312/arts_entertainment/canadian_content/> (accessed 4 May 2004).

——, CBC Radio, 'Sunday Supplement', 26 April 1970 < <http://archives.cbc.ca/IDCC-1-68-1150-6311/arts_entertainment/canadian_content/> (accessed 4 May 2004).

'Canadian Sound Survey', *After Four (Toronto Telegram)*, 16 February 1967.

Cantwell, Robert, *Bluegrass Breakdown: The Making of the Old Southern Sound* (Urbana: University of Illinois Press, 1984).

——, *When We Were Good: Class and Culture in the Folk Revival* (Cambridge, MA: Harvard University Press, 1996).

——, 'When We Were Good: Class and Culture in the Folk Revival', in Neil V. Rosenberg (ed.), *Transforming Tradition: Folk Music Revivals Examined*, (Urbana; Chicago: Illinois University Press, 1993) pp. 35–60.

'CAPAC Proposals incorporated in CRTC's new Radio Regulations', *Canadian Composer/Compositeur Canadien*, September 1970.

Caravan, 1957–60.

Carawan, Guy and Carawan, Candie, *Freedom is a Constant Struggle* (New York: Oak Publications, 1968).

——, *We Shall Overcome! Songs of the Southern Freedom Movement* (New York: Oak Publications, 1963).

Caraway, Steve, 'Robbie Robertson/Rick Danko: Heart and Soul of The Band', *Guitar Player*, December 1976.

Carpenter, Carole Henderson, *Many Voices: A Study of Folklore Activities in Canada and Their Role in Canadian Culture* (Ottawa: National Museums, 1979).

——, 'Politics and Pragmatism in Early North American Folklore Scholarship', *Canadian Folklore*, 13/1 (1991): 11–21.

Carroll, Francis M., *A Good and Wise Measure: The Search for the Canadian-American Boundary, 1783–1842* (Toronto: University of Toronto Press, 2001).

Carroll, Peter N., *It Seemed Like Nothing Happened: The Tragedy and Promise of America in the 1970s* (New York: Holt, Rinehart & Winston, 1982).

Cavallo, Dominick, *A Fiction of the Past: The Sixties in American History* (New York: St. Martin's Press, 1999).

Chafe, William H., *The Unfinished Journey: America Since World War II* (New York; Oxford: Oxford University Press, 1995).

Chauncey, George, *Gay New York: Gender, Urban Culture and the Making of the Gay Male World, 1890–1940* (New York: Basic Books, 1994).

Child, Francis James, *The English and Scottish Popular Ballads*, edited by Helen Child Sargent and George Lyman Kittredge (Boston, MA: Houghton & Mifflin, 1904).

Christopher's Movie Matinee (National Film Board of Canada, 1968).

Churchill, David, 'Coming Out in a Cold Climate: A History of Gay Men in Toronto During the 1950s' (unpublished MA thesis, University of Toronto, 1993).

Cobb, James C. and Namorato, Michael V. (eds), *The New Deal and the South* (Jackson: Mississippi University Press, 1984).

Cocks, Catherine, *Doing the Town: The Rise of Urban Tourism in the United States, 1850–1915* (Berkeley; Los Angeles; London: University of California Press, 2001).

Cocks, Jay, 'Down to Old Dixie and Back', *Time*, 12 January 1970.

Cohen, Andrew and Granatstein, J.L. (eds), *Trudeau's Shadow: The Life and Legacy of Pierre Elliott Trudeau* (Toronto: Random House of Canada, 1998).

Cohen, John, 'A Conversation with Janis Ian', *Sing Out!*, Vol. 18 No. 1 (March/April 1968).

Cohen, Lizabeth, *A Consumer's Republic: The Politics of Consumption in Postwar America* (New York: Knopf, 2003).

Cohen, Ronald D., *Rainbow Quest: The Folk Music Revival and American Society, 1940–1970* (Amherst; Boston: Massachusetts University Press, 2002).

—— (ed.), *Wasn't That a Time!: Firsthand Accounts of the Folk Music Revival* (Metuchen, NJ; London: Scarecrow Press, Inc., 1995).

Collier, Peter and Horowitz, David, *Destructive Generation: Second Thoughts About the Sixties* (New York: Summit Books, 1989).

Coppage, Noel, 'Requiem for the Seventies', *Stereo Review*, July 1979.

Coulson, Robert, 'Commercialism in Folk Music', *Caravan*, October 1957.

Crawdaddy (New York: New Crawdaddy Ventures, 1973–78).

Creem Magazine, 1977–8.

Creighton, Donald, *Canada's First Century* (Toronto: Macmillan, 1970).

——, *The Forked Road: Canada 1939–1957* (Toronto: McClelland & Stewart, 1976).

Crew, Robert, 'Rogers Book Pierces Our Collective Amnesia', *Toronto Star*, 31 July 1993.

Crowder, Richard, *Carl Sandburg* (New York. Twayne Publishers, 1964).

Dancing in the Street: A History of Rock 'n' Roll (BBC television documentary, 1997).

Dane, Barbara and Silber, Irwin (eds and compilers), *The Vietnam Songbook* (New York: *The Guardian*, distributed by Monthly Review Press, 1969).

De Benedetti, Charles and Chatfield, Charles, *An American Ordeal: The Antiwar Movement of the Vietnam Era* (Syracuse, NY: Syracuse University Press, 1990).

D'Emilio, John, *Sexual Politics, Sexual Communities: The Making of a Homosexual Minority in the United States, 1940–1970* (Chicago, IL: University of Chicago Press, 1998, 2nd edn).

Denisoff, R. Serge, *Great Day Coming: Folk Music and the American Left* (Urbana and London: University of Illinois Press, 1971).

——, *Sing a Song of Social Significance* (Bowling Green, OH: Bowling Green University Popular Press, 1972).

—— and Peterson, Richard A. (eds),*The Sounds of Social Change* (Chicago, IL: Rand McNally & Co., 1972).

Denning, Michael, *The Cultural Front: The Labouring of American Culture in the Twentieth Century* (London; New York: Verso, 1996).

Deverill, William, (ed.), *A Companion to the American West* (Malden; Oxford; Victoria: Blackwell Publishing, 2004).

Dorman, Robert L., *Revolt of the Provinces: The Regionalist Movement in America, 1920–1945* (Chapel Hill; London: University of North Carolina Press, 1993).

Dorson, Richard M., *American Folklore and the Historian* (Chicago, IL; London: Chicago University Press, 1971).

Dowd Hall, Jacquelyn, Leloudis, James, Korstad, Robert, Murphy, Mary, Jones, Lu Ann and Daly, Christopher B., *Like a Family: The Making of a Southern Cotton Mill World* (Chapel Hill; London: University of North Carolina Press, 1987).

Doyle, Michael William, 'Debating the Counterculture: Ecstasy and Anxiety Over the Hip Alternative', in David Farber and Beth Bailey (eds), *The Columbia Guide to America in the 1960s* (New York: Columbia University Press, 2001), pp. 143–56.

Duberman, Martin B., *Stonewall* (New York: Penguin Group, 1994).

Duff, Morris, 'After the Marathons, Danceathons, Telethons ... Now It's the Folkathon', *Toronto Star*, 29 June 1963.

——, 'Biggest Hootenanny Was Dullest', *Toronto Star*, 19 October 1963.

——, 'Jazz Declines and Folk Music Soars', *Toronto Star*, 30 December 1961.

Dundes, Alan, *The Study of Folklore* (Englewood Cliffs, NJ: Prentice-Hall, 1965).

Durnell, Hazel, *The America of Carl Sandburg* (Washington, DC: University Press of Washington, DC, 1965).

Dyson, Michael Eric, *Making Malcolm: The Myth and Meaning of Malcolm X* (New York: Oxford University Press, 1995).

Edinborough, Arnold, 'Pierre Elliot Trudeau: The Leader Tomorrow', *Saturday Night*, March 1968.

Einarson, John, *Shakin' All Over: The Winnipeg Sixties Rock Scene* (Winnipeg: Variety Club of Manitoba, 1987).

Farber, David and Bailey, Beth (eds), *The Columbia Guide to America in the 1960s* (New York: Columbia University Press, 2001).

Federal Music Project, California Musicology Music Project (Washington, DC: American Folklife Center Archive, Library of Congress) <http://www.memory.loc.gov/ammem/afccchtml/cowhome.html> (accessed 14 March 2004).

——, Florida Ethnomusicology Project (Washington, DC: American Folklife Center Archive, Library of Congress) <http://www.memory.loc.gov/ammem/flwpahtml/flwpahome.html> (accessed 14 March 2004).

Federal Writers' Project, *Mississippi: A Guide to the Magnolia State* (New York: Hastings House, 1949).

Feintuch, Burt, 'Musical Revival as Musical Transformation', in Neil V. Rosenberg (ed.), *Transforming Tradition: Folk Music Revivals Examined* (Urbana; Chicago: Illinois University Press, 1993), pp. 183–93.

Fetherling, Douglas, *Some Day Soon: Essays on Canadian Singer-Songwriters* (Kingston: Quarry Press, 1991).

Filene, Benjamin, *Romancing the Folk: Public Memory and American Roots Music* (Chapel Hill; London: University of North Carolina Press, 2000).

Finkel, Alvin, Conrad, Margaret and Strong-Boag Veronica, *A History of the Canadian Peoples: Volume II, 1867 to the Present* (Toronto: Copp Clark Pitman/ Longman, 1993).

Fleischhauer, Carl and Brannan, Beverly W. (eds), *Documenting America, 1935–1943* (Berkeley; Los Angeles; London: University of California Press, 1988).

Fleming, Thomas J., 'Greenwich Village: The Search for Identity', *Cosmopolitan*, December 1963.

Flohil, Richard, 'Murray MacLauchlan: Coming to Terms with a New Art Form', *Canadian Composer/Compositeur Canadien*, May 1974.

——, 'Stompin' Tom: Canada's Unlikely National Symbol', *Canadian Composer/ Compositeur Canadien*, November 1973.

'The Foggy, Foggy Don't', *Time*, 21 April 1961.

'The Folk Girls', *Time*, 1 June 1962.

Fong-Torres, Ben, 'David Crosby: The Rolling Stone Interview', *Rolling Stone*, 23 June 1970.

Foreman, Joel (ed.), *The Other Fifties: Interrogating Midcentury American Icons* (Urbana; Chicago: Illinois University Press, 1997).

Fowke, Edith, *The Penguin Book of Canadian Folk Songs* (Harmondsworth, England: Penguin, 1973).

—— and Carpenter, Carole H. (eds), *Explorations in Canadian Folklore* (Toronto: McClelland & Stewart, 1985).

Frager, Ruth A., *Sweatshop Strife: Class, Ethnicity and Gender in the Jewish Labour Movement of Toronto, 1900–1939* (Toronto; Buffalo, NY; London: University of Toronto Press, 1992).

—— and Patrias, Carmela, '"This Is Our Country, These Are Our Rights": Minorities and the Origins of Ontario's Human Rights Campaigns', *Canadian Historical Review*, 82/1 (March 2001): 1–35.

Friedan, Betty, *The Feminine Mystique* (New York: Norton, 1963).

Frith, Simon, 'The Discourse of World Music', in Georgina Born and David Hesmondhalgh (eds), *Western Music and its Others: Difference, Representation, and Appropriation in Music* (Berkeley; Los Angeles; London: University of California Press, 2000).

Fulford, Robert, *This Was Expo* (Montreal: McClelland & Stewart, 1968).

Gardyloo, 1959.

Garreau, Joel, *The Nine Nations of North America* (New York, 1981).

Gaston, Paul M., *The New South Creed: A Study in Southern Mythmaking* (New York: Alfred A. Knopf, 1970)

Gee, Helen, *Limelight: A Greenwich Village Photography Gallery and Coffeehouse in the Fifties* (Albuquerque: New Mexico University Press, 1997).

Gervis, Stephanie, 'The Homosexual's Labyrinth of Law and Social Custom', *Village Voice*, 11 October 1962.

——, 'Politics: A Third Party for the Third Sex?' *Village Voice*, 27 September 1962.

Gilbert, James, *Another Chance: Postwar America, 1945 1968* (Philadelphia, PA: Temple University Press, 1981).

——, *Cycle of Outrage: America's Reaction to the Juvenile Delinquent of the 1950s* (New York: Oxford University Press, 1986).

Gill, Alexandra, 'Canso Reels in Fans of Stan Rogers', *Globe & Mail*, 4 July 1997.

Gill, Andy, *My Back Pages: Classic Bob Dylan, 1962–1969* (London: Carlton Books, 1998).

Gillett, Charlie, *The Sound of the City: The Rise of Rock 'n' Roll* (New York: Outerbridge & Dienstfrey, 1971; London: Souvenir Press, 1996, 3rd edn).

Gitlin, Todd, *The Sixties: Years of Hope, Days of Rage* (Toronto; New York; London: Sydney; Auckland: Bantam Books, 1987).

Glaude, Eddie S., *Is it Nation Time? Contemporary Essays on Black Power and Black Nationalism* (Chicago, IL: University of Chicago Press, 2002).

Gleason, Mona, 'Psychology and the Construction of the 'Normal' Family in Postwar Canada, 1945–60', *Canadian Historical Review*, 78/3 (September 1997): 442–77.

Gleason, Ralph J., 'John Fogerty: The *Rolling Stone* Interview', *Rolling Stone*, 21 February 1970.

——, 'Perspectives: Deathwish of the Hippie Ethos', *Rolling Stone*, 24 August 1968.

Glickman, Lawrence B. (ed.), *Consumer Society in American History: A Reader* (Ithaca, NY; London: Cornell University Press, 1999).

Goddard, J.R., 'Big Turnout for Folksingers, Trouble Feared Next Sunday', *Village Voice*, 27 April 1961.

——, 'Mayor Relents, Opens Square to Folksingers', *Village Voice*, 10 May 1961.

——, '"Right to Sing" Rally Scores Ban by Morris; Ready to Fight', *Village Voice*, 20 April 1961.

Goddard, Peter, 'David Rae Serenades Riverboat's Ghosts', *Toronto Star*, 13 November 1978.

——, 'A Maple Leaf on Every Turntable Means Made-In-Canada Pop Stars', *Maclean's*, November 1970.

Goddard, Peter and Kamin, Philip (eds), *Shakin' All Over: The Rock 'n' Roll Years in Canada* (McGraw-Hill/Ryerson Press, 1989).

Golden, Lotti, 'Whatever Happened to Mike Bloomfield?', *Crawdaddy*, May 1973.

Goldsmith, Peter D., *Making People's Music: Moe Asch and Folkways Records* (Washington, DC and London: Smithsonian Institution Press, 1998).

Goldwasser, Noel, 'Pat Sky: Guaranteed to Offend Everybody', *Crawdaddy*, June 1973.

Gonczy, Daniel J., 'The Folk Music Movement of the 1960s: Its Rise and Fall', *Popular Music and Society*, 10/1 (1985): 15–31.

Gormely, Sheila, 'The Fad's Past But ... Folk's Here To Stay', 'After Four', *Toronto Telegram*, 12 February 1964.

Gottesman, Stephen N., 'Tom Dooley's Children: An Overview of the Folk Music Revival, 1958–1965', *Popular Music and Society*, 5 (1977): 61–78.

Graff, Ellen, *Stepping Left: Dance and Politics in New York City, 1928–1942* (Durham, NC; London: Duke University Press, 1997).

Granatstein, J.L., *Canada 1957–1967: Years of Uncertainty and Innovation* (Toronto: McClelland & Stewart, 1986).

——, *Yankee Go Home? Canadians and Anti-Americanism* (Toronto: HarperCollins, 1996).

Grant, Barry K., 'Across the Great Divide: Imitation and Inflection in Canadian Rock Music', *Journal of Canadian Studies*, 21/1 (1986): 116–27.

Grant, Dale, 'A Sunday Afternoon in the Village', *Toronto Telegram*, 'After Four' section, 8 July 1965.

Grealis, Walt, 'Canadian Songwriters *Are* Making it in Canada', *Canadian Composer/ Compositeur Canadien*, January 1970.

Green, Archie, Review of Ian McKay, *The Quest of the Folk: Antimodernism and Cultural Selection in Twentieth-Century Nova Scotia. Canadian Historical Review*, 77/1, 1996: 122–5.

Green, H. Gordon, *A Heritage of Canadian Handcrafts* (Toronto; Montreal: McClelland & Stewart, 1967).

Green, Sam and Siegel, Bill, *The Weather Underground*. (Free History Project Documentary, 2003).

Greene, Victor, *A Passion For Polka: Old-Time Ethnic Music in America* (Berkeley: California University Press, 1992).

Greenhill, Pauline, '"The Folk Process" in the Revival: "Barrett's Privateers" and "Baratt's Privateers', in Neil V. Rosenberg (ed.), *Transforming Tradition: Folk Music Revivals Examined* (Urbana; Chicago: University of Illinois Press, 1993), pp. 137–59.

——, *Lots of Stories: Maritime Narratives from the Creighton Collection* (Ottawa: National Museums of Canada, 1985).

Greenway, John, *American Folksongs of Protest* (New York: Octagon Books, 1970).

Grissim, John Jr., 'Joan Baez: The *Rolling Stone* Interview', *Rolling Stone*, 7 December 1968.

Groom, Bob, *The Blues Revival* (London: Studio Vista, 1971).

Gruber, J. Richard, *Thomas Hart Benton and the American South* (Augusta, GA: Morris Museum of Art, 1998).

Guest, Christopher (director), *A Mighty Wind* (2003).

Guthrie, Woody, *Bound for Glory* (New York: New American Library, 1983).

Hale, Barrie, 'The Folksong Syndrome', *Toronto Star*, 10 August 1963.

Hays, Matthew, 'Oka Crisis: Worst Moment Revisited', *Globe & Mail*, 21 June 2000.

'Hepatitis Spread Indicated as 'Weekend Hippies' Affected', *Toronto Star*, 7 August 1968.

Hewitt, Steve, *Spying 101: The RCMP's Secret Activities at Canadian Universities, 1917–1997* (Toronto; Buffalo, NY; London: University of Toronto Press, 2002).

Heylin, Clinton, *The Penguin Book of Rock 'n' Roll Writing* (London: Viking, 1992).

Himel, Malka, 'Face to Face: Joni Mitchell in Conversation with Malka', *Maclean's*, June 1974.

Hine, Robert V. and Faragher, John Mack, *The American West: A New Interpretive History* (New Haven, CT; London: Yale University Press, 2000).

Hirsch, Jerrold, 'Benjamin Botkin's Legacy-In-The-Making' <http://www.loc.gov/folklife/botkin/hirsch.html> (accessed 14 March 2004).

——, 'Cultural Pluralism and Applied Folklore: The New Deal Precedent', in Burt Feintuch (ed.), *The Conservation of Culture: Folklorists and the Public Sector* (Lexington: Kentucky University Press, 1988), pp. 46–67.

——, 'Folklore in the Making: B.A. Botkin', *Journal of American Folklore*, 100 (1987): 3–38.

——, 'Modernity, Nostalgia, and Southern Folklore Studies: The Case of John Lomax', *Journal of American Folklore*, 105 (1992): 183–207.

——, *Portrait of America: A Cultural History of the Federal Writers' Project* (Chapel Hill: University of North Carolina Press, 2003).

Hobsbawm, Eric and Ranger, Terence (eds), *The Invention of Tradition* (Cambridge: Cambridge University Press, 1983).

Hobson, Fred, *Tell About the South: The Southern Rage to Explain* (Baton Rouge; London: Louisiana State University Press, 1983).

Hogan, Dorothy, 'Maple Sugar', *Canadian Folk Music Society Newsletter/Bulletin*, Vol. 13 No. 3, Fall 1978.

Holme-Hudson, Kevin (ed.), *Progressive Rock Reconsidered* (New York; London: Routledge, 2002).

Horne, Gerald, *Fire This Time: The Watts Uprising and the 1960s* (Charlottesville: University Press of Virginia, 1995).

Hoskyns, Barney (ed.), *The Sound and the Fury: A Rock's Backpages Reader: 40 Years of Classic Rock Journalism* (London: Bloomsbury Publishing, 2003).

Hoot (Toronto: Guild of Canadian Folk Artists, 1963–66).

Houghan, Jim, *Decadence: Radical Nostalgia, Narcissism and Decline in the Seventies* (New York: William Morrow & Co., 1975).

Howe, Irving with Libo, Kenneth, *World of Our Fathers* (New York: Harcourt Brace Jovanovich, 1976).

Howell, Bill, 'The End of the Maverick', *Canadian Forum*, December 1983.

The Hundredth Year: The Centennial of Canadian Confederation, 1867–1967 (Ottawa: Canadian Centennial Commission, 1967).

Hutcheson, Stephanie, *Yorkville in Bibliography: The Early History of Yorkville/The Hippies of Yorkville* (Toronto: University of Toronto, August 1972).

Irr, Caren, *The Suburb of Dissent: Cultural Politics in the United States and Canada During the 1930s* (Durham, NC; London: Duke University Press, 1998).

Jackson, Bruce (ed.), *Folklore and Society: Essays in Honour of Benjamin A. Botkin* (Hatboro, PA: Folklore Associates, 1966).

——, 'The Folksong Revival', in Neil V. Rosenberg (ed.), *Transforming Tradition: Folk Music Revivals Examined* (Urbana; Chicago: Illinois University Press, 1993), pp. 73–83.

Jackson, Rick, *Encyclopedia of Canadian Rock, Pop and Folk Music* (Kingston, Ontario: Quarry Press, 1994).

Jacobs, Ron, *The Way the Wind Blew: A History of the Weather Underground* (London; New York: Verso, 1997).

'James Taylor: One Man's Family of Rock', *Time*, 1 March 1973.

Jennings, Nicholas, *Before the Gold Rush: Flashbacks to the Dawn of the Canadian Sound* (Toronto; London; New York; Victoria; Auckland: Penguin, 1997).

Jensen, Merrill (ed.), *Regionalism in America* (Madison: Wisconsin University Press, 1951).

'Jewish Folk Lab Gets Yiddish Songs', *Sing Out!*, Vol. 1 No. 6 (1951).

Johnson, Charles, *Discussion paper No. 28: The Preservation of Yorkville Village* (Toronto: York University Press, 1984).

Johnston, Denis W. *Up the Mainstream: The Rise of Toronto's Alternative Theatres* (Toronto: Toronto University Press, 1991).

Jones, Alfred Haworth, 'The Search for a Usable American Past in the New Deal Era', *American Quarterly*, 23/5 (1971): 710–24.

'Juno Awards: Pop Music Up Front', *Canadian Composer/Compositeur Canadien*, April 1971.

Kahn, Ashley, George-Warren, Holly, and Dahl, Shawn (eds), *Rolling Stone: The Seventies* (Boston, MA; New York; Toronto: Little, Brown and Company, 1998).

Kaiser, Charles, *1968 in America: Music, Politics, Chaos, Counterculture, and the Shaping of a Generation* (New York: Weidenfeld and Nicolson, 1988).

Kaplan, Judy and Shapiro, Linn, *Red Diapers: Growing Up in the Communist Left* (Urbana: University of Illinois Press, 1998).

Keats, John, *The Crack in the Picture Window* (New York: Ballantine Books, 1962).

Kendall, Brian, *Our Hearts Went Boom: The Beatles' Invasion of Canada* (Toronto: Viking Press, 1997).

Kindler, Jan, 'Cops, "Beatniks", and Facts', *Village Voice*, 13 April 1961.

Kirkpatrick, Ernest Stanley, *Tales of the St. John River and Other Stories* (W. Briggs, 1904).

Kitromilides, Paschalis M. and Varouxakis, Georgios, 'The "Imagined Communities" Theory of Nationalism', in *Encyclopedia of Nationalism* (New Brunswick, NJ: Transaction Press, 2001).

Klymasz, Robert, '"Sounds You Never Heard Before": Ukrainian Country Music in Western Canada', *Ethnomusicology*, 16 (1972): 372–80.

Knobler, Peter, 'Bob Dylan: A Gut Reaction', *Crawdaddy*, September 1973.

——, 'On the Nature of Rock Journalism', *Crawdaddy*, February 1973.

Knowles, Norman, *Inventing the Loyalists: The Ontario Loyalist Tradition and the Creation of Usable Pasts* (Toronto; Buffalo, NY; London: University of Toronto Press, 1997).

Korinek, Valerie J., *Roughing It in the Suburbs: Reading Chatelaine Magazine in the Fifties and Sixties* (Toronto; Buffalo, NY; London: University of Toronto Press, 2000).

Kostash, Myrna, *Long Way From Home: The Story of the Sixties Generation in Canada* (Toronto: James Lorimer & Co., 1980).

——, 'The Pure, Uncluttered Spaces of Bruce Cockburn', *Saturday Night*, June 1972.

Krim, Seymour, 'Life in a Coffeehouse', *Cosmopolitan*, December 1963.

Kurlansky, Mark, *1968: The Year that Rocked the World* (New York: Ballantine, 2004).

Kusch, Frank, *All American Boys: Draft Dodgers in Canada from the Vietnam War* (Westport, CT: Praeger, 2001).

Kuznick, Peter J. and Gilbert, James (eds), *Rethinking Cold War Culture* (Washington, DC; London: Smithsonian Institution Press, 2001).

Lankford, George E., *Bearing Witness: Memories of Arkansas Slavery – Narratives from the 1930s WPA Collections* (Fayetteville: University of Arkansas Press, 2003).

Lasch, Christopher, *The Culture of Narcissism: American Life in an Age of Diminishing Expectations* (New York: W.W. Norton & Co., 1978).

'Learning to Live With Canadian Content', *Canadian Composer/Compositeur Canadien*, February 1971.

Lears, T.J. Jackson, *No Place of Grace: Antimodernism and The Transformation of American Culture, 1880–1920* (New York: Pantheon Books, 1981).

Ledbetter, Huddie (Leadbelly), Correspondence (Washington, DC: American Folklife Center Archives, Library of Congress) <http://lcweb4.loc.gov/service/afc/afc1933001> (accessed 17 February 2004).

Lederman, Anne, '"Barrett's Privateers": Performance and Participation in the Folk Revival', in Neil V. Rosenberg (ed.), *Transforming Tradition: Folk Music Revivals Examined* (Urbana; Chicago: University of Illinois Press, 1993), pp. 160–75.

Lee, Dennis, 'Getting to Rochdale', in Gerald F. McGuigan with George Payerle and Patricia Horobin (eds), *Student Protest* (Toronto; London; Sydney; Wellington: Methuen, 1968), pp. 64–87.

Lehr, John, 'As Canadian as Possible … Under the Circumstances: Regional Myths, Images of place and National Identity in Canadian Country Music', in Beverley Diamond and Robert Witmer (eds), *Canadian Music: Issues of Hegemony and Identity* (Toronto: Canadian Scholars' Press, 1994), pp. 269–81.

Lemon, James, *Toronto Since 1918: An Illustrated History* (Toronto: James Lorimer & Co., 1985).

Leoussi, Athena S. (ed.), *Encyclopedia of Nationalism* (New Brunswick, NJ: Transaction Publishers, 2001).

Lester, Julius, 'The View from the Other Side of the Tracks', *Sing Out!*, 14/4 (September 1964).

Levine, Lawrence, *Highbrow/Lowbrow: The Emergence of Cultural Hierarchy in America* (Cambridge, MA: Harvard University Press, 1988).

——, 'The Historian and the Icon', in Carl Fleischhauer and Beverly W. Brannan (eds), *Documenting America, 1935–1943* (Berkeley; Los Angeles; London: University of California Press, 1988).

Levitt, Cyril, *Children of Privilege: Student Revolt in the Sixties. A Study of the Student Movements in Canada, the United States, and West Germany* (Toronto; Buffalo, NY; London: University of Toronto Press, 1984).

Limerick, Patricia Nelson, *The Legacy of Conquest: The Unbroken Past of the American West* (New York; London: WW Norton & Co., 1987).

——, 'The Realization of the American West', in Charles Reagan Wilson (ed.), *The New Regionalism* (Jackson: Mississippi University Press, 1998), pp. 71–98.

Lipset, Seymour Martin, *Continental Divide: The Values and Institutions of the United States and Canada* (New York: Routledge, Chapman and Hall, 1990).

Lipsitz, George, *Time Passages: Collective Memory and American Popular Culture* (Minneapolis: Minnesota University Press, 1990).

List, Dan, 'Gaslight's Night-of-Travail Sparked by False Alarm', *Village Voice*, 12 January 1961.

Little Sandy Review (Minneapolis, 1959–65).

Lomax, John A., *Adventures of a Ballad Hunter* (New York: MacMillan, 1947).

——, and Lomax, Alan, *American Ballads and Folk Songs* (New York: Dover, 1994).

—— (eds, compilers and transcribers), *Negro Folk Songs as Sung By Lead Belly* (New York: MacMillan, 1936).

Long, Barbara, 'Argue the Case for a New Definition of Folk Music', *Canadian Folk Music Society Bulletin*, Vol. 10 Nos. 1 and 2 (December 1975).

Lott, Eric, *Love and Theft: Blackface Minstrelsy and the American Working Class* (New York: Oxford University Press, 1993).

Lund, Jens and Denisoff, R. Serge, 'The Folk Music Revival and the Counter Culture: Contributions and Contradictions', *Journal of American Folklore*, 84 (1971): 394–405.

Lydon, Michael, *Flashbacks: Eyewitness Accounts of the Rock Revolution* (New York; London: Routledge, 2003).

Makin, Kirk, 'The Death Knell Sounds for Folk', *Toronto Globe*, c. November 1978.

Malcolm X and Alex Haley, *The Autobiography of Malcolm X* (New York: Grove Press, 1965).

Malone, Bill C., *Country Music, USA* (Austin: University of Texas Press, 2002).

Mangione, Jerre, *The Dream and the Deal: The Federal Writers' Project, 1935–1943* (Boston, MA; Toronto: Little, Brown & Co., 1972).

Mann, W.E. (ed.), *The Underside of Toronto* (Toronto; Montreal: McClelland & Stewart, 1970).

Marcus, Greil, *Mystery Train: Images of America in Rock 'n' Roll Music* (New York: Plume, 1990, 3rd rev. edn).

Margolin, George, 'Sidewalk Hootenanny', *People's Songs*, Vol. 2 Nos. 1 & 2 (February/March 1947).

Mariposa Folk Festival, Programmes, 1960s–80s.

Markle, Robert, 'Early Morning Afterthoughts: Gordon Lightfoot and the Canadian Dream', *Maclean's*, December 1971.

Massey, Vincent, *Great Canadians: A Century of Achievement* (Canadian Centennial Publishing Company, 1965).

Matusow, Allen, *The Unraveling of America: A History of Liberalism in the 1960s* (Cambridge, MA; Philadelphia, PA; San Francisco, CA; London; Mexico City; Sao Paolo; Sydney; New York: Harper & Row, 1984).

'Maverick Stan Rogers Was "a Folksinger and Proud of it"', 5 June 1983 (no source or author provided).

Maynard, Steven, '"Horrible Temptations": Sex, Men and Working Class Male Youth in Urban Ontario, 1890–1935', *Canadian Historical Review*, 78 (June 1997): 191–235.

McCracken, Melinda, 'They Think They can Make Me a Star: And These Guys Might Even Do It!', *Canadian Composer/Compositeur Canadien*, April 1969.

MacFarlane, J., 'What if Anne Murray were an American?', *Maclean's*, May 1971.

McGee, Timothy J. (ed.), *Taking A Stand: Essays in Honour of John Beckwith* (Toronto: University of Toronto Press, 1995).

McGuigan, Gerald F. with Payerle, George and Horrobin, Patricia (eds), *Student Protest* (Toronto; London; Sydney; Wellington: Methuen, 1968).

MacGregor, Roy, 'To Hell with Bob Dylan: Meet Rush – They're In It For the Money', *Maclean's*, 23 January 1970.

McKay, Ian, *The Quest of the Folk: Anti-modernism and Cultural Selection in Twentieth-Century Nova Scotia* (Montreal; Kingston; London; Buffalo, NY: McGill-Queen's University Press, 1994).

Maclean's (Toronto: Maclean Hunter, 1965–80), selected editions.

200 *The North American Folk Music Revival*

MacManus, Sheila, *"The Line Which Separates": Race, Gender, and the Alberta-Montana Borderlands, 1862–1892* (PhD Thesis, York University, Canada, 2001).

MacMechan, Archibald, *Tales of the Sea* (Toronto: McClelland & Stewart, 1947).

McNaughton, Janet, 'John Murray Gibbon and the Inter-War Folk Festivals', *Canadian Folklore Canadien*, 3 (1981): 67–73.

McNeil, Mark, 'Stan Rogers, Ten Years Gone', *Ottawa Citizen*, 11 July 1993.

McWilliams, John C., *The 1960s Cultural Revolution* (Westport, CT: Greenwood Press, 2000).

Melhuish, Martin, *Oh What A Feeling: A Vital History of Canadian Music* (Kingston, Ontario: Quarry Press, 1996).

Melosh, Barbara, *Engendering Culture: Manhood and Womanhood in New Deal Public Art and Theatre* (Washington, DC; London: Smithsonian Institution Press, 1991).

Melton, Barry, 'Everything Seemed Beautiful: A Life in the Counterculture', in Alexander Bloom (ed.), *Long Time Gone: Sixties America Then and Now* (Oxford; New York: Oxford University Press, 2001), pp. 146–57.

Meyerowitz, Joanne, 'Beyond the Feminine Mystique: A Reassessment of Postwar Mass Culture, 1946–1958', *Journal of American History*, 79/4, (1993): 1455–82.

Michener, Wendy, 'Too Serious, But Success At Singin' and Strummin'', *Toronto Star*, 23 May 1961.

Mietkiewicz, Henry and Mackowycz, Bob, *Dream Tower: The Life and Legacy of Rochdale College* (Toronto: McGraw-Hill/Ryerson, 1988).

Miller, Douglas T., *On Our Own: Americans in the Sixties* (Lexington, MA: D.C. Heath & Co., 1996).

Miller, James, *"Democracy is in the Streets": From Port Huron to the Siege of Chicago* (New York: Simon & Schuster, 1987).

Miller, Mark, 'Singer's Loss Stuns Folk Scene', *Toronto Star*, 4 June 1983.

Miller, Terry, *Greenwich Village and How It Got That Way* (New York: Crown Publishers, 1990).

Miller, Timothy, *The Hippies and American Values* (Knoxville: University of Tennessee Press, 1991).

Mills, C.Wright 'Letter to the New Left', in Alexander Bloom and Wini Breines (eds), *Takin' It to the Streets: A Sixties Reader* (New York and Oxford, 2003, 2nd edn), pp. 61–6.

'The Mirage that Drew Gloria, 16, to Yorkville … and the Streets', *Toronto* Star, 4 June 1967.

Mishler, Paul C., *Raising Reds: The Young Pioneers, Radical Summer Camps and Communist Political Culture in the United States* (New York: Columbia University Press, 1999).

Mitgang, Herbert (ed.), *The Letters of Carl Sandburg* (New York: Harcourt, Brace & World, 1968).

Morgan, Edward P., *The Sixties Experience: Hard Lessons About Modern America* (Philadelphia, PA: Temple University Press, 1991).

Morris, Pat, 'Guthrie the Goatherd', *Crawdaddy*, June 1973.

Morton, Desmond and Granatstein, J.L., *Victory 1945: Canadians from War to Peace* (Toronto: Harper Collins, 1995).

Moytl, Alexander J. (editor in chief), *Encyclopedia of Nationalism: Volume II: Leaders, Movements and Concepts* (San Diego, CA; San Francisco, CA; New York; Boston, MA; London; Sydney; Tokyo: Academic Press, 2001).

Nadle, Marlene, 'Joan Baez: The Pop Idol Who Wouldn't', *Village Voice*, 21 August 1969.

Nagel, Julian (ed.), *Student Power* (London: Merlin Press, 1969).

Natambu, Kolfi, *The Life and Work of Malcolm X* (Indianapolis, IN: Alpha Books, 2002).

Negus, Keith, *Popular Music in Theory* (Cambridge: Polity Press, 1996).

Nelles, H.V., *The Art of Nation-Building: Pageantry and Spectacle at Quebec's Tercentenary* (Toronto; Buffalo, NY; London: University of Toronto Press, 1999).

Nelson, Paul, 'Newport: The Folk Spectacle Comes of Age', *Sing Out!*, 14/5 (November 1964).

Newport Folk Festival, Programmes, 1959–69.

Nicols, Mary Peart, 'Morris Ban on Singers in Square Divides Village', 27 April 1961.

Nissenbaum, Stephen, 'Inventing New England', in Charles Reagan Wilson (ed.), *The New Regionalism* (Jackson: Mississippi University Press, 1998).

Niven, Penelope, *Carl Sandburg: A Biography* (New York; Oxford; Singapore; Sydney: Maxwell Macmillan International/New York: Charles Scribner's Sons/ Toronto: Maxwell Macmillan Canada, 1991).

Nowry, Lawrence, *Man of Mana: Marius Barbeau* (Toronto: NC Press, 1995).

Odum, Howard W. and Estill Moore, Harry, *American Regionalism: A Cultural-Historical Approach to National Integration* (New York: Henry Holt and Company, 1938).

O'Neil, Doris C., *Life: The 1960s* (Boston, MA; Toronto; London: Little, Brown and Company/Bullfinch Press, 1989).

Owram, Doug, *Born at the Right Time: A History of the Baby Boom Generation in Canada* (Toronto; Buffalo, NY; London: Toronto University Press, 1996).

Paredes, Americo and Stekert, Ellen J. (eds), *The Urban Experience and Folk Tradition* (Austin; London: University of Texas Press for the American Folklore Society, 1971).

Patterson, James T., *Grand Expectations: America, 1945–1974* (New York; Oxford: Oxford University Press, 1996).

People's Songs (New York, 1946–49).

Polenberg, Richard, *One Nation Divisible: Class, Race and Ethnicity in the United States Since 1938* (New York: Viking Press, 1980).

Porter, John, *The Vertical Mosaic: An Analysis of Social Class and Power in Canada* (Toronto: University of Toronto Press, 1965).

Porterfield, Nolan, *Last Cavalier: The Life and Times of John A. Lomax* (Urbana; Chicago: Illinois University Press, 1996).

Posen, I. Sheldon, 'On Folk Festivals and Kitchens: Questions of Authenticity in the Folk Revival', in Neil V. Rosenberg (ed.), *Transforming Tradition: Folk Music Revivals Examined* (Urbana; Chicago: Illinois University Press, 1993), pp. 127–36.

Potter, Paul 'The Incredible War', in Alexander Bloom and Wini Breines (eds), *Takin' It To the Streets: A Sixties Reader* (New York; Oxford: Oxford University Press, 2003, 2nd edn.

Potts, Lyman, 'Horizons Expanded for Our Musicians', *RPM*, 9 January 1971.

Powers, Robert, 'The Rise and Fall of Barry Sadler', *Crawdaddy*, August 1973.

Promenade (New York: American Square Dance Society, 1940–42).

Quarter, Jack, *The Student Movement of the Sixties: A Social-Psychological Analysis* (Toronto: Ontario Institute for Studies in Education, Occasional Papers, No. 7, 1972).

Reid, Tim and Reid, Julyan (eds), *Student Power and the Canadian Campus* (Toronto: Peter Martin Associates, 1969).

Reiner, Rob (director), *This is Spinal Tap*, Film, 1984.

Resnick, Philip, 'The New Left in Ontario', in Dimitrios J. Roussopoulos (ed.), *The New Left in Canada* (Montreal, 1970), pp. 92–100.

Reuss, Richard A. with Reuss, JoAnne C., *American Folk Music and Left-Wing Politics, 1927–1957* (Lanham, MD; London: Scarecrow Press, 2000).

Rice, Timothy and Gutnik, Tammy, 'What's Canadian About Canadian Popular Music? The Case of Bruce Cockburn', in Timothy J. McGee (ed.), *Taking a Stand: Essays in Honour of John Beckwith* (Toronto: University of Toronto Press, 1995), pp. 238–56.

Ritchie, Jean, *The Newport Folk Festival Songbook* (New York: Alfred Music, 1964).

Riesman, David, with Denny, Reuel and Glazer, Nathan, *The Lonely Crowd: A Study of the Changing American Character* (New Haven, CT: Yale University Press, 1962).

'Robert Plant Finds Blues Roots in the Sahara' on the 'Eye for Talent' website <http://www.eyefortalent.com/index.cfm/fuseaction/artist.articlesdetail/artistid/70/articleid/42.cfm> (accessed 13 October 2005).

Rochdale College Closure, CBC Television News, 8 August 1977. <http://archives.cbc.ca/IDCC-1-69-580-3224/life_society/hippies/> (accessed 4 May 2004).

Rodgers, Tim, 'Focus on Festival', *Canadian Folk Music Society Newsletter/Bulletin*, Vol. 16 No. 3 (July 1982).

Rodnitzky, Jerome L., *Minstrels of the Dawn: The Folk-Protest Singer as Cultural Icon* (Chicago, IL: Nelson-Hall, 1976).

——, 'Popular Music as a Radical Influence, 1945–1970', in Leon Borden Blair (ed.), *Essays on Radicalism in Contemporary America* (Walter Prescott Webb Memorial Lectures) (Austin; London: Texas University Press, 1972).

——, 'The Sixties Between the Microgrooves: Using Folk and Protest Music to Understand American History, 1963–1973', *Popular Music and Society*, 23 (1999): 105–23

Rolling Stone (San Francisco, CA; New York (1977–present): Straight Arrow Publishers, 1967–present).

Rooney, Jim, and Von Schmidt, Eric, *Baby Let Me Follow You Down: The Illustrated History of the Cambridge Folk Years* (Garden City, NY: Anchor Books/Doubleday, 1979).

Rosenberg, Neil V., *Bluegrass: A History* (Urbana: University of Illinois Press, 1985).

——, *Country Music in the Maritimes: Two Studies* (Newfoundland: Memorial University Department of Folklore Studies Reprint Series No. 2, 1976).

——, 'Overview', in Ronald D. Cohen (ed.), *Wasn't That a Time! First-Hand Accounts of the Folk Music Revival* (Metuchen, NJ: Scarecrow Press, 1993)

——, 'Starvation, Serendipity, and the Ambivalence of Bluegrass Revivalism', in Neil V. Rosenberg (ed.), *Transforming Tradition: Folk Music Revivals Examined* (Urbana; Chicago: Illinois University Press, 1993), pp. 194–202.

——, *Transforming Tradition: Folk Music Revivals Examined.* (Urbana; Chicago: University of Illinois Press, 1993).

Rossinow, Doug, 'The New Left: Democratic Reformers or Left-Wing Revolutionaries?', in David Farber and Beth Bailey (eds), *The Columbia Guide to America in the 1960s* (New York: Columbia University Press, 2001).

Roussopoulos, Dimitrios J (ed.), *The New Left in Canada* (Montreal: Our Generation Press – Black Rose Books, 1970).

Rubin, Ruth, *Voices of a People: The Story of Yiddish Folksong* (New York: McGraw-Hill, 1973).

Rutherford, Paul, *When Television Was Young: Prime Time Canada, 1952–1967* (Toronto; Buffalo, NY; London: University of Toronto Press, 1990).

Salamone, Frank A., *Popular Culture in the Fifties* (Lanham, MD; New York; Oxford: University Press of America, 2001).

Sandburg, Carl, *American Songbag* (San Diego, CA; New York; London: Harcourt Brace Jovanovich, 1990, 2nd edn).

——, *Slabs of the Sunburnt West* (New York: Harcourt, Brace & World, Inc., 1922).

Sarlin, Bob, 'Eric Andersen: I Was Always Scared of Success', *Crawdaddy*, December 1972.

——, 'Janis Ian at 24', *Crawdaddy*, February 1976.

Saturday Night, Toronto. 1965–80, selected editions.

Satyrday, 1967–68.

Scheurer, Timothy E., *Born in the USA: The Myth of America in Popular Music from Colonial Times to the Present* (Jackson; London: Mississippi University Press, 1991).

Schiff, Marvin, 'A Blaring Bandwagon Rolls Towards Obscurity', *Globe and Mail*, 25 April 1964.

——, 'Canadian Talent: As Instrumentalists Ramblers Are Exciting', *Globe*, 25 October 1966.

——, 'Modern Writers Blowing Cobwebs from an Old Idea', *Globe*, 17 April 1965.

——, 'A Night of Tedium Unrelieved', *Globe and Mail*, 19 October 1963.

Schur, Edwin M., *The Awareness Trip: Self-Absorption Instead of Social Change* (New York: Quadrangle, New York Times Book Co., 1976).

Scorsese, Martin (director), *Bob Dylan: No Direction Home* (2005).

Seeger, Pete, *The Incompleat Folksinger,* edited by Jo Metcalf Schwartz (New York: Simon & Schuster, 1972).

——, *Where Have All The Flowers Gone: A Singer's Stories, Songs, Seeds, Robberies*, edited by Peter Blood (Bethlehem, PA: Sing Out, 1993).

Sellick, Lester B., *Canada's Don Messer* (Kentville, Nova Scotia: Kentville Publishing Co., 1969).

Sharpe, David, *Rochdale, the Runaway College* (Toronto: Anansi, 1987).

Shepherd, John et al. (eds), *The Continuum Encyclopedia of Popular Musics of the World* Vol. 1. (London; New York: Continuum, 2003).

'Ship of Fools Stages Tribute', *Toronto Star*, 10 November 1978.

Siegmeister, Elie, 'Folk Song and Symphony', *People's Songs*, Vol. 3 No. 5 (June 1948).

——, 'Peace Hop', *Sing Out!*, Vol. 1 No. 5 (September 1950).

Siggins, Maggie, 'Yorkville: The Inside Story', *Toronto Telegram*, 'After Four' section, 28 July 1966.

Silber, Irwin, 'Open Letter to Bob Dylan', *Sing Out!*, Vol. 14 No. 4 (September 1964).

——, Review of Newport Folk Festival. *Sing Out!*, Vol. 17 No. 5 (October–November 1967).

——, 'Traditional Folk Artists Capture the Campus', *Sing Out!*, Vol. 14 No. 2 (April–May 1964).

Simpson, Jeffrey, *Star-Spangled Canadians: Canadians Living the American Dream* (Toronto: HarperCollins, 2000).

Sing Out! (New York: Oak Publications, selected editions, 1950–present day).

Skolnick, Arlene, *Embattled Paradise: The American Family in an Age of Uncertainty* (New York: HarperCollins, 1991).

Slobin, Mark (ed.), *American Klezmer: Its Roots and Offshoots* (Berkeley: California University Press, 2002).

——, 'The Neo-*Klezmer* Movement and Euro-American Musical Revivalism', *Journal of American Folklore*, 97 (1984): 98–104.

——, 'Rethinking "Revival" of American Ethnic Music', *New York Folklore*, 9 (1983): 37–44.

Smart, Reginald George, with Ampur, Gopala and Jackson, David, *The Yorkville Subculture: A Study of Lifestyles and Interactions of Hippies and Non-hippies* (Toronto: Addiction Research Foundation, 1969).

Smith, Anthony D., 'Nationalism', in Athena S. Leoussi. (ed.), *Encyclopedia of Nationalism* (New Brunswick, NJ: Transaction Publishers, 2001), pp. 222–5.

'Special Section' (CRTC Canadian Content.), *Canadian Composer/Compositeur Canadien*, May 1970.

Stambler, Irwin, *Encyclopedia of Rock, Pop and Soul* (New York: St. Martin's Press, 1989, rev. edn).

Stansell, Christine, *American Moderns: Bohemian New York and the Creation of a New Century* (New York: Metropolitan Books/Henry Holt & Co., 2000).

Stein, David Lewis, 'Lazy Days of Communist Camping in Brampton', *Toronto Star*, 10 August 2000.

Stekert, Ellen J., 'Cents and Nonsense in the Urban Folksong Movement', in Neil V. Rosenberg (ed.), *Transforming Tradition: Folk Music Revivals Examined* (Urbana; Chicago: Illinois University Press, 1993), pp. 84–106.

Strange, Carolyn, *Toronto's Girl Problem: The Perils and Pleasures of the City, 1880–1930* (Toronto: University of Toronto Press, 1995).

Stott, William, *Documentary Expression and Thirties America* (New York: Oxford University Press, 1973).

Strong-Boag, Veronica, 'Home Dreams: Women and the Suburban Experiment in Canada', *Canadian Historical Review*, 72/4 (1991): 471–504.

——— and Gerson, Carole, *Paddling Her Own Canoe: The Life and Texts of E. Pauline Johnson (Tekahionwake)* (Toronto; Buffalo, NY; London: University of Toronto Press, 2000).

'Students Form Folksong Club at Downsview', *Globe*, 27 October 1962.

Stuessy, Joe, *Rock & Roll: Its History and Stylistic Development* (Englewood Cliffs, NJ: Prentice Hall, 1990).

Sukenick, Ronald, *Down and In: Life in the Underground* (New York: Beech Tree Books, 1987).

'Sunday Serenade in Square Causes Morris to Yield', *Village Voice*, 13 April 1961.

Susman, Warren, *Culture as History: The Transformation of American Society in the Twentieth Century* (New York: Pantheon Books, 1984, 2nd edn).

Thody, Ron, 'A Peek Through the Mousehole', *Satyrday*, December 1966.

———, 'US Draft Chills Youth: "Ashamed to be an American"' *Satyrday*, Vol. 1 (1967).

———, 'Yorkville Needs its Heads Examined', *Satyrday*, Vol. 2 No. 4 (1967).

Thomas, Cal, 'The 1960s Damaged American Culture', in Mary E. Williams (ed.), *Culture Wars: Opposing Viewpoints* (San Diego, CA: Greenhaven Press Inc, 1999), pp. 69–75.

Temple Kirby, Jack, *Media-Made Dixie: The South in the American Imagination* (Baton Rouge; London: Louisiana State University Press, 1978).

Time magazine, selected editions, 1960–80.

Tippett, Maria, *Making Culture: English Canadian Institutions and the Arts Before the Massey Commission* (Toronto; Buffalo, NY; London: Toronto University Press, 1990).

Tipton, Steven M, *Getting Saved from the Sixties: Moral Meaning in Conversion and Cultural Change* (Berkeley; Los Angeles; London: University of California Press, 1982).

Titon, Jeff Todd, 'Reconstructing the Blues: Reflections on the 1960s Blues Revival', in Neil V. Rosenberg (ed.), *Transforming Tradition: Folk Music Revivals Examined* (Urbana; Chicago: University of Illinois Press, 1993), pp. 220–40.

Toronto '59: One Hundred and Twenty-Fifth Anniversary (Toronto: City Administration, 1959).

Toronto Happening, CBC Television, 17 February 1963. <http://archives.cbc.ca/IDCC-1-69-1587-3080/life_society/60s/> (accessed 3 May 2004).

Tower, Courtney, 'The Heartening Surge of a New Canadian Nationalism', *Maclean's*, February 1970.

Truscott, Lucian, 'Gay Power Comes to Sheridan Square', *Village Voice*, 3 July 1969.

Tuesdaily (Toronto: Rochdale College), 1969–72.

Tuft, Harry M., *The Denver Folklore Center Catalogue and Almanac of Folk Music Supplies and Information for the Fiscal Year 1966* (Denver, CO: Denver Folklore Center, 1966).

Tulchinsky, Gerald, *Taking Root: The Origins of the Canadian-Jewish Community* (Toronto: Lester Publishing, 1992).

Tye, Diane, '"A Very Lone Worker": Woman-Centred Thoughts on Helen Creighton's Career as a Folklorist', *Canadian Folklore Canadien*, 15/2 (1993): 107–17.

Tyler May, Elaine, 'The Commodity Gap: Consumerism and the Modern Home', in Lawrence B. Glickman (ed.), *Consumer Society in American History: A Reader* (Ithaca, NY; London: Cornell University Press, 1999).

——, *Homeward Bound: American Families in the Cold War Era* (New York: Basic Books, 1988).

Usher, Bill and Page-Harpa, Linda, *For What Time I Am In This World: Stories from Mariposa* (Toronto: P. Martin Associates, 1977).

Vallely, Fintan (ed.), *The Companion to Irish Traditional Music* (Cork: University of Cork Press, 1999).

Vertical Files, (Various Subjects) (Ottawa: National Library of Canada).

——, (Various Subjects) (Toronto: Toronto Public Library, Central Branch).

——, (Various Subjects) (Toronto: Urban Affairs Library).

——, (Various Subjects) (Washington, DC: American Folklife Center, Library of Congress).

Village Voice (New York: 1959–present), selected editions.

Wakefield, Dan, *New York in the Fifties* (Boston, MA; New York; London: Houghton Mifflin/Seymour Lawrence, 1992).

Walden, Keith, *Becoming Modern in Toronto: The Industrial Exhibition and the Shaping of Late Victorian Culture* (Toronto: University of Toronto Press, 1997).

Ware, Caroline Farrar, *Greenwich Village, 1920–1930: A Comment on American Civilization in the Post-War Years* (Boston, MA: Houghton Mifflin, 1935).

Watroba, Matt, 'Guy and Candie Carawan: Keeping Their Eyes on the Prize', *Sing Out!*, Vol. 44 No. 3 (Spring 2000).

Waxman, Chaim L., *Jewish Baby Boomers: A Communal Perspective* (New York: New York State University Press, 2001).

Waxman, Ken, 'Stan Rogers's Music Goes Abroad – Thanks to Himself' (pre-1983 – no source provided.)

Whelton, Clark, 'MacDougal and Bleecker: The Scene that Ended', *Village Voice*, 9 January 1969.

Whisnant, David, *All That is Native and Fine: The Politics of Culture in an American Region* (Chapel Hill: University of North Carolina Press, 1983).

Whitefield, Stephen J., *The Culture of the Cold War* (Baltimore, MD; London: Johns Hopkins University Press, 1991).

Wiley Hitchcock, H. and Sadie, Stanley, *The New Grove Dictionary of American Music* (New York: MacMillan Press, 1986).

Williams, Mary E. (ed.), *Culture Wars: Opposing Viewpoints* (San Diego; CA: Greenhaven Press, 1999).

Williams, Richard, *Dylan: A Man Called Alias* (London: Bloomsbury, 1992).

Winick, Steve, 'The Musical Life of Mick Moloney', *Dirty Linen*, 48 (October–November 1993).

Winkleman, Donald M. and Browne, Ray B., 'Folklore Study in Universities', *Sing Out!*, Vol. 14 No. 4 (September 1964).

Wolfe, Paul, 'Dylan's Sell-Out of the Left', in R. Serge Denisoff and Richard A. Peterson (eds), *The Sounds of Social Change* (Chicago, IL: Rand McNally, 1972),

Wolliver, Robbie, *Bringing it All Back Home: Twenty-Five Years of American Music at Folk City* (New York: Pantheon Books, 1986).

Wood, Michele, 'Music and the "Mayor" of the Village', *Cosmopolitan*, December 1963.

Woods, Fred, *Folk Revival: Rediscovery of a National Music* (Poole, Dorset: Blandford Press, 1979).

'A World of LSD, Drugs, and … Sex', *Toronto Telegram*, c. April 1967

Wright, Charles, 'Two Queens, Unfurling', *Village Voice*, 22 May 1969.

Wright, Robert A., 'Dream, Comfort, Memory, Despair: Canadian Popular Musicians and the Dilemma of Nationalism, 1968–1972', in Beverley Diamond and Robert Witmer (eds), *Canadian Music: Issues of Hegemony and Identity* (Toronto: Canadian Scholars' Press, 1994), pp. 283–301).

Yankelovich, Daniel, *New Rules: Searching for Self-Fulfillment in a World Turned Upside-Down* (New York: Random House, 1981).

Yannella, Philip R., *The Other Carl Sandburg* (Jackson: University of Mississippi Press, 1996).

Yorke, Ritchie, *Axes, Chops and Hot Licks: The Canadian Rock Music Scene* (Edmonton: M.G. Hurtig, 1971).

——, 'Canada's Role in World Music Industry: Silent No Longer', *Billboard*, 24 May 1969.

——, 'They're All Pop', *Canadian Composer/Compositeur Canadien*, February 1969.

Yorkville (documentary), Criterion Videos, 1986.

Yorkville Sit-In, CBC Television News, *Metro Extra*. 21 August 1967 <http://archives.cbc.ca/IDCC-1-69-580-3224/life_society/hippies/> (accessed 4 May 2004).

Yorkville Yawn, 1967.

Young, Bob and Ruddy, Jon, 'Neil Young: My Brother The Folk Singer', *Maclean's*, May 1971.

Young, Israel, *Autobiography: The Bronx, 1928–1938* (New York: Folklore Center Press, 1969).

——, Interviews with Richard Reuss, 1965–69. Tape Recordings (Washington DC: American Folklife Center Archives, Library of Congress).

Young, Ian, *The Stonewall Experiment: A Gay Psychohistory* (London; New York: Cassell, 1995).

Zeldin, Arthur, 'A Pre-Centennial Folk Session', *Toronto Star*, 4 November 1966.

Zumwalt, Rosemary Levy, *American Folklore Scholarship: A Dialogue of Dissent* (Bloomington: Indiana University Press, 1988).

Selected Discography

Au-Go-Go Singers, The, *They Call Us the Au-Go-Go Singers*. Collectors' Choice Music CCM-0112-2, 1999.

Baez, Joan, *Greatest Hits*. A&M Records 314540510 2, 1996.

Band, The. *The Band*. Capitol 74235-25389-2-8, 2000.

——, *The Last Waltz*. Warner Bros 7599-27346-2, 1978.

——, *Music From Big Pink*. Capitol 72435-25390-2-4, 2000.

Bluegrass Super Hits. Columbia CK 67735, 1973.

Byrds, The, *The Very Best of The Byrds*. Columbia CK 91179, 1998.

Chieftains, The, *The Wide World Over*. RCA/Victor 09026-63917-2, 2002.

Cockburn, Bruce, *Bruce Cockburn*. True North TNBD 0001, 1970.

Creedence Clearwater Revival, *Chronicle: The 20 Greatest Hits*. Fantasy FCD-623, 1976.

Dylan, Bob, *Bob Dylan Live 1966: The 'Royal Albert Hall' Concert*. Columbia COL 491485 2, 1998 (1966).

——, *The Freewheelin' Bob Dylan*. Columbia CD 32390, 1989.

Guthrie, Arlo, *The Best of Arlo Guthrie*. Warner Bros. 7599-27340-2, 1977.

Guthrie, Woody, *Dust Bowl Ballads*. Camden 74321 578392, 1998.

Hammond, John, *I Can Tell*. Atlantic 7 82369-2, 1992.

Harris, Emmylou, *Pieces of the Sky*. Reprise 7599-27244-2, 1975.

Havens, Richie, *Mixed Bag*. Polydor 835 210-2, 1967.

Hillbilly Blues: 25 Country Classics, 1929–1947. ASV CD AJA 5361, 2000.

Incredible String Band, The, *The Incredible String Band*. Hannibal HNCD 4437, 1966.

Kingston Trio, The, *The Original: The Kingston Trio*. EMI TO 864342, 1996.

Klezmorim, The, *The Klezmorim: First Recordings, 1976–78*. Arhoolie CD 309, 1989.

Leadbelly, *My Last Go Round*. Snapper Music SMDCD 240, 1999.

MacIsaac, Ashley, *Hi How are you Today?* A&M Records, 1996.

McLauchlan, Murray, *Greatest Hits*. True North TNK 35, 1990.

McLean, Don, *Tapestry*. Capitol BGO CD 232, 1994.

McMaster, Natalie, *In My Hands*. WEA, 1999.

Mitchell, Joni, *Ladies of the Canyon*. Reprise CD 6376, 1970.

——, *Joni Mitchell*. Reprise RS 6293, 1968.

New Orleans Klezmer Orchestra, The, *Flesh Out the Past*. Shanachie 9015, 1999.

Page, Jimmy and Robert Plant, *No Quarter: Jimmy Page and Robert Plant Unledded*. Fontana 526 362-2, 1994.

Peter, Paul and Mary, *Ten Years Together: The Best of Peter, Paul and Mary*. Warner Bros. CD 3105, 1970.

Rogers, Stan, *Between the Breaks ... Live!* Fogarty's Cove Music FCM-002D, 1979.

Simon, Paul, *Graceland*. Warner Bros., CDW 46430, 1986.

——, *Shining Like a National Guitar: Greatest Hits*. Warner Bros. WTVC 47721, 2000.

Statman, Andy, (The Andy Statman Klezmer Orchestra). *Klezmer Suite*. Shanachie 21005, 1984.

Taylor, James, *Mud Slide Slim (And The Blue Horizon)*. Warner Bros. 2561-2, 1971.

——, *Sweet Baby James*. Warner Bros. 7599-27183-2, 1970.

Terry, Sonny and Brownie McGhee, *Blowin' the Fuses*. Tradition TCD 1013, 1996 (1961).

A Tribute to Woody Guthrie, Warner Bros. 9 26036-2, 1972.

Weavers, The, *The Best of the Weavers: Wasn't That a Time?* Half Moon HMNCD 012.

Woodstock: Three Days of Peace and Music: The Twentieth Anniversary Collection. Atlantic 82636-2, 1994.

Index